Very Respectfully, &c.
W. G. Brownlow

OUGHT

AMERICAN SLAVERY

TO BE PERPETUATED?

A Debate

BETWEEN

REV. W. G. BROWNLOW AND REV. A. PRYNE.

HELD AT PHILADELPHIA, SEPTEMBER, 1858.

PUBLISHED FOR THE AUTHORS
BY J. B. LIPPINCOTT & CO.,
PHILADELPHIA.

PREFACE.

As a book must not go out without a PREFACE, the undersigned herewith introduce the correspondence between them, which gave rise to the debate in which they have been engaged, and which is substantially contained in the following pages.

In presenting the following work to the American public, no apologies are offered. We live under a Government which tolerates liberty of thought, liberty of speech, and freedom of the press; and in this expression of our honest views and feelings — differing widely as we do — upon the subject of Domestic Slavery in the United States — a subject relating to the general welfare of the country, we are but exercising a right which belongs to every American citizen. The age of proscription for opinion's sake, is past, and, as we trust, never again to return. The liberal genius of our free institutions, allows to all unrestricted interchange of thought and sentiment; while men's opinions are received or rejected, according as they possess merit or demerit.

For the imperfections of this volume, the undersigned offer no apology. The Lectures of each were prepared for the occasion, under the pressure of other important, and frequently distracting avocations. We both claim to have spoken honestly, and with a sincere desire to do good. One of us a Southern man, the other a Northern man—both prejudiced, as we frankly admit, at least to some extent, in our educations, habits, and associations, in favor of the institutions, and usages of the respective section of the country we hail from—the reader will appreciate our principles and opinions, as he may deem them entitled to favor.

W. G. Brownlow.
Abram Pryne.

Philadelphia, Sept. 14, 1858.

PRELIMINARY CORRESPONDENCE.

[From the Knoxville Whig.]

OUR DISCUSSION IN SEPTEMBER.

The reader will see from the following correspondence, that the battle spoken of in many of the newspapers, comes off on Tuesday, the seventh of September, in the city of Philadelphia, between the Editor of this paper and Rev. Abram Pryne, a Congregational minister, and the Editor of an anti-slavery paper, published in McGrawville, Courtland county, New York, styled the "Central Reformer." The following challenge appears in his *Reformer* for March 10, 1858.

REV. MR. BROWNLOW AND SLAVERY.

The public will remember that this gentleman has challenged the friends of freedom in the North to debate with him the merits or demerits of slavery. His very elaborate challenge has not been accepted, unless it be a conditional acceptance, from Frederick Douglas. I now propose to reduce the question to a single proposition, sweeping the entire area of the subject, and in that form I challenge him to its discussion. The proposition I would state as follows: —

"Ought American Slavery to be abolished?"

This question to be reversed when the debate is half through, and to be stated as follows: —

"Ought American Slavery to be perpetuated?"

He may select the time and place of holding the debate. I only stipulating that it shall be in the State of New York, and that I shall have four weeks' notice between his acceptance of my challenge and the commencement of the debate.

As my name may not have reached him, I may state that like Mr. Brownlow I am a clergyman, and an editor, and will take the liberty to refer him to Hon. Gerritt Smith, Hon. J. R. Giddings, Dr. Mark Hopkins, President of Williams College, and Rev. L. G. Calkins, President of New York Central College.

ABRAM PRYNE.

McGRAWVILLE, NEW YORK.

CENTRAL REFORM OFFICE,
McGRAWVILLE, New York, April 14, 1858.

Dear Sir — I sent you some time since a challenge to debate the question of the rightfulness of American Slavery with me. I have not heard from you — I write to express the hope that after your blustering announcement that you would meet the entire North on this question, you will not back out from the first debate offered you. Yours, &c., A. PRYNE.

MORRISTOWN, TENN., April 20, 1858.

REV. ABRAM PRYNE —

Sir — In your issue of an abolition paper, of the 10th ult., styled the "Central Reformer," and of which you seem to be the ostensible editor, you challenge me to meet you in debate on the slavery question. You say you are "a clergyman and an editor," and for your character, you refer me to several distinguished abolitionists.

There are two points of information I wish from you, before I respond to your challenge. First, what church are you connected with? Next, are you a white man, or a gentleman of color? Respectfully, &c., W. G. BROWNLOW,
Editor of Knoxville Whig.

MORRISTOWN, TENN., April 20, 1858.

HON. J. R. GIDDINGS—

A clergyman at McGrawville, Courtland county, who edits an abolition paper, styled the "Central Reformer," proposes a discussion with me on the subject of Slavery, and refers me to you, and others, for his character. His name is *Abram Pryne.* Is he a gentleman, in good standing in his church? What church is he connected with? *Is he a white man, or a man of color?*

Your early reply will oblige,

Very respectfully, &c.,

W. G. BROWNLOW.

HALL OF REP., U. S., April 24, 1858.

Dear Sir—I have heard Abram Pryne preach several times. I understand him to be a preacher in good standing with the Congregational Church — at least I never heard aught against him, as a Christian, a gentleman, a scholar. Very respectfully,

J. R. GIDDINGS.

W. G. BROWNLOW, Esq.

KNOXVILLE, April 26, 1858.

Rev. Mr. Pryne — Your letter of the 14th inst. is before me, and I hasten to reply. My failing to answer your "challenge" of March 10th, as set forth in the "Central Reformer," an Abolition paper, of which you seem to be the ostensible editor, has induced you to believe that I have "backed out," after my "blustering announcement" that I was willing to meet the entire North.

I was in New Orleans when your characteristic, not to say "blustering," challenge came to hand, and upon my return, I started east of here, taking my exchange papers with me; and so soon as I opened your paper, and discovered your "challenge," I addressed you from Morristown, in this State, and also your friend, Hon. Joshua R. Giddings. That letter I have no doubt has reached you before this time, and if so, has given you to understand that I am not going to "back out," as you no doubt *desire* me to do!

I think you have been a little too hasty in attributing *cowardice* to me in this matter. I was one thousand miles distant, in the sunny South, when your "challenge" came here to my address, on a tour of observation among the negroes, and sugar and cotton plantations of Mississippi, Arkansas, Louisiana, and Alabama, and I answered you with promptness, so soon as I returned and flashed my eye upon your very fair, liberal, and one-sided "challenge," prescribing the *terms* and *place* of our discussion!

In my letter to you, of the 20th inst., I requested to know, as a preliminary step towards engaging with you in "mortal combat," whether you were a white man or a gentleman of color. I must still know this fact, and I hope you will impart the information to me. My reason for desiring this information is, that I have heretofore understood there is an Abolition College in McGrawville, and that an educated negro is at its head. I thought it likely that *you* might be that man, and if so, it is due to me that I know the fact.

To be candid with you—and I deal so with all men—the same mail bringing me your insolent letter, also brings one from Mr. Giddings; and while he stated that you are a minister in good standing in the Congregational Church, he is silent as to your *color*, the only question I propounded to him with *emphasis*. This silence on his part has increased my suspicions as to your *color*.

Hoping to hear from you soon, I am,

Very respectfully,

W. G. Brownlow,

Editor of the Knoxville Whig.

McGrawville, N. Y., April 28.

Rev. W. G. Brownlow—

Sir—I have your note of April 20th, and hasten to reply. The churches with which I act, are known as Union Churches. They are Independent Congregational in organization and government, and Evangelical in doctrine and practice. They differ from Congregationalism as to total independency, and on the subject of Christian union only. But of course you do not deem this point important, for in your first challenge you call out Theodore Parker by name, and you are not likely to meet a greater heretic than he in all the North!

Your second inquiry I can answer, by stating that my father is a Hollander by descent, and my mother's father was a Scotchman, and though not a *very white man*, there is not a drop of negro blood in my veins.

I shall hope to hear from you again by return mail.

Yours, &c., ABRAM PRYNE.

McGRAWVILLE, N. Y., May 6th, 1858.

REV. MR. BROWNLOW —

Sir—Your letter of the 26th came this morning. You have, probably, received my last before this, and are satisfied as to my color; your excuse for not replying sooner to my challenge, is satisfactory, and I withdraw any intimation contained in my letter as to your "backing out." Your hint that I desire you to "back out," I shall answer in deeds rather than words.

You may select the place anywhere in the North, or Northwest, from Augusta, Maine, to Chicago, as you please.

Let me suggest one or two incidental questions: —

1. Shall the debate be published?
2. Shall admission be free or otherwise. A fee at the door to pay expenses is common at the North.

Yours in hope of a speedy and definite reply,

A. PRYNE.

KNOXVILLE, May 15th, 1858.

Rev. Abram Pryne—Your letters of April 28th, and May 6th, are both before me. My delay in answering is because of my absence from home again, in attendance at the meeting of the General Conference of the Methodist Church, South, still in session at Nashville.

Your statements as to your *Church relations* and *color*, are perfectly satisfactory, and you may prepare to meet me; but you will have to wait on me for a short time on account of engagements I must comply with. This will only give you the more time for preparation; and you will please not accuse me of *egotism* when I advise you to be fully ready, as I purpose to give you battle after a style you have not been accustomed to—

not intending to be outdone by you, however, in courtesy and fairness.

1. I will claim the right of meeting you on Mason and Dixon's Line, say in the great Free Soil city of Philadelphia, which will give me twice the distance to travel that you will have. Pennsylvania is a Northern State — Philadelphia can accommodate us with a suitable Hall — and I presume you cannot object to the place.

2. As I do not go into this fight as the representative of any Church or political organization, South, but upon my own hook, as a Southern man, and the advocate of Southern institutions, I will not be limited to any *particular form of discussion,* but will claim the right to discuss the whole Slavery question, contrasting the morality and integrity of Northern men, with the morals and integrity of those of the South.

3. I am willing to open the debate, and give you the concluding speech, but I will protract it until I announce to you and the audience, that I am through. I will not be limited to any time under an hour, in each of my speeches, allowing you the same time that I occupy in reply; and when, in some instances, I chance to exceed one hour, it shall not be to the extent of more than thirty minutes, say, in all, one hour and a-half.

4. While I am speaking, I will deny the right of interrupting me, but will concede to you the right to correct any and everything I may say. On the other hand, while you are speaking, I will not interrupt you, nor tolerate it in any friend of mine, or of the South.

5. I will not suffer any other person to participate in the debate, but I will concede to you the privilege of surrounding yourself with all the anti-Slavery leaders at the North, and with counselling them, and being prompted by them at intervals; and when we are through, if any one of them shall think you have not done me or the South justice, I will renew the contest with him.

6. As it regards *publishing* the debates, I propose to print in a book, all that I say, and *just as I say it.* I suggest that the whole be published under one cover.

7. As it regards "a fee at the doors," I would prefer that it be "a free fight;" but if we are required to pay hall rent, and

other incidental, but necessary expenses, we shall have to require the doors to be closed, and sell tickets of admission. I am too poor myself, to be at any other expenses than my tavern bills and travelling expenses. But this we will agree upon when we meet, which must be a few days in advance of the discussion.

Hoping you will accept the fair and liberal terms laid down, and respond without delay, I will, upon receipt of your reply, publish the intended debate, and the *time* at which it is to come off. Your obedient servant, W. G. Brownlow.

Editor of the Knoxville Whig.

McGrawville, June 1st, 1858.

Rev. W. G. Brownlow —

I have your letter of May 15th, and hasten to reply. One or two paragraphs of your letter need explanation; you say you "will not be limited to any particular form of discussion." Am I to infer from this, that you now decline debating the question which I challenged you to debate; namely, whether American slavery ought to be abolished or perpetuated? Or am I to understand this paragraph to mean, that *under that question*, you simply ask a wide range of debate? If the latter is all you mean, still agreeing that the question shall stand as I first proposed, I have no fault to find.

2. As to the length of time the debate shall continue, I have nothing to say.

3. I should much prefer that the length of the speeches should be agreed upon on the start — and not varied from.

4. I agree to your proposition as to interruptions.

5. I will not consent that any other person shall take part in the debate on either side.

6. As to publishing, I propose that each of us employ a verbatim reporter — and each revise his own speeches after the reporter has written them out — and that the book be *published*, stereotyped, and each edition be equally divided between us, each paying half the expense.

7. I am equally obliged, with yourself, to make the debate

pay its expenses—and think a fee at the door will secure as large an audience as any room will hold.

I should prefer going to New York, but will not object to going to Philadelphia.

If then, I understand right, that you accept my challenge, and that the question shall be stated—"Ought American Slavery to be perpetuated," or "Ought American Slavery to be abolished," with the added agreement that the debate shall give you the widest latitude, to discuss all phases of the slavery question—with this understanding, I say, you may give notice of the debate. But there must be a well defined question, under which I agree to give you the widest latitude.

Your notice as to where the debate shall take place, must reach me four weeks before the time appointed.

Please answer immediately.

My reply has been delayed a few days by my absence in Ohio. Yours, &c., A. PRYNE.

KNOXVILLE, June 10, 1858.

Rev. A. Pryne—Your letter of the 1st inst, post-marked same date, came to hand to-day, nine days out, and I reply by the first mail going east.

I mean in my letter to you, of the 15th ult., that *under the question you proposed*, "Ought American slavery to be perpetuated?" I shall claim a wide range in the debate. In other words, I mean that I will go into an investigation of the WHOLE SUBJECT OF SLAVERY, contrasting the consistency and morality of the North, with that of the South. I mean, further, that in my speeches, *I* will be the judge of what is to the point, and will not be ruled out of order, or off of the subject, by any moderators, or judges of the debate. As we are both preachers, I will use a figure that we fully understand: You may select any *Text* you please, but in my *sermons* upon that text, I will preach what seems to me to be gospel. If I say nothing to the purpose, and dodge the issues, it will be to your advantage, both before the audience, and in the published debates; for I will see that my speeches appear in the book just as I deliver them, and I hope you will do the same.

If the proprietors of the largest Hall in Philadelphia, will require pay from us, for its use, &c., as they doubtless will, we of course must charge an entrance fee, or for a season ticket. I am a poor man, and not able to pay out several hundred dollars for Hall rent, for a week, to accommodate others. I have served the public all my lifetime, and have never turned my attention to the business of making money.

As I suppose we now understand each other fully, write me that all is right, and I will announce the time, giving you as long a notice in advance as you desire.

I have the honor to be, &c.

W. G. BROWNLOW,

McGRAWVILLE, N. Y.. June 18.

REV. W. G. BROWNLOW:

Dear Sir: — I have your letter in reply to my last. It is quite satisfactory on the point of my inquiry, and you may give notice of the debate, according to our understanding.

I have said but little to you about my course of argument. I now desire to say, that with me, the debate is quite other than a contest between the two sections of the Union. I shall by no means undertake to defend the North, or condemn the South, in all things. It is the institution of slavery, and not the South, upon which I make war. I look upon the course of many Northern men, both in politics and religion, with shame and scorn, and shall only defend what is right in the North. — But of course I accord to you the right to discuss side issues as much as you please, reserving to myself the right to reply or not as I may think best.

I represent no party in politics or religion, and am alone responsible for my views. As to expenses, I presume that I am far less able to bear them than yourself. A fee at the door is quite proper, and if more than enough to pay expenses can be thus raised, it will be right and just, and no drawback in a Northern audience. I think we need feel no delicacy about that matter. As to the time, I have only this to say, that my health is not robust, and I am about going to a Water Cure for two or three weeks. But if I have four weeks after your final notice, it will be enough.

2

I must not debate all day, every day.—Afternoons and evenings will be all that I can do, leaving us the mornings for rest. You will have the advantage of me in physical strength, to say nothing of your superior mental abilities.

One thing about the Hall. It must be open to *all*, of every grade and *color* who buy tickets. You will see at once, that I cannot consent to any restrictions here. This must be stated in our contract for a Hall.

You will be quite as free from any prejudice from a Philadelphia audience as myself. Every Northern audience will hear you with entire respect, and no effort of mine shall be wanting in that direction. My sense of honor would prompt this course.

I should prefer 30 minutes as the general length of speeches because I think it would suit the audience better. But I will not contend for this.

Of course, if we can mutually agree when the debate shall close, that would be well, but if not each one must quit when he thinks best.

I suppose that it would not be best to permit the entire debate to be reported for the press, for that would injure the sale of our book. But upon that we can consult.

Write me freely anything that strikes you.

Respectfully yours,

A. PRYNE.

KNOXVILLE, July 8th, 1858.

Rev. A. Pryne—Returning from the counties below me, I hasten to yours of the 18th ult. You say your purpose is, in our forthcoming debate, not to make war upon the South, but upon "the institution of slavery." We are unable in the South, to distinguish between a war upon the South, and this institution. However, as our general arrangements have been agreed upon, you and I must make these fine-spun distinctions, when we come to measure arms in debate.

The debate must be carried on in day time, and I purpose to make only one speech each day. As to the length, I cannot be limited, as heretofore agreed upon, but it shall be of reasonable length. I am willing that it be in the after part of the day.

As to the *time of closing,* I can only say, I will wind up, when in my own judgment, I have covered the whole ground. As to reporting our debate for the newspapers, we can't prevent that if we would. But we must first secure the copyright, and prevent any other publication than newspaper reports.

The debate will open on Tuesday, the seventh of September, and I hope we may able to conclude the same week.

Very respectfully, &c.

W. G. Brownlow.

American House, Sept. 3d, 1858.

Rev. A. Pryne.—I arrived in this city this afternoon, and learned you were here. By speaking both too long and too loud, and by over-heating myself in a controversy during the last summer, I have brought upon myself bronchitis, rendering it impossible for me to speak, or even converse, without an effort somewhat painful. I have resorted to cupping, to the external use of Croton Oil, and other remedies, prescribed by physicians, and thus far all to no purpose. With the exception of this almost incurable hoarseness, I am well. I come here to let you know of my condition, and to suggest, and even ask a postponement of our discussion of the Slavery question. I regret the disappointment as much as any one living; and I will add, that it is the first time in thirty years I have been without a strong and powerful voice.

But if you think we must have it over, now that we are here, I am willing to go into it, and employ some competent man to read for me, as great as the disadvantages will be to me. I look more to the result of the publication of our speeches, in the same volume, than to any momentary effect upon a Philadelphia audience. In other words, I am willing to stand or fall by the matter of my speeches, as, from first to last, they shall cover the whole ground, concluding each speech with such replies to your remarks, as I may deem necessary.

Very respectfully, &c.,

W. G. Brownlow.

PHILADELPHIA, Sept. 3d.

Rev. W. G. Brownlow.—I have this moment received your note and hasten to reply. I deeply regret your loss of voice, but as we have both travelled far to meet in this debate, and as public expectation will be sadly disappointed if it fail, I readily accept your very honorable proposition to employ a second person to read your speeches, and am ready to do all in my power to accommodate myself to your misfortune. Permit me to express the hope that you will be able to produce a reader who will do justice to your speeches in the rendering.

Very respectfully, yours, &c.,

ABRAM PRYNE.

SLAVERY DISCUSSION.

"OUGHT AMERICAN SLAVERY TO BE PERPETUATED?"

AFFIRMATIVE, I.—BY W. G. BROWNLOW.

RESPECTED AUDITORS: Before I enter on the discussion of this important question, and various other kindred topics connected with, and growing out of this question, I wish to apprise this audience of what they will have discovered before I take my seat — namely, that in my public addresses, no matter what my topics may be, I do not present my themes with an eloquence that charms, with that critical acumen that fascinates, or with that richness of diction that captivates an audience. This I regret, as there is no power like that of oratory. Cæsar controlled men by exciting their fears; Cicero by captivating their affections and swaying their passions. The influence of the one perished with its author; that of the other continues to this day, and will continue with public speakers to the end of time.

Believing that I address an appreciative audience, who are here to learn facts in reference to "the peculiar institution," and the great question of the Nineteenth Century, I shall look more to *what* I say, than to my *manner* of saying it — more, if you please, to the *subject matter* of my speeches, during this discussion, than to any exhibition of rare powers of analysis, wit, satire, or remarkable force and beauty of language. I deem this the more important, at least on my part, since this whole discussion is to go out to the world in the same bound volume, and be read by thousands, even after my reverend competitor and I shall "cease at once to walk and live."

In advocating the affirmative of this question, it is not meant that I am to be restricted to the narrow limits that technically accurate terms would fix, defining the limits of the debate. I may be allowed to remark, that in the correspondence which brought about this discussion, and which has been read in your hearing, I resisted the efforts of the gentleman — if indeed he intended such a thing — to tie up the discussion by limiting me to his *text*, by the strict rules of sermonizing.

Not only will I throughout this discussion openly and boldly take the ground that *Slavery as it exists in America, ought to be perpetuated*, but that slavery is an established and inevitable condition to human society. I will maintain the ground that God always intended the relation of master and slave to exist; that Christ and the early teachers of christianity, found slavery differing in no material respect from American slavery, *incorporated into every department of society;* that in the adoption of rules for the government of society, and of the church, they provided for the rights of *owners*, and the wants of *slaves;* that slavery having existed ever since the first organization of society, it will exist to the end of time. And in the wide range I propose to take in this debate, I shall defend the South, and make war upon the abolitionism of the North — covering, if you please, the whole ground of difference between the two sections.

Whoever, then, reflects upon the nature of man, will find him to be almost entirely the creature of circumstances; his habits and sentiments are, in a great measure, the growth of adventitious circumstances and causes — hence the endless variety and condition of our species. That race of men in our country, known as abolitionists, free soilers, or as black republicans, look upon any deviation from the constant round in which *they* have been spinning out the contentious thread of their existence, as a departure from nature's great system; and from a known principle of our nature, the first impulse of these unmitigated fanatics is to condemn.

It is thus that a man born and reared in a free state, looks upon slavery as unnatural and horrible, and in violation of every law of justice and humanity! And it is not unusual to hear bigots of this character, in their churches at the North, imploring the Divine wrath to let fall the consuming fires of heaven upon that great Sodom and Gomorrah of the New World — all that vast extent of territory, south of Mason and Dixon's Line, where this horrible practice is known to prevail! I hope my worthy competitor, who will follow me in this discussion, has never been steeped to the nose and chin in unwarrantable prejudices against the South.

When an unprejudiced and candid mind examines

into the past history of our race, and learns the fact which history develops, as the honest enquirer will, that a majority of mankind were *slaves*, he will be driven to the conclusion I have long since reached; namely, that the world, when first peopled by God himself, was not a world of *freemen*, but of SLAVES — the Declaration of American Independence, as usually construed, to the contrary notwithstanding.

Slavery was really established and sanctioned by Divine authority, among even God's chosen people — the favored children of Israel. Abraham, the founder of this interesting nation, and the chosen servant of the Most High, was the lawful owner, at one time, of more slaves than any cotton-planter in South Carolina, Georgia, Alabama, or Mississippi; or any tobacco or sugar planter in Virginia or Louisiana. This may strike you as a bold assertion, at first glance; but my competitor, who is familiar with the Scriptures, will *regret*, that there is more truth than poetry in the declaration.

That magnificent shrine, the gorgeous temple of Solomon, commenced and completed under the pious promptings of religion and ancient free-masonry, was reared alone by the hands of slaves! Involuntary servitude, reduced to a science, existed in ancient Assyria and Babylon. Egypt's venerable and enduring pyramids were all reared by the hands of slaves, and black negroes at that! The ten tribes of Israel were carried off to Assyria by Shalmanezar, and the two strong tribes of Judah were subsequently carried in triumph by Nebuchadnezzar to end their days in Babylon *as slaves*, and to labor to adorn the city. Ancient

Phœnicia and Carthage, were literally overrun with slavery; the slave population outnumbering the free and the owners of slaves, nearly three to one! The Greeks and Trojans, at the siege of Troy, were attended with equal numbers of their slaves, to themselves. Athens, and Sparta, and Thebes — indeed, the whole Grecian and Roman worlds — had more slaves than freemen. And in those ages which succeeded the extinction of the Roman empire in the West, slaves, abject and degraded slaves, were the most numerous class. Even in the days of civilization and christian light, which revolutionized governments, laboring serfs and abject slaves were distributed throughout Eastern Europe, and Western Asia — showing that slavery existed throughout these boundless regions. In China, the worst forms of slavery have existed since the earliest history of the "Celestial Empire." And when we turn to Africa, we find slavery, in all its most revolting forms, existing throughout its whole extent, the slaves outnumbering the free-men three to one! Looking then, to the whole world, I may with confidence assert, as I do to-day in your midst, that slavery in its worst forms, subdues by far the largest portion of the human race.

Now, my respected auditors, the inquiry is, how has slavery thus risen and spread over our whole earth? I answer — by the *laws of war* — the *state of property* — the *feebleness of governments* — the thirst for *bargain and sale* — the *increase of crime* — and last, but not least, *by and with the consent, knowledge, and approbation of Almighty God!* Slavery, then, is an established and inevitable condition to human society.

I do not speak of the *name*, but the *fact*. But the Abolition philanthropists of the United States care nothing for facts. They deal in terms and fictions. It is not the institution of American slavery, but the *word* "slavery" which shocks their tender sensibilities, and their fruitful imaginations associate it with "hydras and chimeras dire."

In "that sacred book from Heaven bestowed," usually called the Bible, this call is made upon *slaves*, or *servants*, as you may choose to regard them:

> "Let as many servants as are under the yoke count their own masters worthy of all honor, that the name of God and his doctrine be not blasphemed."— 1 *Tim.* vi: 1.

The Scriptures, for the most part, were written in the Hebrew and Greek languages, and I flatter myself that my worthy competitor is familiar with these languages. If so, he knows that the word here rendered *servants* means SLAVES converted to the Christian faith; and the word *yoke* signifies the *state of slavery*, in which Christ and the Apostles found the world involved, when the Christian Church was first organized.

By the word rendered *masters*, we are to understand the heathen masters of those christianized slaves. Even these, in such circumstances, and under such domination, are commanded to treat their masters with all honor and respect, that the name of God, by which they were called, and the doctrine of God, to wit: Christianity, which they had professed, might not be blasphemed — might not be evil spoken of in consequence of their improper conduct. Civil rights are never abolished by any communication from God's

Spirit; and those fiery bigots at the North, who propose to abolish the institution of slavery, as it exists in the South, are not following the dictates of God's spirit or law. And if the Rev. gentleman who is to follow me in this debate, will allow me to instruct him in political economy, and Christian theology, I will here distinctly announce to him, that the civil state in which a man was before his conversion, is not altered by that conversion; nor does the grace of God absolve him from any claims which the State, his neighbor, or lawful owner may have had on him. All these outward things continue unaltered; hence, if a man be under the sentence of death for a capital offence, and God see fit to convert him, which is sometimes the case, he is not released from suffering the extreme penalty of the law!

The Church of Christ, when originally constituted, claimed no right, *as an ecclesiastical organization*, to interfere with the civil government, as the united Churches of New England are now doing. This was the principle upon which the Church was founded, as distinctly announced by its immortal Head. When Christ was doomed by a cruel Roman law to its most ignominious condemnation, he did not so much as resist it, *because it was law*, nor did he complain of it as oppressive. I hope my reverend adversary will bear this in mind!

"Then Pilate entered into the judgment-hall again, and called Jesus, and said unto him, Art thou the King of the Jews? . . . Jesus answered, My kingdom is not of this world; if my kingdom were of this world, then would my servants fight, that I should not be delivered to the Jews; but now is my kingdom not from hence. . . . To this end was I born, and for this cause came I into the world, that I should bear witness to the truth."—*John* xviii. 33–37.

Sir (*turning to Mr. Pryne*), when Christ came into the world on the business of His mission, He found the Jewish people subject to the Roman kingdom; and in no instance did he counsel the Jews to rebellion, or incite them to throw of the Roman yoke, as do the *vagabond philanthropists* of the Free States of this Confederacy, in reference to the existing laws of the United States, in reference to slavery. Christ was by lineal descent "THE KING OF THE JEWS," but he did not assert his temporal power; so far from it, he actually refused to be crowned in that right.

Under the Roman law, human liberty was held by no more certain tenure than the whim of the sovereign power, protected by no definite constitution whatever. Slavery constituted the most powerful and essential element of the government; and that slavery was of the most cruel character, and gave the masters absolute discretion over the lives of the slaves.

This is not the case in any Slave State in this Union, and never can be. On the contrary, laws exist in all the Southern States punishing cruel treatment of slaves, as other misdemeanors; and in some of our States, my own beloved Tennessee among the rest, owners of slaves are liable to an indictment before a grand jury, for failing to clothe them decently. And for the murder of a slave, unless it be done in self-defence, masters and overseers have been frequently executed. This was done, but a few years since, in South Carolina!

But to return to the argument. Notwithstanding all this, under the Roman laws, Christ did not make war upon the existing government, nor did He denounce the rulers for conferring such powers; though He looked upon cruel legislation in the light in which the character of His mission required. And although the *Church itself* was not what it should have been, in no instance did Christ denounce *that.* The only denunciations the Saviour ever uttered, were those against the doctors and lawyers, the ministers and expounders of the Jewish code of ecclesiastical law. For this he was crucified. And the *Jewish anti-slavery gamblers*, who put him to death, divided out his garments, as you recollect, casting lots for them. And from that day to this, whenever you meet with one of these *Abolition* Jews, he is engaged in the *clothing business*, either retailing or wholesaling "ready-made clothing."

But allow me to present the case of the inspired apostle to the Gentiles, as proof more palpable and overwhelming, on this very point. He had been falsely accused, cruelly imprisoned, and unjustly arraigned; and that, too, before a licentious governor, a tyrannical and dissipated ruler, and an unprincipled infidel. The Roman law in force at the time arrested the freedom of speech, denied the rights of conscience, and even forbade the free expression of opinion in all matters conflicting with the provisions of the laws of the Roman government. In his defence before Felix, Paul never so much as speaks of *Roman law*, though well versed in it; but "he reasoned of *righteousness*, and *temperance*, and the *judgment to come.*" Here was a suitable occasion to condemn the regulations, and to question the authority, of the *villanous statutes* of Rome; but, instead of this, Paul plead his rights *under* the unjust regulations of the law. He charged

Felix with *official* delinquency, with *personal* crime, and, as a *man*, he held him up to public scorn, and threatened him with the vengeance of a justly offended God! He appealed *to the law*, and justified himself *by the law*. He claimed the rights of a "*Roman citizen*" — demanded the protection due to a Roman citizen — and he scorned to find fault with the law, cruel and unjust as he knew it to be. And the consequence was, that the licentious infidel who ruled, "*trembled*" in his presence.

The views I have here submitted, are not at all new, but have been uniformly acted upon by evangelical Christians in all ages of the world. Since the days of St. Paul and Simon Peter, no reformer has appeared who was more violent than that great and good man, MARTIN LUTHER. JOHN CALVIN possessed a revolutionary spirit; he fought everything he believed to be wrong; he was unmitigated in his severity. Yet neither of these great and justly distinguished men ever made war upon the existing laws of their respective countries.

JOHN WESLEY was the great reformer of the past century: he reformed the whole machinery of the modern Church of Christ; and his doctrines and manner of conducting revivals are now leading elements of American Christianity. But Mr. Wesley never made war upon the English government, under which he lived and died. On the other hand, it is a matter of serious complaint among sectarians not friendly to the spread of Methodism, that Mr. Wesley wrote elaborately against the war of the Revolution. Mr. Wesley believed it to be religiously his duty to sustain the government under the reign of George III.; and had I been placed in his circumstances, I should most unquestionably have imitated his pious example. And although devoted to law and order, and opposed to all resistance to existing laws, Mr. Wesley's letter to LORD NORTH, as British Premier, and a similar one to the Earl of Dartmouth, as Secretary of these Colonies, dated June 15, 1773, but recently brought to light by GEORGE SMITH, Fellow of the Royal Society of Great Britain, show that Mr. Wesley did not entertain towards the American colonies the hostilities that have been attributed to him. In those letters he *condemns the policy of Great Britain towards the American colonies*, and predicted just what came to pass—actually sympathizing with the Colonies!

JOHN WESLEY, in his troubles at Savannah, Georgia — like Paul before the licentious governor, appealed *to the law*, and sought by every means in his power to be tried *under the law*, asking only the privilege of being heard in his own defence! And as a propagator of gospel truth, he thus adhered to existing laws, "*that the name of God and his doctrine be not blasphemed.*"

One word more as to Mr. Wesley: He is quoted by Abolition Methodists at the North, against the Methodists of the South. And for aught I know to the contrary, the Reverend gentleman who debates with me here, may be intending to confront me with some quotation from the pen of Mr. Wesley. What Mr. Wesley has said upon this subject, relates chiefly to the African slave trade, an iniquitous traffic I shall by no means attempt to justify. But it is a matter of record, that when Mr. Wesley returned from Savannah to England, after a residence of two years in Georgia, in his Report to the London Board of Missions who sent him out *he advised the purchase of more negroes for the use of the American Missions* — saying that a small experiment in that way had worked well — that while they were adapted to the climate, and their labor proved valuable, the Missionaries could be serviceable to them in a spiritual point of view! Am I asked for my authority for making this statement, I refer to the Report of Mr. Wesley to the Board, after his return to London, which was in 1739. I also refer to the minutes of the Board, before whom he appeared in person, and where a record is made of this fact!

The essential principles of the great Moral Law delivered tō Moses by God himself, are set forth in what is called the Tenth Commandment, and will be found in the 20th chapter of the book of Exodus:

"Thou shalt not covet thy neighbor's house, thou shalt not covet thy neighbor's wife, nor his *man-servant,* nor his *maid-servant,* nor his ox nor his ass, nor any thing that is thy neighbor's."

The only true interpretation of this portion of the word of God is, that the species of property herein mentioned, are *lawful,* and that all men are forbid to disturb others in the lawful enjoyment of their property. "Man-servants and maid-servants," are distinctly *consecrated as property,* and guaranteed to man for his exclusive benefit—proof that slavery was ordained by God himself. I have seen learned dissertations from the pens of Anti-slavery men—and I expect to *hear* one equally learned, before this discussion closes—setting forth that the term "*servant*" and not "*slave*" is used here. To this I reply, once for all, that both the Hebrew and Greek words translated "*servant*," mean "*slave*" also, and are more frequently used in this sense than in the former. Beside, the Hebrew Scriptures teach us, that God especially authorized his peculiar people to *purchase* "BOND-MEN FOR EVER"; and if to be in *bondage for ever*, does not constitute *slavery* as *perpetual as American slavery*, I yield the point to the gentleman who proposes to abolish the latter!

The visionary notions of piety and philanthropy entertained by many men at the North, lead them to resist the *Fugitive Slave Law* of this government, and even to *violate the tenth Commandment*, by stealing our "men-servants and maid-servants" and running them into what they call free territory, upon their "under-ground railroads!" Nay, the *villanous piety* of some has led them to contribute *Sharp's rifles* and *Holy Bibles*, to send the *uncircumcised Philistines* of our New England States, into "bleeding Kansas," to shoot down the Christian owners of slaves, and then to perform religious ceremonies over their dead bodies! Clergymen lay aside their Bibles at the North, and apply *forty parson power* to the President of the United States, to induce him to reverse his decrees in reference to Kansas matters! Even females, as in the case of that model beauty, *Harriet Beecher Stowe*, unsex themselves, to aid in carrying on this horrid and slanderous warfare against the slaveholders of the South! English travellers, steeped to their very eyebrows in prejudices against this government, and our domestic and political institutions, have written books upon this subject, and our Northern neighbors have circulated them. The

Halls, Hamiltons, Trollopes, Thackerays, and Misses Martineaus, *et id omne genus*, all have slandered the South, and misrepresented her institutions. These English writers all denounce Slavery and eulogize *Democracy*, as though an Englishman could be a Democrat, in the modern, vulgar, bogus sense of that much-abused term, and still be a consistent man!

But, as already stated, I do not propose in this discussion to enter into any defence of the African slave trade, although the evils of it are greatly exaggerated. Its evils, and cruelties, its barbarities, which are bad enough at best, are not justified by the most ultra Southern slaveholder. The vile traffic — for such I characterize it — was abolished by the United States, even before the Parliament of Great Britain prohibited it. All the civilized governments in the world have subsequently prohibited this trade — some of the more influential and powerful of them having declared it *piracy*, and covered the African seas with armed vessels to prevent it!

This trade, which seems so shocking to the feelings of mankind, dates its origin as far back as the year 1442. Antony Gonzales, a Portuguese mariner, while exploring the coast of Africa, was the first to steal some *Moors*, and was subsequently forced by Prince Henry of Portugal to carry them back to Africa. In the year 1502 the Spaniards began to steal negroes, and employ them in the mines of Hispaniola, Cuba, and Jamaica. In 1517 the Emperor Charles V. granted a *patent* to certain privileged persons, *to steal exclusively* a supply of 4000 negroes annually for these islands!

At the commencement of the present century, the slave trade was carried on by Turkey, Holland, England, France, Spain, Denmark, Portugal, the United States, and Central America. In all of those countries, however, the trade has been suppressed, except in the Island of Cuba, and it is carried on there, as it has been for years, only by the evasion of law. And it is due to the truth of history to state, that no two men now dead or alive, have done more to put an end to this brutal and unchristian commerce, than Lords Palmerston and John Russell, for neither of whom have I ever entertained any great regard.

In 1807 the American Congress passed a law, which effectually put a stop to the slave trade, by imposing a fine of $20,000 and a forfeiture of the vessel, upon all persons concerned in fitting out any vessel for the slave trade; while the importer of a negro from a foreign country, if convicted of selling him in the United States, was, by that Act, subjected to a fine of $10,000, and imprisonment for a term of years, not less than *five*, nor exceeding *ten*.

And now, after a lapse of half a century of prohibition, an attempt was made in Congress, last winter was a year ago, to revive this trade, which was negatived by a vote of 183 to 8, in the popular branch of our National Legislature, in the adoption of the following resolution, offered by COL. JAMES L. ORR, of South Carolina, and at present the Democratic Speaker of the House:

"*Resolved, That it is* INEXPEDIENT, UNWISE, AND CONTRARY TO THE SETTLED POLICY OF THE UNITED STATES, *to repeal the laws prohibiting the African Slave Trade.*"

With pride and pleasure, I announce that this resolution came from South Carolina — that out of the thirteen slave states represented in Congress, there were but *eight* votes against this resolution — and that these were *ultra* Southern men, from Alabama, Mississippi, and Louisiana, strongly tinctured with fire-eating and disunion sentiments. I may possibly be told that repeated efforts have been made in the several sessions of the "SOUTHERN COMMERCIAL CONVENTION," to revive the African slave trade. In reply, I have to say, that these efforts as repeatedly failed. I was at different times a member of that body, and I therefore speak advisedly.

African slaves were first imported into America in 1620, a century after their introduction into the West Indies. The first cargo of 20 Africans, by a Dutch vessel, was brought up the James River, into Virginia, and sold out as slaves. *Las Casas*, a Spanish priest, superintended the sale of the first cargo, and shared largely in the profits.

England then being the most commercial of European nations, engrossed the trade; and from 1680 to 1780, one hundred years, there were imported into the British Possessions alone, *two millions of slaves* — making an average annual importation of more than 20,000!

The States of this Union, north of Mason and Dixon's Line, commonly called the New England States, alias the *Free States*, were never, to any great extent, *slaveholding*. No sir-ee, (*turning to Mr. Pryne*) their virtuous and pious minds were chiefly exercised in *slave-stealing* and *slave-selling!* To *Old* England, the mother country, our Pilgrim Fathers of the New England States, are indebted for their knowledge of the art of *slave-stealing;* and to the pious, God-fearing, and liberty-loving *New* England States, are we of the South, wholly indebted for our slaves! They *stole* the African from his native land, and sold him into bondage for the sake of gain. In 1711, there was a slave depot established in New York, in what is now known as Wall Street, and slaves captured on the Western coast of Africa, were landed there by New England vessels, to supply the Southern market! About the same time, another slave depot was opened in the God-fearing and liberty-loving city of Boston, near to where the "Franklin House" now stands! They kept but few of their captives among themselves, because it was not profitable to use negro labor in the cold and sterile regions of New England. And when they enacted laws in the New England States, abolishing slavery, they hurried their negroes round South, in sail vessels, and sold them into bondage to Maryland, Virginia, and the Carolinas, before their laws could go into operation! What an unmitigated generation of hypocrites! They *stole* and sold into *perpetual bondage*, a race of human beings it was not profitable to keep, and for whom they now, like so many graceless pirates, refuse all warranty. And what few American ships are in the trade now, at the peril of piracy, are New England ships.

Nay, it is asserted—and I have nowhere seen it contradicted, that as many as *seventy-five* vessels were fitted out for the slave trade in the United States, during the year 1857, and every one of these in northern ports! I have no doubt — though I cannot prove the fact—that a portion of these are owned and manned by the hypocritical freedom-shriekers of the Northern States, who desire to recover the several sums of money they have contributed, under excitement, to aid the cause of "bleeding Kansas."

But I cannot dismiss this branch of my subject, without going somewhat into detail, as it regards the course pursued by northern men. From 1804 to 1807, a period of three years, there were imported into the little town of Bristol, in the State of Rhode Island—a seaport that did not then contain a population of 2000 souls — as many as 3914 slaves, all from the coast of Africa! During the same period, there were brought into Newport, a town within twelve or fifteen miles of Bristol, in the same State, now the famous and attractive watering-place, 3488 slaves, all from the coast of Africa! Providence, in the same State, received 559, also from the coast of Africa, and *feloniously* obtained at that! Hartford, in Connecticut, the ancient head-quarters of Federalism, whose extreme piety and "Blue Laws" led them to fine a man for kissing his wife on Sunday—this town received 250 of these *stolen negroes* from the coast of Africa, and was as *importunate* in her demand for more, as was the celebrated beggar of London, in soliciting charities! And the transcendantly pious, and God-fearing city of Boston, received 1000 in the same length of time, on *consignment*, all from the coast of Africa!

The slaves brought into Rhode Island, were but a small portion of the number *her citizens* were stealing from the coast of Africa, and carrying directly to the

West Indies, and into the ports of Maryland, Virginia, the Carolinas, and Georgia! As many as *fifty-nine* slave ships belonged, at the time, to the little State of Rhode Island, not larger than some of our counties in Tennessee. Some of the largest fortunes which have descended to her citizens, were created by this nefarious traffic; and but a few years ago, there were men in that State, among the most honored and wealthy of the inhabitants, who had been active participants in the trade, and owned the identical ships that brought these human cargoes to our shores! One of her Senators in Congress, as late as 1827, commenced his career in life *as a slaver*, between the coast of Africa and the West India islands; and he had ships engaged in the traffic, until it was suppressed by the Act of Congress already cited! He died but a few years ago, bequeathing a fortune of millions to his children and grandchildren, who are at this day classed in the highest ranks of society, and are among the bitterest opponents of negro slavery! Some one may be curious to know who this Senator was. To mention names would be *personal.* I will just say, that in 1827, Rhode Island was represented in the Senate by NEHEMIAH R. KNIGHT and ASHER ROBINS!

Now, too, the little State of Rhode Island has run mad upon the subject of slavery, and will promote no man to a post of honor who is not the advocate of what is falsely called freedom. She spurned Buchanan on account of his *Democracy*, and Fillmore, because of his conservative views touching the Southern question, and cast her vote for *Fremont and Dayton!*

The pious and religious portion of northern abolitionists, I take it, are the better portion, and in these the people of the South can repose no sort of confidence. Take, for example, the case of that great man, and powerful pulpit orator, DR. OLIN, who visited Georgia more than thirty years ago, as a school-teacher, and was kindly treated by BISHOP ANDREW and others — ultimately became a minister — and married an estimable Georgia lady, owning quite a number of slaves. He cashed those negroes at fair prices, pocketed the money, and returned to his congenial North; and when Bishop Andrew was arraigned before the General Conference of 1844, in New York, because he had married a widow lady owning a half dozen slaves, DR. OLIN appeared on the floor of that conference, and both spoke and voted against the Bishop! I might multiply instances of this kind, but it is not necessary. I will name the cases of two distinguished Presbyterian ministers — DR. BEMAN, who married in Georgia, and DR. HALL, who was the pastor of a church in Tennessee — who exchanged their negroes for money, returned to their congenial North, and became the zealous advocates of "Freedom," in the *abolition* sense of the term. These gentlemen, like DR. OLIN, washed their hands of the sin and scandal of slavery, pocketed the money their negroes sold for, and employed their time and talents in pleading for the rights of the poor Africans of the South! May I not exclaim, "Lord! what is man?"

But the gentleman who follows me in this discussion, as well as many who hear me to-night, may feel disposed to complain that I am not adhering to the question in controversy —"*Ought American Slavery to be perpetuated?*" I purpose to meet that question, and to march square up to it—but I have not reached the point in this controversy, at which I design to meet this issue. Gentlemen will please exercise a little patience.

I am personally acquainted with many of the abolitionists of the North, connected with the Methodist Church; and although I suppose they are about as pious and reliable as abolitionists of other denominations, I have but little confidence in their pious sympathies for Southern negroes. Their clergymen will enter their fine churches on the Sabbath, preach and pray against the sin of slavery, shed their tears over the wrongs of the "servile progeny of Ham" in the South; and, on the next day, in a purely business transaction, in a dry-goods store, or a candy shop, in closing up a book account, they would cheat a Southern slave out of the *pewter* that ornaments the head of his walking-stick! But, then, they have this redeeming quality, they would do it *religiously*, and in the *sacred name of the Lord!*

What was the course pursued by the *pious* Methodists of the North, toward their brethren of the South, when the Church divided in 1844? The General Conference agreed upon a "Plan of Separation;" commissioners were subsequently appointed to adjust and settle all matters relating to a fair and equitable division of the Church property and funds. The Southern Conferences met in Louisville, Kentucky, in May, 1845, in convention, and resolved themselves into a "SEPARATE AND DISTINCT ECCLESIASTICAL CONNECTION." Instead of abiding by this *sacred compact,*

4

entered into after much prayer and deliberation, the Northern Church came down upon the Southern organization, as a *pro-slavery* Church, intending only to strengthen slavery in the South, and to protect slave-holding in the ministry.

And, sir, with characteristic hypocrisy, and anti-slavery dishonesty, the Northern Methodist Church *repudiated* the "Plan of Separation" they had agreed upon, and the adjustment in reference to the Church property and funds — thus forcing the Southern commissioners to institute legal proceedings against them in the United States Courts at Cincinnati and New York, where the Church property was located. These suits, conducted on the part of the South, by such lawyers as LORD, of New York, REVERDY JOHNSON, of Maryland, STANSBURY and CORWIN, of Ohio, and BRYEN, of Tennessee, cost the Church, South, OVER SIXTEEN THOUSAND DOLLARS; but the South recovered about HALF A MILLION!

This Church now has a mammoth publishing house in successful operation at Nashville; and dispersed throughout her bounds are her *seven* Christian Advocates, weekly organs of the Church, with their 100,000 subscribers, and from *three* to *five* hundred thousand readers. She has her "Missionary" organization, now contributing as much money for Missionary purposes as the entire Church did before the separation in 1844. She has her *ninety* literary institutions — such as colleges and high-schools, male and female, under her care — more than the entire Church had at the time of the separation!

What next? This Church has 24 annual conferences, extending from the Potomac to California, and 2300 travelling preachers. Beside these, she numbers in her ranks 5000 *local preachers*. Within the bounds of these 24 annual conferences, she has a membership of SIX HUNDRED AND FIFTY THOUSAND, 200,000 of whom are COLORED PERSONS, and slaves at that, with but few exceptions!

At another time I will speak of the Southern slaves in connexion with other Christian denominations. At present, I will content myself with the remark, that the Methodist Church, South, is dispensing more labor, and expending more money, to improve the spiritual condition of the slaves; nay, she is doing more for the souls and bodies of the negro race; than all the Wendell Phillipses, Josh Giddingses, Horace Greelys, Ward Beechers, Loyd Garrisons, Theodore Parkers, Madam Stowes, and other freedom-shriekers, now out of the infernal regions!

What next? A distinguished statesman and patriot, now no more, delivered a speech in the United States Senate, on the 4th of March, 1850, and it was *his dying speech*, for he never spake thereafter. He was posted on this slavery question, in all its bearings; and for a quarter of a century, while in the public councils of the country, he watched the movements of parties with sleepless vigilance. Speaking of the effect of the Abolition agitation upon the religious cords which assisted in holding the Union together, this dying statesman said:

"The first of these cords which snapped under its explosive force (Abolitionism) was that of the powerful Methodist Episcopal Church. The numerous and strong ties which held it together are all broken, and its unity gone."

These were among the last words of that great and towering intellect, and tried patriot, JOHN C. CALHOUN, who literally died in *Southern harness*, battling for the rights of the South, under the Constitution. A man of unblemished private character, a consistent member of the Church, and a firm believer in the truths of the Bible, I hope, nay I believe he has found a calm and welcome retreat from the cares and anxieties of political strife, in the paradise of our God, where the harsh epithets, and rude insults of unprincipled freedom-shriekers, and false-hearted Abolitionists, will never fall upon his ear! for that class of men, after death, never travel in the direction of God's habitation!

The explosive force of Abolitionism has snapped asunder the cords and strong ties of other Churches, as well as that of the "powerful Methodist Episcopal Church," which have long been holding this Union together. The Southern portion of the New School Presbyterian Church, have seperated from their Abolition brethren, on account of their ceaseless and graceless agitation of the slavery question, and have organized an independent synod!

The Baptists split with their Northern brethren upon this issue, years ago, and the Southern portion of them occupy the only position that Southern Christians can occupy, that of independent ground—denying the right of any ecclesiastical body to meddle with our domestic institutions!

The Episcopal Church is moving in the same direction, in getting up a great Southern University; and although no formal split has taken place in that Church, the reckless Abolitionists within her pale, will sooner or later create a schism of the worst sort!

As churches, at the South, we cannot affiliate with men who fight under the dark and piratical flag of Abolitionism, and whose infernal altars smoke with the vile incense of Northern fanaticism! I have no confidence in either the *politician* or the *divine* at the North, constantly engaged in the villanous agitation of the slavery question. There are true, reliable, conservative, pious, and patriotic men in the North, and there are similar men in the South, who came from the North, but they are not among these graceless agitators. And if I find any of these agitators in heaven—where I expect to go after death—I shall conclude they have entered that world of joy, by practising a gross fraud upon the door-keeper!

There is much in the political papers of our country, and especially at the North, calculated, if not *intended*, to fan a flame of intense warfare upon the subject of slavery, between the North and the South, which can result in no possible good to either section. Those politicians, and bad men, who are exciting the whole country, and fanning society into a livid consuming flame, particularly at the North, have no sympathies for the *black man*, and care nothing for his comfort. They seek their own—not the negro's good. My competitor may retort, that I am a leading newspaper editor in one of the Southern States, and that I am violent upon this subject. I am violent in defence of the rights of the South, as I understand them. A glance at my history, will acquit me of the charge of *sectionalism*. A native of the "Old Dominion," I have resided in Tennessee for the last thirty years, and have been that long connected with the politics of the country. In 1828, I supported JOHN QUINCY ADAMS in opposition to ANDREW JACKSON. Subsequently I supported CLAY, HARRISON, and TAYLOR. In opposition to SCOTT and PIERCE, I went for DANIEL WEBSTER. Last, but not least, I supported FILLMORE. Thus I have supported patriots and statesmen, without any regard to their *local habitations*. But, this political disquietude and commotion, I regret to say, is giving birth to new and loftier schemes of agitation and disunion, among the vile Abolitionists of the country, and to bold and hazardous enterprises in the States and Territories; and many of our Southern altars smoke with the offensive incense of Abolitionism. We have scores of these men in the South, in disguise — designing men: some filling our pulpits — some occupying high positions in our colleges — some editing political, and some religious papers — some selling goods — some retailing pills--some keeping hotels—and some following one calling, and some another, who, though among us, are not of us, but are in many instances, our worst enemies.

But the reverend gentleman who follows me, would no doubt like to hear what I have to say in answer to his question, "*Ought American slavery to be perpetuated?*" This question I will *affirm*, when, in the progress of this controversy, I reach it. For the present, I have only to say, that the institution of slavery was established for the benefit of that class of the human family who had not the *capacity to provide for their wants*—and of this class are the entire African race—

a class that existed in the days of Moses—has existed ever since—and will continue to exist as long as man is clothed with the infirmities of mortality. Yes—the decree has gone forth, that fully *two-thirds* of the civilized race of man shall work for the rest in the capacity of *bond* or *hired* servants. It is a decree that pervades the dominions of civilization, not as the edict of duty, but of fallen humanity; and to meliorate the sufferings of the *dependant*, by affording them a competency during sickness and aged infirmity, *bondage* was instituted by Moses, under the inspiration of God! This form of slavery, then, is in perfect accordance with the will of God. And I shall be able to show that "American slavery" does not differ in *form* or *principle*, from that of the chosen people of God.

I endorse, without reserve, that much-abused sentiment of an eminent Southern statesman, now no more, Gov. McDuffie, that "slavery is the corner-stone of our republican edifice;" while I repudiate, as ridiculously absurd, that much lauded, but nowhere accredited dogma of Thomas Jefferson's, that "all men are born equal." God never intended to make the negro the equal of the white man, either morally, mentally, or physically. He never intended to make the *butcher* a judge, nor the *baker* a president, but to protect them according to their claims as butcher and baker. Pope has beautifully expressed this sentiment, in these lines:

> "Order is heaven's first law, and this confess'd,
> *Some are*, and MUST BE, greater than the rest."

I have gone among the free negroes of the North—I have visited their miserable dwellings in New York,

Providence, Boston, and other large towns. I have more than once visited the *negro localities* of this, the "Quaker City," and twenty-five years ago, I preached to them in this city; and in every instance, I have found them more miserable and destitute, as a whole, than the slave population of any portion of the South. And this must necessarily be the case, while time shall last, and the regulations of human society remain as they are, and have been. In our Southern States, where negroes have been set at liberty, in nine cases out of ten, their condition has been made worse; while the most wretched, indolent, immoral, and dishonest class of persons to be found in the Southern States, are *free persons of color.* But more of this hereafter, as an argument to prove that "*American slavery ought to be perpetuated!*"

The freedom of negroes in even your *Free States*, is, in all respects, only an empty name. Your citizen negro does not vote, and takes good care not to do so. The law does not interdict him this privilege, in some of your States, but if he attempt to avail himself of the privilege, should he differ in his choice of candidates with your white "lords of creation," he is apprehensive of apostolic blows and kicks," which pious Abolitionists will administer to him!

All the social advantages, all the respectable employments, all the honors, and even the *pleasures* of life, are denied the free negroes of the North, by pious Abolitionists full of sympathy for the down-trodden African! The negro cannot get into an omnibus, cannot enter a bar-room frequented by whites, nor a church, nor a theatre; nor can he enter the cabin of a steamboat, on one of your Northern rivers or lakes, or enter a first-class passenger car on one of your railroads. When a negro has dared to do so, in New York, he has been unceremoniously thrown out, and has taken his case into court, as you very well know: the court has held that the conductor served him right! As a general thing, in New England, negroes are not suffered to enter a stage coach with whites, but are forced upon deck, whether it shall rain or shine, whether it be hot or cold. Industry is closed to them, and they are forced to live as *servants* in hotels, or adopt the profession of barber, or boot-black, or open oysters in saloons, or sell villanous liquors to the lower classes of foreign emigrants, who throng our large cities and towns. The negroes even have their *own streets*, and their own low-down kennels, as is the case here in Philadelphia, even! In nearly all the Northern States, they have their own hospitals, their churches, their cars, upon which, in many instances, are written in large letters, "FOR COLORED PEOPLE."

Finally, as many of you well know, they are forced to have their own *grave-yards*—the *yellow* remains of Northern Abolitionists, and pious white men, refusing to mingle with the bleaching bones of the dead negro, after death! Not so in the South: they crowd the galleries and back-seats in our churches, travel in our passenger-cars and stage-coaches; and, in our cemeteteries, they are frequently buried with the whites, in their owners' lots. I know this to be true.

In ancient Jerusalem, which is nought but a heap of mouldering bones and shattered houses, eastern travellers tell us, that the promenades are *cemeteries*, and the very seats are whited sepulchres, where whole generations of Jews have been buried. But — unlike our Northern anti-slavery men — there are the bones of the Assyrian, the Egyptian *negro*, the Chaldean, the Persian, the Greek, the Syrian, the Roman, the Crusader, and the Turk! There they have all met together, acting out the principle that "the Lord is the Maker of us all."

During the past year, I have seen the particulars of a movement in the Canadian Parliament, looking to the removal from that province of all free negroes and fugitive slaves, who, as alleged, have proven positive *nuisances*.

The notorious *Gerritt Smith*, who, for a quarter of a century, has been a rabid Abolitionist, and has bestowed many farms upon free negroes, in his great zeal to promote the happiness of the colored race, has become disgusted with the recipients of his bounty. He published in the New York *Tribune*, that "*the colored people are generally idle, worthless, and vicious*," and that his "*expectations of their reformation have* IN NO DEGREE BEEN REALIZED." He asserts that half of those to whom he "gave farms have sold their lands, or have been so worthless as to allow them to be sold for taxes." And *Gerritt Smith* is not the only anti-slavery man in the North who has made the discovery that white men subsist comfortably and make money, while negroes are ignorant and thriftless! Suffer me to edify you with a brief article from the Cincinnati *Enquirer*, for July, 1857, the great political organ of Ohio:

"There is a remarkable and very suggestive fact in regard to the negro emigration into this State. It is this: Of the twenty-five thousand free negroes in the State, the vast majority reside in counties where there are very few Abolitionists, and which have been chiefly settled by emigrants from the Southern States. These negroes appear to have a great dread of the Abolition counties; they give them a wide berth. Thus, for example, Ashtabula has a negro population of forty-three; Geauga, seven; Trumbull, sixty-five. The other counties on the lake have a proportionate number of negroes. These counties are settled almost exclusively by New England emigrants. On the other hand, Ross county, a Virginia settlement, has one thousand nine hundred and six negroes; Gallia has one thousand one hundred and ninety-eight; and Hamilton county has over four thousand.

"In these counties the negro is regarded as inferior, socially and politically; and the Abolitionist has but a slight hold. What is the cause of this striking discrepancy? Is it that the negro feels and knows his inferiority, and naturally attaches himself to the population which is disposed to regard him as an inferior? or is it that the whites in the lake shore counties are Abolitionists from an ignorance of the real character of the negro? Certainly there is no better mode of curing a neighborhood of Abolitionism than by inflicting on them a colony of free negroes. The only way in which Giddings can be defeated will be by a few more such philanthropic efforts as those of Col. Mendenhall, in settling a few hundred North Carolina or Kentucky negroes in Ashtabula. If our Southern friends will send us their surplus negro population, let them provide that they may be located among their kind and generous friends in the Western Reserve. Such earnest philanthropy as they profess ought not to be 'wasted on the desert.'"

The New York *Times*, good anti-slavery authority, in publishing the proceedings of a meeting held in Kingston, Jamaica, on the 23d of April last, in reference to persons of color, sets forth the following facts in the two brief extracts I read you:

"One gentleman who visited this country so long ago as 1840, with a view to procure colored laborers, spoke very highly of the character and capacity of the free negroes he saw at the South; but those he met in New York did not impress him favorably at all. Neither their habits of industry nor their morals were such as he desired to see."

"The island of Jamaica, the largest of the British West India possessions, is one hundred and fifty miles long, and averages about forty in width. Its area is 4,250 square miles — about two-thirds the size of the State of New Jersey. The population in 1848 was 380,000, of whom only 16,000 were whites. The emancipated slaves have, to a great extent, wholly refused to work; and, consequently, hundreds of estates all over the island have been abandoned. It is to remedy this evil that free colored emigration is solicited. What the result of the movement may be remains to be seen."

The following paragraph is from the pen of a Northern correspondent of the New York *Times*, for 1858, writing from New Orleans:

"Bad as we of the North believe slavery to be, I have yet to see the first sign of the squalid wretchedness, poverty, and degradation among the blacks here, which we daily see among the blacks and the foreigners of the North.

"I have been in several of of the churches built for the slaves, and I have seen crowds of them worshipping with their masters in the same great congregation. They are wonderfully impressible, uttering their feelings in the very midst of the services — sometimes by a simple 'yes, yes,' sometimes by a long low wail, or a sweet plaintive musical sound that goes all over the congregation, and often by a shriek from some female voice, followed with a spasmodic uplifting of the hands, and then a slight swoon, which draws together a crowd of sympathizing negroes, who attend to the subject until she is restored to consciousness. All the while the services go on as if nothing was the matter, the preacher evidently satisfied with this evidence of his power over his audience."

The Philadelphia *North American*, one of the ablest and most influential journals of this city, and bitterly opposed to slavery, has a long article in one of its issues for 1858, upon the condition and prospects of the free negro population of the Free States. I subjoin a few short paragraphs from its article, as they fully sustain my charges:

"If there is any one fact established by steadily accumulating evidence it is that the free negro cannot find a congenial home in the United States. He is an exotic amongst us; and all the efforts of philanthropists to naturalize him on American soil and under American skies, have failed."

"Ninety-nine in a hundred make a precarious living by contentedly performing the most menial offices, or live in idleness and wretchedness.— *We can hardly fail to attribute this to characteristics of their own.* We see the blacks daily driven from avocations once almost exclusively their own. It is long since they have flourished in any of the trades, if they ever pursued them with success."

"Whatever explanation may be given of these facts, the facts themselves cannot be denied; and what is to be done with our colored population, unless they can be induced to return as colonists to the native land of their race, or seek some other tropical region, baffles the wisest of us to say."

The *North American* then refers to the aversion which has been exhibited by the North-western States to free negroes, and the measures which they have taken to exclude this class of population, and says:

"In a Free State, where emigration is invited by holding out every inducement to the inhabitants of the old States and to foreigners, this aversion to the presence of colored people can only be explained by the opinion that has obtained, almost universally, that they cannot become useful citizens of the United States; or, in other words, that they cannot compete on equal terms with the white race."

Last, but not least, the New York *Herald*, for July 8, 1858, in its notice of the public meeting and free negro meeting at Kingston, in Jamaica, says:

"The state of affairs shown to exist, and the admissions made by the speakers at this meeting, in relation to the free negro communities generally, are of an extraordinary character. Jamaica itself is acknowledged to continue its recession towards barbarism; Liberia is pronounced to be a humbug, both as a country and as a social community; the free negroes of the North are rejected as vicious and worthless, and those of the South are pronounced to be the only ones fitted to become colonists. In this admission a strong but indirect compliment is paid to the effect of Southern legislation and education upon the negro nature, and it is not the less significant that it comes from the colored humanitarians themselves."

It will not do to meet me with an "Oh! these are only newspaper paragraphs, and the newspapers of the country are very unreliable." They give *facts*, known to be such by every intelligent man who hears me. Besides, these are the more significant, as they come from the acknowledged organs of "the colored humanitarians," as the Herald styles them!

In a Republican Convention in Minnesota, only one year ago, the vote was *two to one* against the negro! The Convention resolved, by a unanimous vote, "that negroes were born free and equal with white men;" and then, by a vote of *two to one*, refused to admit the negroes to that equality, and to the enjoyment of those rights they had resolved that they were "born" heir to! And this is but in keeping with Abolition consistency, wherever they are found.

My time has expired, and I must close, yielding the stand to the gentleman who presents the negative side of the question. This, my introductory address, is intended to prepare the mind of the gentleman, and of the audience, for what is to come! Thanking you for your patient and respectful attention, I will now join you in an equally patient hearing of Mr. Pryne.

"OUGHT AMERICAN SLAVERY TO BE PERPETUATED?"

NEGATIVE, I.—BY ABRAM PRYNE.*

LADIES AND GENTLEMEN: I enter upon this debate profoundly impressed by the magnitude of the subject which depends upon my poor powers to-night. No greater question, no sublimer cause, can come before the human mind than the one we are to investigate before you. The civil rights of four million human beings depend, in this debate, upon my feeble advocacy. Their appeal to the justice, humanity, and Christianity of the civilized world for freedom speaks with the trembling tones of my poor voice. I am to do my best to render vocal their unwritten, unspoken wrongs, and arouse your souls to do them justice. I am to defend a pure religion, and a true philanthropy, against the assaults of the most gigantic crime of human history. I speak for humanity crushed under iron-shod oppression; for religion murdered in her own sanctuary; for law trampled under foot in her own temple of justice; for government prostituted by national crime; and in behalf of civilization, progress, order, and national development.

Combined against me is a mighty wrong, hoary with age and deeply imbedded in the history of the past.

---

* All of my speeches were faithfully reported by Mr. De Wolf Brown of Philadelphia.

Very truly yours
A. Pryne

To argue down American slavery, I must meet 1200,000,000 of dollars, with logic and ethics; must overturn the precedents of our national administrations, the forms of American law, the teachings of our past literature, and the sanctions of our religion. And when I reflect that with all these, in popular estimation, against me, I am to meet the reputed Ajax of slavery propagandism in this debate, you will agree with me that I may well stand appalled. Besides, I come to you an unknown man, with no trumpet of fame to announce me, no confident national reputation to inspire me with courage. I cannot boast of learning or eloquence, but am only a plain man, with a heart faithful to the cause of freedom, and a will to do some service in her behalf.

On the other hand there are many things which gather around this debate to give me courage. My cause is itself an inspiration. I speak for voiceless maidens sold in the shambles; for millions of strong men rendered mute by chains; for religion, justice, law, and an outraged God; circling out from this hall, the vast audience of the civilized world will listen for the words of this debate. Thousands of freemen in the North will bend their ears and abate their breath to learn how their self-elected champion bears himself in this controversy. Thousands of oppressors in the South will listen for the words of this debate; and if I fail with such a cause to plead, I shall be followed to a shameful grave by the deep-voiced execrations of my countrymen; but if I succeed I shall carry to my grave the proud consciousness of having struck one good blow for God and freedom. Appealing therefore to the justice of my cause for aid, and to the great God of all peoples for inspiration, I launch forth upon the stormy waves of this debate.

I am to maintain, not that American slavery ought to be limited, regulated, or restricted, but that it ought to relax its ruffian grasp from the throat of every victim on this continent and DIE. With me, in this debate, slavery has no rights but one, and that is the right to a grave so deep that it shall never have a resurrection. I have nothing to do with any schemes for its amelioration or restriction; but, in the name of God and humanity I demand its annihilation.

Shall slavery live? This question is up — up in church and state—up in senate-hall and sabbath-school — up at the communion-table and the council-room— up in school-house and court-room—up from the golden sands of California to the stormy shores of the Bay of Fundy — from Cape Sable to the mouth of the Columbia River—and, like the ghost of Banquo, it will not "down," though priest and politician bid it "void" their presence; and I am here to meet it and question it.

> "Though hell itself should gape,
> And bid me hold my peace."

My first argument against American Slavery is that it began in robbery, piracy, and murder; and having this indescribably wicked beginning, it ought to die. It was born of rapacity and cruelty, without the sanctions of law for its birth, and every step of its existence since has been a criminal existence, in defiance of the just rights of the hangman and the halter.

The first Englishman who committed the rape of

one continent, and entailed ages of prostitution upon another, by opening the African slave trade, was Sir John Hawkins, an adventurous buccaneer in the reign of Queen Elizabeth. The English queen gave him a license to trade to Africa, and import to America such natives as he could *persuade* (!) to accompany him; expressly enjoining in the license, that he should not use *force, or fraud, or violence,* to induce them to accompany him. Now, in the first place, the very giving of such a license was a violation of the law of civilized nations. Queen Elizabeth had no more right to give a license to her subject to trade in Africans, than has Queen Victoria a right to license her subjects to trade in Tennesseeans. She could have no sovereignty over Africa, and could only license lawful trade, subject to treaties with the African kings; and this trade being, in its very nature unlawful and piratical, could not be licensed, according to any civilized law, human or divine.

But whatever shadow of sanction this license seemed to give to the murderous traffic, is dissipated by the history of the expeditions of Hawkins. He violated the very terms of his license every voyage, and in the case of every slave. He did use "force, violence, and fraud," contrary to the express prohibitions of his license. He desolated the coast with fire and sword; he kidnapped the inhabitants, and loaded them with chains, at their own doors; he burned their dwellings, stole men, women, and children, and drove them at the point of the pike into the hold of his vessel, and thus at every step violated the license under which he professed to act.

When the death hour of this inhuman traffic came, when Clarkson and Wilberforce, and last of all, Pitt, had roused the British nation to its enormity — and Wilberforce, of whom Lamartine said, "at his death he went up to the Throne of God with a million broken fetters in his hands" — had for the last time moved in the British parliament the abolition of this trade, Pitt startled its defenders, and electrified the House with the following brave words:

> "*Any* contract," he said, "for the promotion of this trade *must*, in his opinion, have been VOID FROM THE BEGINNING, for if it was an outrage upon justice, and only another name for fraud, robbery, and murder, what pledge could devolve on the legislature to incur the obligation of becoming principals in the commission of such enormities, by sanctioning their continuance?
>
> "But he would appeal to the acts themselves. That of 23 George II. c. 31, was *the one upon which the greatest stress was laid.* How would the House be surprised to hear that these very outrages, committed in the prosecution of this trade, had been *forbidden* by that act! 'No master of a ship trading to Africa,' says the act, 'shall, by fraud, force, or violence, or by any indirect practice whatever, take on board or carry away from that coast any Negro, or native of that country, or commit any violence upon the natives, to the prejudice of said trade; and every person so offending shall, for every such offence, forfeit one hundred pounds.' But the whole trade had been demonstrated to be a system of fraud and violence, *and therefore the contract was daily violated*, under which *the Parliament allowed it to continue.*"
> — *Clarkson's History*, p. 314.

Thus did the great English statesman sweep down every vestige of a legal foundation for the Slave Trade, and reveal the whole system as naked piracy. This trade was the fountain from which slavery proceeded — the infernal womb from which the haggard monster was born; and having such a birth, it could have no legitimate life in civilized society; no rights but the right to be hunted to its death like the fabled dragons of old.

Here I am happy to stand on common ground in this debate, and to start the first proposition of my argument against American slavery on ground in which my opponent and myself agree. Having had the premises of my first argument most fully admitted and argued by my opponent, I need offer no further argument to prove these premises, but only lead you to the legitimate, inevitable conclusion from the premises that he himself has furnished me. If the slave trade was piracy at its beginning — if it was villanous in its inception and its carrying out — then, as it and American slavery drew their first breath simultaneously, and as American slavery never could have had an existence without the slave trade, and has drawn from that trade the new blood with which it has covered the soil of our own land, I have only to take the premises of my opponent to a conclusion which no man can dodge — that that which necessarily and legitimately grew out of what he joins with John Wesley in denouncing as "the sum of all villanies," is itself also villanous. Slavery and the slave trade rise or fall together. The trade was the grand trunk artery of the whole system in its beginning, and will be in the continuance of its existence; and I am astonished that a mind so logical as that of my opponent did not strike deeper, and defend the trade, as the only premises upon which slavery can plant its foot, outside the infernal regions. I fully expected him to do this, and in failing to do it, and in condemning the origin of slavery, he has blasted its character forever with the dark crime of its birth; and no forms of legislation, no baptisms of religion, no sanctions of time, or lapse of ages, can render innocent in its after life that which committed a foul crime at its very birth.

The slave trade having been conceded to be illegal, and wrong, and villanous, I shall go on to the inference. Slavery having had its birth in that trade — that trade being its mother — and the man who first invented and carried out that trade, committing the rape of one continent, and centuries of prostitution for another, being held up here before us as a violator of all law, human and divine, and as a scourge of his race — the children of that trade, and the products of that trade, and the results of that trade, all the way up to the ripe fruit of plantation discipline, all partake of the illegitimate character of the trade itself. Between the middle-passage, with all its horror, and the plantation discipline, there is an iron-linked, logical connection, that even the Ajax of pro-slavery propagandism will in vain attempt to break.

Right and wrong are not subject to territorial boundaries. Morality has no geographical limits. If the slave trade is wrong on the coast of Africa, it is wrong in America. It is no greater crime to rob a mother of her babe on the Guinea coast, than in the streets of Richmond. The domestic slave trade is the same in morals, the same before God as the foreign slave trade. To rob a father of his daughter, or a mother of her son, on the Niger, or the Big Boom, in Africa, is no worse than to do this same deed on the Potomac, or Tombigbee, in America. Trading in human beings is the same unmatched crime, whether done by brutal buccaneers, on the African coast, or canting priests and whining deacons, from the bosom of a Southern church. Whether this crime be prefaced by a prayer or an oath, by a psalm or a pirate's song, the crime still stands unrivalled in its enormity—and as every day's continuance of slavery involves the continuance of the domestic trade, with all its horrors, slavery ought to die. Why should a sailor be hung for being caught in the slave trade, fifty miles at sea, and a priest be applauded and petted, while engaged in the same kind of trade on land? Does cant cover crime, or will the mockery of hypocritical words blind the eyes of God? Will pious grimace cloak bloody wrong? Will you drown the voice of justice by a psalm, and mob down the cry of murdered innocence with drawling prayers? Ah! God can see through the smoke of hypocritical sacrafice, and hear the cry of the poor along with the din of brawling cant!

But I go further, gentlemen, than to argue that American slavery ought to die because it had its origin in a confessedly villanous trade, and in an outrage and a wrong upon humanity. I say that, in its historical development from that day to this, every progressive step in its career has been equally outrageous in the eye of the law of nations, the laws of our own land, and the laws of God. Its entire life, from its villanous birth to this night, has been in defiance of the just claims of God's outraged justice.

And now I am about to take a bold position—one that will startle Free Soilers and Republicans—one for which I stand here to-night alone responsible. I proclaim the doctrine that, according to all just notions of human law, there never was and never can be a slave legally held on the American continent. As my opponent tells me that he is a friend of law and order, that he is a friend of constitutions and government, that he is no enemy of the laws of the land—when I shall have proved to you, as I will, that American slavery, from beginning to end, is a system of lawlessness, then I shall have him on my side, for he is pledged to the support of law and order.

The Slave States of this Union have never established slavery by direct and positive legal enactments. No statute establishing it can be found. The positive law refuses to interfere, and leaves the master to catch the slave if he can, while, as we shall see, the common law is out against the institution, with its thunders of condemnation, and the lightning of its wrath. We have the testimony of southern statesmen themselves, that slavery has no enactments on which to stand. John C. Calhoun, my opponent's model statesman, says:

"They were brought here as slaves, sold as slaves, and held as slaves, long before any enactment made them slaves. *I even doubt whether there is a single State in the South that ever enacted them to be slaves.* There are hundreds of acts that recognize and regulate them as such, but none, I apprehend, that undertake to *create* them slaves. Master and slave are constantly recognized as prëexisting relations."—*John C. Calhoun, Reply to T. H. Benton*, 1849.

"No legislative act of the Colonies can be found in relation to it," (the introduction of Slavery.)—See *Wheeler's Law of Slavery*, p. 8–9; *Am. Slave Code*, p. 268.

"If the record of any such act exists, we have not been able to find any trace of it."—*Judge Matthews; Wheeler's Law of Slavery*, p. 15; *Am. Slave Code*, 267.

Senator Mason, of Virginia, objected to a jury trial for fugitives, on the ground that such a process would require

> "Proof to be brought forward that Slavery is established by existing laws;" and, said he, "it would be impossible to comply with the requisition, *for no such law could be produced.*"—*Goodel's Slavery and Anti-Slavery*, pp. 570, 571.

Mr. Bayly, M. C. of Va. agreed with him.

Senators Douglas and Toombs, in the debate on the Nebraska Bill, contended that no statute was necessary to establish slavery in Kansas, because no statute had established it in any of the States.

Gen. Stringfellow, of Missouri, used the same argument in a letter, in which he said:

> "The veriest schoolboy must know, *as a matter of history*, that although slavery existed in all the old States, *in not one of them was a law ever enacted to establish it.*"

The following gentlemen, namely, Messrs. S. C. Brooks and John McQueen, of South Carolina, William Smith, of Virginia, and Thomas L. Clingman, of North Carolina, (members of Congress,) addressed a joint-letter to General Stringfellow, strongly commending his statements.

The Southern doctrine all through is, that slavery is a natural condition—a creature of natural laws—that your tenure to your slave is the same as to your horse, —because you can catch him; that you hold him by virtue of conquest alone; that you drive him into your field as you drive your ox,—because you have broken him and can manage him. The legislature has given you no promise to put him in your hands or to make him work. The legislature never stands behind him driving him up to his work. It has only stood by and enabled you to lay your hands upon him and make him a slave, never enacting a law giving you the legal right to do it, but basely allowing you to catch him if you can. So that, gentlemen, American slavery has not, for its support, even that shabby notion of law that we call legislation. No legislature has yet dared to defy Heaven by passing an act to condemn a freeman to slavery.

But even if it had, it would not help the case. For let me tell you that everything cannot be framed into law. Law has a character of its own. Certain elements enter into it; and whatever enactments lack these elements are no laws at all. They are not bad law, but they are no law — are null and void, and are oftentimes conspiracies against law. An enactment, to have the authority and force of law, must be founded in justice and reason — must draw its life principles from the government of God — must grow out of the nature of man — must bear relation to the Divine government and come into harmony with it. The mere votes of a legislature can no more make a law than they can make a God, unless those votes are cast for the development and manifestation and revelation of a law that God Almighty wove into the structure of the universe at the beginning.

Suppose, gentlemen, (this is an abstract argument, but you will see the sweep of it in a moment) — suppose, if you please, that a company of ten thousand natural philosophers should get together and undertake to legislate that water should cease to run down-hill and hereafter shall run up-hill; suppose they should solemnly vote that this should be a law of nature — that the brooks should turn round, that the streams should run up towards their fountain — would the streams obey them? or would they laugh on in their course and disregard them?

Suppose all the mathematicians in the world should gather themselves together, and enact, as a law of mathematics, that instead of twice two making just four, it should make just four and a half — would that make it a law? would that make it a rule in mathematics? Every boy that could count his fingers would tell you when the matter was proposed to him, "Let all the mathematicians in God's world declare that this is law, I have only to count my fingers to prove that it is not true, and does not govern the case, and therefore cannot be law." Now for the application: God inscribed upon man's forefront the law of self-ownership as clearly and distinctly as he revealed the fact that twice two makes four. He gave each man two hands and one head: and if all the legislatures to be gathered together on earth, should legislate that a man should own two dozen hands and one dozen heads, the law of God stands forever revealed against them; and instead of such an enactment being law, it is a villanous legislative conspiracy against law, and deserves no other name. So that, were you able, even, to find enactments in favor of the institution of American slavery—were you able to find enactments in favor of murder, of robbery, of adultery, of any crime that I could name — you would not feel bound to bow down to these crimes, because of these enactments, but would say that you had come into a land of legislative criminals, and that what they enacted was not law, but multiform crime, stealing the sacred garb of law, under which to hide its villany.

Now, gentlemen, to prove to you that I have not been talking mere fanaticism — that the principle which I have laid down is the principle sanctioned by all legal writers of any note, allow me to quote a few authorities:

"The law of nature is that which God, at man's creation, infused into him, for his preservation and direction, and this is an eternal law, and may not be changed."—2 *Shep. Abr.*; *also Jac. Law Dict.*

"Of law no less can be acknowledged, than that her seat is the bosom of God, her voice the harmony of the world. All things in heaven and earth do her homage; the least as feeling her care, and the greatest as not exempted from her power."—*Hooker.*

"This law of nature being coeval with mankind, and dictated by God himself, is of course superior in obligation to any other. It is binding over all the globe, in all countries, and at all times; no human laws are of any validity, if contrary to this; and such of them as are valid, derive all their force, and all their authority, mediately, or immediately, from this original."—*Blackstone, Vol.* 1, *p.* 41.

"Jurisprudence is the science of what is just and unjust." —*Justinian.*

"The primary and principal objects of the law are rights and wrongs."—*Blackstone.*

"Justice is the constant and perpetual disposition to render to every man his due."—*Justinian.*

"The precepts of the law are to live honestly; to hurt no one; to give to every one his due."—*Justinian & Blackstone.*

"LAW. The rule and bond of men's actions; or it is a rule for the well governing of civil society, to give to every man that which doth belong to him."—*Jacob's Law Dictionary.*

"All laws derive their force from the law of nature; and those which do not, are accounted as no laws."—*Fortescue, Jac. Law Dict.*

"No law will make a construction to do wrong; and there are some things which the law favors, and some it dislikes; it favoreth those things that come from the order of nature." —1 *Inst.* 183, 197.—*Jac. Law Dict.*

"Lord Chief Justice Hobart has also advanced, that even an act of Parliament made against natural justice, as to make a man judge in his own cause, is void in itself, for *jura naturæ sunt immutabilia*, and they are *leges legum*"—(the laws of nature are immutable—they are the laws of laws.)—*Hob.* 87.

"Those human laws that annex a punishment to murder, do not at all increase its moral guilt, or superadd any fresh obligation in the forum of conscience to abstain from its perpetration. Nay, if any human law should allow or enjoin us to commit it, we are bound to transgress that human law, or else we must offend both the natural and the divine."—*Blackstone*, Vol. 1, p. 42, 43.

"Those rights then which God and nature have established, and are therefore called natural rights, such as are life and liberty, need not the aid of human laws to be more effectually invested in every man than they are; neither do they receive any additional strength when declared by the municipal laws to be inviolable. On the contrary, no human legislature has power to abridge or destroy them, unless the owner shall himself commit some act that amounts to a forfeiture."—*Blackstone*, Vol. 1, p. 54.

"Now we must entirely take leave of our senses, ere we can suppose that law and justice have no foundation in nature, and rely merely on the transient opinions of men."—*Same*, B. 1, p. 56–57.

"Whatever is just is always the true law; nor can this true law either be originated or abrogated by any written enactments."—*Same*, B. 2, p. 83.

"It appears in our books, that in many cases, the common law will control acts of parliament, and sometimes adjudge them to be utterly void; for when an act of parliament is against common right or reason, the common law will control it, and adjudge such act to be void."—*Coke, in Bonham's case;* 4 *Coke's Rep.*, Part 8, p. 118.

"If the will of the people, the decrees of the senate, the adjudications of magistrates, were sufficient to establish justice, the only question would be how to gain suffrages, and to win over the votes of the majority, in order that corruption and spoliation, and the falsification of wills, should become lawful. But if the opinions and suffrages of foolish men had sufficient weight to outbalance the nature of things, might they not determine among them, that what is essentially bad and pernicious should henceforth pass for good and beneficial? Or why should not a law, able to enforce injustice, take the place of equity? Would not this same law be able to change evil into good, and good into evil?"—*Cicero.*

I would, were it important, give you multiplied quotations upon this point.

Have I to prove that American slavery is not in harmony with the law of nature, but contravenes the law of nature? No; I shall not stop for such an argument to-night. But let us look for a moment to see how it stands in the light of statutes.

In 1772, the Court of King's Bench of Great Britain decided that no slave could be held under the English Constitution. This was four years before the Declaration of American Independence. That decision was equally of binding force wherever the British Constitution bore sway, and applied to the colonies as well as to the mother country, for their charters were all subordinate to the laws of England. It consequently settled the question that, in the American colonies, there could no more be legal slavery than in Great Britain itself. After the decision of Lord Mansfield, in 1772, the next great legal step that swept slavery from the country, was the Declaration of American Independence.

Gentlemen, when the old bell that now stands, cracked, in Independence Hall—an object of reverence to every American patriot—rang out upon the startled air her first peal after the Declaration of American Independence, the language to the nation was that inscribed upon her own form, "Proclaim liberty throughout all the land to all the inhabitants thereof." And that sentiment was put in other language into the Declaration itself; when it declared all men — not all white men—not all men of a certain color, but all men —to be entitled to life, liberty and the pursuit of happiness. That Declaration, I take it, is the basis, the corner-stone of all American law—the constitution of the American Constitution — and lies at the foundation of everything that comes after in the form of an organized and legislating government; and that Declaration swept away every legal vestige of American slavery from the whole breadth of the land.

I shall be answered, perhaps, that slavery continued to exist after that — that it still exists. It does. In the State of New York we had a few months ago a "Maine liquor law," making illegal the sale of intoxicating drinks anywhere in the State. Yet the sale went on. But did that fact make the sale legal? or did it only show that there was a power sustaining the sale that could override the law? So, when the Declaration of American Independence swept away every legal foundation for slavery, the fact of its continued existence no more proves its legality than the fact of a continued sale of intoxicating drinks in spite of a "Maine Law," proves the legality of such sale. Because all thieves are not caught and punished, is theft therefore lawful?

So far as this argument is concerned, then, I shall

— as my opponent has declared himself a friend of law and order and government, and in favor of sustaining the law — call upon him to come up with me to the support of the Declaration of American Independence — the basis of American law; I shall ask his aid in the effort to carry it out strictly in the country and proclaim, in the language of the old bell, "liberty throughout all the land and to all the inhabitants thereof."

But another step is necessary in this argument against the legal existence of slavery. I take my friend on his own premises. He is in favor of the law and the Constitution; so am I, and I shall spend a few moments in proving to him that the Constitution of the United States itself is a document all instinct with Abolitionism from beginning to end, and that in harmony with that Constitution and in the carrying out of its principles, every slave in this nation should be set free. And when I shall have proved this, I shall be sure to have him on my side; for he is in favor of the law and in favor of the Constitution.

I will only start this argument to-night by quoting the preamble of the Constitution of the United States —its own declaration of its intention and its purposes. The preamble of any law is the declaration of its intention, as made by the legislators themselves—its breadth and scope, and width and design, as mapped out in the minds of those who frame it. And I take it that the preamble of the Constitution of the United States is to be regarded by lawyers, as well as by all men of common sense, as the statement made by the adopters of that Constitution, of what they intended to do with it and by it. On this point I quote authorities:

Chief-Justice Jay regards the *Preamble of the Constitution* of the United States an authoritative guide to a correct interpretation of that instrument.—2 *Dallas*, 419.

Story says, "The importance of examining the preamble, for the purpose of expounding the language of a statute, has been long felt, and universally conceded in all juridical discussions. It is an admitted maxim in the ordinary course of the administration of justice, that the preamble of a statute is a key to open the mind of the makers, as to the mischiefs which are to be remedied, and the objects which are to be accomplished by the provisions of the statute. We find it laid down in some of our earliest authorities in the common law, and civilians are accustomed to a similar expression, *cessante legis præmio, cessat et ipsa lex.* (The preamble of the law ceasing, the law itself also ceases.) Probably it has a foundation in the exposition of every code of written law, from the universal principle of interpretation, that the will and intention of the legislature is to be regarded and followed. It is properly resorted to where doubts or ambiguities arise upon the words of the enacting part; for if they are clear and unambiguous, there seems little room for interpretation, except in cases leading to an absurdity, or to a direct overthrow of the intention expressed in the preamble.

"There does not seem any reason why, in a fundamental law or constitution of government, an equal attention should not be given to the intention of the framers, as expressed in the preamble. And accordingly we find that it has been constantly referred to by statesmen and jurists to aid them in the exposition of its provisions."—1 *Story's Comm. on Const.*, pp. 443–4.

That preamble reads thus:

"We, the people of the United States, in order to form a more perfect union, establish justice, ensure domestic tranquillity, provide for the common defence, promote the general welfare, and secure the blessings of liberty to ourselves and our posterity, do ordain and establish this Constitution for the United States of America."

Now I shall assume that the framers of the Constitution did not lie—that, when they stated that their object was to form a more perfect union, to establish justice, to promote the general welfare, to secure the blessings of liberty, they told the truth. If this be the fact, then, that preamble is to be regarded as a declaration that the Constitution is against slavery.

One of their objects was "to form a more perfect union." What endangers the Union? What has disturbed the Union? What has rocked and heaved the Union from Cape Sable to the mouth of the Columbia River, and from the stormy shores of the Bay of Fundy to the golden sands of California? What but the introduction and determined perpetuation among us of the gigantic wrong of American slavery? I ask, shall this Union be made more perfect until it shall cease to stand rocking and heaving, as it does, on the bosom of the poor slave? A Union that is held together by planting the iron heel of the National administration on the bosom of four million innocent men—who expects such a Union to be tranquil? Who expects it to rest a moment? God, breathing into the heart of humanity the nobler and higher impulses of our common nature, demands of every man living under such a Union that he shall rock it from centre to circumference until it shall cease to rest upon the bosom of four million crushed slaves. The humanity of the age is sure to secure the freedom of these slaves, either through the union of these States or over the union of these States. Though I am a friend to the Union—though I would not have the South leave the Union, but would grapple her to it as with hooks of steel, until she shall be obliged to let her bondmen go free and to do justice to the slave—nevertheless, I cannot fail to see, as does every man, that the disturbing force which prevents a perfect union of these States is the institution of slavery. Abolish it, and your Union will be perfect.

Another object stated in the preamble is, "to establish justice." Justice is it, that in God's bright world, in the noon of the nineteenth century, one man should take the child of another from the cradle and reduce him to life-long slavery? Justice is it, that one man should take the sister of another, and hold her upon the auction block, and auctioneer off her beauty? Justice is it, that one man should drive a hundred of his fellows into the cotton-field, in order that he himself may be enriched out of their unpaid toil? If that is justice, then, in the name of humanity, let wild anarchy commence its reign, and let us have something else than that form of justice. Oh, gentlemen, when the objects declared in the preamble of the Constitution of the United States shall be carried out, and when justice shall be established in this nation, there will go up a glad shout to Heaven from millions of slaves, rejoicing that the day of freedom has at last dawned for them.

Another object stated in that preamble is to "ensure domestic tranquillity." Why is the South untranquil now? Why dare she not let every man in this land go forth, speaking his free thoughts, over her hills and valleys? Why would she, if she were able, inflict upon me, for the utterance of these thoughts that I have spoken, the direst punishment that the wrath of her citizens could invent. Simply because she has an element in her society that renders freedom and domestic tranquillity impossible together; and she can only secure what to her appears to be quiet, (but which is, in fact, but sleeping over a volcano) by suppressing freedom of speech, by crushing out freedom of debate, by driving her John C. Underwoods from Va., and casting out the book of Frederick Douglass from Alabama, and driving from her borders every man of a free and faithful utterance; and so long as this element of slavery continues, her masters will continue to sleep with pistols under their bolsters, and as they go out in the night time or the day, the ghost of their own horrid system will conjure up among them fears and phantasies, and dread of insurrection, thick as the men of Roderick Dhu, in the brake, and the day will never come when they will have domestic tranquillity in the South, until slavery be abolished.

Having, in proceeding thus far with my argument, carried with me the law and the Constitution, I shall ask my opponent to-morrow night, he being a law-abiding and Constitution-loving man, to make a speech on my side of the question.

But I will not this evening go further in this argument, founded on the American Constitution, but turning from that point, I will give my attention for a few moments to the speech of my opponent. My reference to it shall be brief, for my friend tells me that he has not yet reached the main issue — and I was aware of it without his telling me. He being on the affirmative, I shall defer beginning anything like a serious reply to his speeches until he digs his way up within, at least some reasonable proximity of the question that we have come here to debate.

My friend has urged as authority in support of slavery — the Bible. When he shall bring forward his proof, then, if I am not able to meet it, and meet it successfully, I will give up my opposition to the institution of slavery. But I am not to be drawn into the ingeniously set trap of making a negative argument against a position which he simply declares, and does not deign to argue. Let him give us his argument, and then, if I do not meet it, you may say that I am unable to do so. He tells us that slavery has always existed. Sad as it may be to confess it, I have not the slightest disposition to deny it. So, since the day when Cain and Abel met unfortunately by the altar of God, and Cain raised his club and slew his brother, murder has always existed. But does that make it right?

Because a hoary wrong has, with stern and iron tread, walked down the line of centuries, crushing millions under its ponderous heel, does length of time baptize it with sacredness, make it innocent, and give it sanctity? or does it add by every revolving century and each rolling year and each diurnal revolution of the earth, the deeper damnation of a deeper condemnation to every age and hour of its outrageous existence!

Slavery is defended by the length of time which it has existed. Ay! and that length of time has projected the groan of humanity in one long wail down the stream of centuries, and it has gone up to God evermore crying for vengeance upon oppressors and the outragers of the poor; and though men may, by time, have become familiar with the crime, in Heaven's eye, it has not bated a jot nor tittle of its frightful mien since its introduction on the face of the earth.

My friend refers to Abraham as a slaveholder. When he tries to prove it I will meet his argument. He tells you that Babylon and Egypt were built by slaves. Yes! and when God Almighty, with the outstretched arm of his vengeance, thundered on Babylon in her iniquity, one of the reasons that the prophet gives why it was done, was that she dealt in "slaves and the souls of men." And Egypt now lies buried under the ruins of the same greatness which she builded by oppression, and the retributive waves of ages of vengeance have nearly buried her gigantic works of art built by slaves. God manifested his wrath for her slavery, when he once threw her king and his slave-catching hosts in the waves of the Red Sea, where "the horse and his rider" perished together!

My opponent tells us that slaves were held and are still held in Africa. The poor African, he tells us, after two hundred years of amelioration and cultivation under Southern piety, and plantation godliness, is not yet fit for freedom. Yet he refers us to the African in his darkness and heathenism centuries back as a model for us: we are to hold slaves because he did!

I pass over many of the points which I have noted, bearing on this Bible argument, because I shall pursue this subject further to-morrow evening.

The last half nearly of my friend's speech was taken up with abusing — no, I will not use that word — with saying hard things of Northern men and Northern society. It is unfortunate that in some of these hard things I shall be compelled to partly join with him. Of the scorn and indignation which he projects at New England slave-holders and slave-owners, and New York slave-holders and slave-traders, I take, so far as I am concerned for those States, my full share. But if New England was hypocritical in buying slaves and working slaves — if New York is to be hooted at and scorned for having been a slave-dealing and a slave-holding State a hundred years ago — what is to be said of Tennessee, that continues the practice in the noon of the nineteenth century. If New England and New York were hypocritical in stealing men from Africa to make them slaves, and selling them at the South, what has become of the old adage, that the "partaker is as bad as the thief." The man who buys stolen goods, knowing them to be stolen, lacking the enterprise and the courage to steal them himself, gets them into his hands in a lazier, but not a nobler way.

If Northern men have bowed in base and toadying subserviency to the spirit of villanous politics, the reason is to be found in the fact that the national capitol is on slave-holding territory; and the vilest slave-holding spirit, demoralizing as it does whatever it touches, has oftentimes overborne the bulwarks of Northern virtue. I shall charge the delinquencies of Northern men upon the seductions of American slavery as presented by the South; so,

"Lay on, Macduff,
And —"

I will not complete the sentence.

By every argument which proves that Northern men have bowed in cringing subserviency to American slavery, you prove that slavery is the spirit of ruffian tyranny, and holds such sway with its instrumentalities, as to destroy the virtue of such Northern men as come under its power. If Northern men have ever been sneaks, slavery has made them so. If Northern men have shown themselves lacking in virtue when they got to Congress, it was after they had been subjected to the corrupt influences with which they are surrounded by the South.

My friend tells us — of course it is of no account to the argument — that some Northern Abolitionists are so mean that they would steal the pewter ornament off the cane-head of the negro. Let me retort that the law of the South is so tyrannical that it permits the slave-holder to steal the negro, cane, and all!

Ladies and gentlemen! I thank you that you have given me, an unknown stranger, a patient hearing and a cordial reception; and I hope by to-morrow night my opponent will reach the heart of this question, and lead the way, so that the discussion may be made worthy of the audience, and worthy of the ponderous gravity of the subject under debate.

"OUGHT AMERICAN SLAVERY TO BE PERPETUATED?"

AFFIRMATIVE, II. — BY W. G. BROWNLOW

RESPECTED AUDITORS! It is usual, if it is not even an established rule in all scholastic discussions, that the respondent shall confine himself to the arguments of the affirmant, on whom the *onus probandi* rests. However, I am willing to overlook the *aberrations* observable in the truly *desultory* remarks of my worthy friend on yesterday evening, and for two good and sufficient reasons. First, in our correspondence, we agreed upon the largest liberty, in the way of a margin; and next, introductory speeches are usually more *general* than *special* in their character. I may be allowed to add, that not having been demolished by the rejoinder, I have no cause to repine. This I venture to say, without assuming the office of umpire in this debate. I hope the gentleman has recovered his composure after the discussion of yesterday evening. And if the *joints* of his *armor crack* under the power of the truth to-night, it shall not be my fault; nor his: but the fault of the *cause he advocates.*

In my remarks to-night I aim to consult the Holy Scriptures, to see whether or not they sustain or condemn the institution of slavery. The opposers of slavery profess to be governed alone by the teachings of the Bible, in their war upon the institution. My friend and competitor, being a Protestant minister, will endorse what the Bible teaches: we may differ when we come to *interpret* its teachings, and doubtless will, upon this grave subject!

It is vain to look to Christ or any of his Apostles to justify the blasphemous perversions of the word of God, continually paraded before the world by those graceless agitators known as Abolitionists. Although slavery in its most revolting forms was everywhere visible around them, no visionary notions of piety, or mad schemes of philanthropy, ever tempted either Christ or one of his Apostles to gainsay the LAW, even to mitigate the cruel severity of the slavery system then existing. On the contrary, finding slavery *established by law*, as well as an *inevitable and necessary consequence*, growing out of the condition of human society, their efforts were to sustain the institution. Hence St. Paul actually apprehended a "*fugitive slave*," and sent him home to his lawful owner, and earthly master!

I shall first appeal to the authority of the Old Testament Scriptures, before I appeal to the irresistible authority of the New Testament, where we learn that slavery existed in the earliest days of the Christian Church, and that both *masters* and *slaves* were members of the same Christian congregations. Slavery was an institution of the State, in the Roman empire, just as it is in the Southern States of this Confederacy; and the inspired Apostles, and first teachers of Christianity did not feel at liberty to denounce it, if, indeed, they felt the least opposition to it—a thing I utterly deny.

Listen to me while I read you some truly sensible passages from the Bible:

"And he said, I *am* Abraham's servant."—*Gen.* xxiv : 34.

"And there was of the house of Saul a *servant*, whose name was Ziba; and when they had called him unto David, the king said unto him, Art thou Ziba? And he said, *Thy servant is he.*"—2 *Sam.* ix : 2.

"Then the king called to Ziba, Saul's *servant*, and said unto him, I have given unto thy *master's* son all that pertained to Saul, and to all his house."—*Verse* 9th.

"Thou, therefore, and thy sons, and thy *servants*, shall till the land for him, and thou shall bring in *the fruits*, that thy *master's* son may have food to eat, &c. Now Ziba has fifteen sons and TWENTY SERVANTS."—*Verse* 10th.

"I got my *servants* and maidens, and had *servants born in my house;* also, I had great possessions of great and small cattle, above all that were in Jerusalem before me."—*Eccles.* ii : 7.

"And he said, Hagar, Sarai's maid, whence camest thou? And she said, I flee from the face of my *mistress* Sarai."—*Gen.* xvi : 8.

"And the Angel of the Lord said unto her, *Return to thy mistress*, and submit thyself to her hands."—*Verse* 9th.

I have but few comments to offer upon these passages from Holy Writ; still, I wish to impress upon your minds one or two points which you may overlook. First, then, one individual acknowledges himself to be the owner of 20 slaves! Another was raising slaves—acknowledges that he was a regular *slave breeder*—was having them born in his house, no doubt intending them for the *best market* he could find—and all this, mark you, was under the sanction of the Almighty! And last, but not least, the *Angel of God* arrested a fugitive slave and forced her to return to her lawful owner. High authority this, for apprehending *runaway negroes!* And when I tell you, as I now do, in all candor, that the Angel of God, on this occasion, was acting in the capacity of a *United States Marshal*, under the then existing fugitive slave laws of the Old Testament, and arresting a *fugitive slave*, the anti-slavery portion of you, either think me crazy, or guilty of a profanation of sacred things!

In reference to *bad* servants, we read in Prov. xxix : 19—

"A servant will not be corrected by *words;* for though he understand, he will not answer."

Here we are taught that a servant will not be corrected by *words*, and the inference is, that *stripes* must be inflicted. The Scriptures look to the correction of servants, and really enjoin it, as they do in the case of children. I esteem it the duty of Christian masters to feed and clothe their negroes well—to work them well, that is, constantly, but in moderation—and in cases of disobedience, to *whip well.* And upon this principle we proceed in the South! I may be inquired of to say whether I approve the cruelty exercised by masters and overseers in the South, and the starvation and nakedness displayed there — and whether or not the Scriptures tolerate this! I have to say in reply, that this cruelty, starvation, and nakedness, does not exist in the South, but in the disordered imaginations of Abolition preachers, travellers, and slanderers, who pass hurriedly through the South, getting up materials for book-making.

Born and raised in the South, I have lived there a half a century — I have travelled through all the Southern States but Florida and Texas, and to this good day I have never seen a negro whipped, hanged, or burned at the stake. I have seen negro children whipped, for disobedience, just as I have seen the white children corrected on the same premises! I have seen many negroes who deserved basting for their disobedience and bad conduct. *Madam Stowe*, in one brief tour through the South, was annoyed with the appalling vocabulary of "cruel overseer," "unfeeling driver," "clanking chains," &c., but I, who have travelled through these States for thirty years, visiting cotton and sugar plantations, have never met with anything of the kind!

In the book of Joel iii: 8, the *slave trade* is even recognized as of Divine authority:

> "And I will sell your sons and your daughters into the land of the children of Judah, and they shall sell them to the Sabeans, to the people far off; FOR THE LORD HATH SPOKEN IT!"

DR. CLARKE informs us in his comments on this passage, that as many as *thirty thousand* of these people were *sold* into bondage—first to the children of Judah, and then to the Sabeans, or *Arabs*, a people far off! The geography of the country shows that they removed them about as far from their kindred and friends, as we do our negroes when we drive them from *Virginia* and the *Carolinas*, to *Alabama*, *Mississippi*, and *Louisiana!*

But I now appeal to the irresistible authority of the New Testament:

> "Let every man abide in the same calling wherein he was called. Art thou called, being *a servant?* Care not for it; but if thou mayest be made free, use it rather. For he that is called in the Lord, being *a servant*, is the Lord's freeman;

likewise also he that is called, being free, is Christ's servant." 1 *Cor.* vii: 20–22.

"*Servants*, be obedient them that are your *masters according to the flesh*, with fear and trembling, in singleness of your heart, as unto Christ. Not with eye-service, as men-pleasers; but as the servants of Christ, doing the will of God from the heart. With good-will doing service, as to the Lord, and not to men: knowing that whatsoever good thing any man doeth, the same shall he receive of the Lord, whether he be bond or free. And, *ye masters*, do the same things unto them, forbearing threatening: knowing that your Master also is in heaven: neither is there respect of persons with him."— *Eph.* vi: 5–9.

"*Servants*, obey in all things your *masters according to the flesh:* not with eye-service, as men-pleasers; but in singleness of heart, fearing God. And whatsoever ye do, do it heartily, as to the Lord, and not unto men: knowing that of the Lord ye shall receive the reward of the inheritance; for ye serve the Lord Christ."—*Col.* iii: 22–25.

"*Masters*, give unto *your servants* that which is just and equal: knowing that ye also have a Master in heaven."—*Col.* iv: 1.

"Let as many *servants as are under the yoke* count their *own masters* worthy of all honor, that the name of God and his doctrines be not blasphemed. And they that have *believing masters*, let them not despise them, because they are brethren; but rather to do them service, because they are faithful and beloved, partakers of the benefit. These things teach and exhort."—1 *Tim.* vi: 1, 2.

"Exhort *servants* to be obedient unto their *own masters*, and to please them well in all things; not answering again; nor purloining, but showing all good fidelity; that they may adorn the doctrine of God our Saviour and all things."—*Titus* ii: 9, 10.

"*Servants*, be subject to *your masters* with all fear; not only to the good and gentle, but also to the froward. For this is thankworthy, if a man for conscience toward God endure grief, suffering wrongfully."—1 *Peter* ii: 18, 19.

I have but a few words of comment to offer upon these passages of Scripture. The original words used by the Greek, both sacred and profane, to express *slave*—the most abject condition of slavery—to express the *absolute owner* of a slave, and the *absolute control* of a slave — are the strongest that the language affords, and are used in the passages I have quoted. If the inspired Apostles understood — if they knew what they were talking about, and desired to convey these ideas, and to recognize the relations of *master* and *slave*, they would naturally enough employ the very words they used. To say that they did not know the primary meaning and *usus loquendi* of the original words, is paying them a compliment I have no wish to participate in!

There is one other strong point I wish to make in this controversy. Christ says of a Roman Centurion, upon his confession to him that he held slaves, "*I have not seen so great faith, no, not in Israel.*" The Centurion, mark it, was a *Roman* Centurion, not a *Jew*, and held slaves under the Roman law, that admitted of enormities and excesses before which the worst features of "*American Slavery*" appear but as tender mercies, when compared with their diabolical cruelties. Still Christ, by this act, although he condemned injustice and cruelty, acknowledged and established the fact that a man could be a Christian and yet hold slaves, even under the tenor of the law that admitted of so great enormities. Should not, therefore, every unbiassed mind come to the conclusion, that anti-slavery men of the North, who are *no better* than Christ and his Apostles, ought not to attempt to exclude Christian Tennessee, Georgia, Alabama, &c., from the kingdoms of grace and glory, who live under, and hold slaves under a far more human and Christian law, governing the institution of slavery!

But, to show that I am not singular in my views of the meaning expressed in the passages quoted—showing that they express in one case *slaves*, and in the other *masters* or *owners*, actually holding them as *property*, under the sanction of the laws of the State, I quote from the following *distinguished* authorities.

That great commentator, DR. ADAM CLARKE, on 1 Cor. vii. 21, says:

> "Art thou converted to Christ while thou art a slave—the property of another person, and bought with his money? *Care not for it.*"

The learned DR. NEANDER, in his work entitled "Planting and Training the Church," in referring to *Onesimus*, mentioned in the Epistle to Philemon, says of him:

> "It does not appear to be at all surprising that a *runaway slave* should betake himself at once to Rome."

The gentleman who follows me in this debate, knows very well that to the foregoing I might add any number of authorities, of equal weight and importance.

Historians all agree that slavery existed, and was general throughout the Roman empire, at the time the Apostolic Churches were instituted. I have at my command the authorities to prove this; but no well-informed gentleman will expose himself by calling the fact in question. I will cite the authorities only; and Abolitionists denying my position can examine for themselves. See Gibbon's "Decline and Fall of the Roman Empire," vol. i. See "Inquiry into Roman

Slavery," by Wm. Blair, Edinburg edition of 1833. See vol. iv. of "Lardner's Works," p. 213. See vol. i. of "Dr. Robertson's Works," London edition.

These authorities, if consulted, show that slavery was a civil institution of the State; that the Roman laws held slaves as *property*, at the disposal of their *masters;* that the slaves, whether white or black, had no civil rights or existence, and contended for none; and that there were, throughout the empire, *three slaves to one citizen*—showing an exact similarity between the Roman empire and the tobacco, cotton, and sugar-growing States of this Confederacy! Gibbon says that "slavery existed in every province and every family," and that they were bought and sold according to their capacities for usefulness, and the demand for labor—selling for hundreds of dollars, and from that down to the price of a beast of burden!

Now, it is notorious that the Gospel made considerable progress among the citizens of the Roman empire; and, as every family owned slaves, it follows that slaveholders were converted to God, and admitted into the Church. It will not do to allege, as some anti-slavery men do, that the *poor*, including the *slaves*, were alone converted to God, because the apostles make frequent allusions to the receiving into the Church of intelligent, learned, professional, and opulent persons. The learned DR. MOSHEIM, in his "Church History," vol. i., relating to the *first three centuries*, settles this question. He says:

"The apostles, in their writings, prescribe rules for the conduct of the rich as well as the poor, for *masters* as well as *servants*—a convincing proof that among the members of the Church planted by them were to be found persons of opulence and masters of families. St. Paul and St. Peter admonished Christian women not to study the adorning of themselves with pearls, with gold and silver, or costly array. 1 Tim. ii. 9; 1 Peter iii. 3. It is, therefore, plain that there must have been women possessed of wealth adequate to the purchase of bodily ornaments of great price. From 1 Tim. vi. 20, and Col. ii. 8, it is manifest that, among the first converts to Christianity, there were men of learning and philosophers; for, if the wise and the learned had unanimously rejected the Christian religion, what occasion could there have been for this caution? 1 Cor. i. 26 unquestionably carries with it the plainest intimation that persons of rank or power were not wholly wanting in that assembly. Indeed, lists of the names of the various illustrious persons who embraced Christianity, in its weak and infantile state, are given by Blondel, p. 235 De Episcopis et Presbyteris; also by Wetstein, in his Preface to Origen's Dia. Con. Mar., p. 18."

This is an important argument; for it is safe to go to Christ and his inspired apostles to learn the truth in reference to slavery. In concluding what I term my scriptural argument in favor of the institution of slavery, I desire to present for the consideration of the gentleman who replies to me, *Five Points*, which I hold to be legitimate deductions from what has gone before. His Church relations have acquainted him with the "Five Points of Calvinism," and his local habitation in the Empire State has made him familiar with the "Five Points in New York," where the degradation of free white and colored persons falls far below the degradation of the slaves in any portion of the South. But I will present him with *Five Points*, in the close of this scriptural argument, which he may characterize the FIVE POINTS OF THE SOUTH.

First Point.—There is not a single passage in the New Testament, nor a single act in the records of the Church, during her early history, for even centuries, containing any direct, professed, or *intended* denunciation of slavery. The apostles found the institution existing, under the authority and sanction of law; and, in their labors among the people, *masters* and *slaves* bowed at the same altar, communed at the same table, and were taken into the same church together—the apostles exhorting the one to treat the other as became the Gospel, and the other to obedience and honesty, that their religious profession might not be evil spoken of!

Secondly.—The early Church of Christ, not only admitted the existence of slavery, but in various ways, by her teachings and discipline, expressed her *approbation* of it, enforcing the observance of certain "*Fugitive Slave Laws,*" which had been enacted by the State. And in the various acts of the Church, from the times of the Apostles downward, through several centuries, she enacted laws and adopted regulations, touching the duties of masters and slaves, *as such.* This, apart from all other considerations, amounts to a justification and defence of the institution of slavery.

Thirdly.—My investigations of the subject have led me to where similar investigations must lead all candid and unprejudiced men—namely, to the conclusion that God intended the relation of master and slave to exist, both in and out of his Church. Hence, when God opened the way for the organization of the Church, the Apostles and first teachers of Christianity found slavery *incorporated with every department of society;*

and, in the adoption of rules for the government of the members of the church, they provided for the *rights* of owners, and the *wants* of slaves.

Fourthly. — Slavery, in the days of the Apostles, had so penetrated society, and was so intimately interwoven with it, that a religion *preaching freedom to the slave*, would have arrayed against it the civil authorities, armed against itself the whole power of the State, and destroyed the usefulness of its preachers. St. Paul knew this, and did not assail the institution of slavery, but labored to get both masters and slaves to heaven, as all ministers should do. That St. Paul was himself *favorable* to slave-holding, is manifest from the fact, that in the case of the *runaway slave* he apprehended, he modestly asked the wealthy owner for the slave, for his own domestic purposes!

Fifthly. — Slavery having existed ever since the first organization of the Church, the Scriptures clearly teach that it will exist to the end of time. Rev. vi. 12–17 points to "The Day of Judgment," "The Last Day," "The Great Day," and the condition of the human race at that time, as well as the *classes of persons* to be judged, rewarded, and punished! A portion of this text reads:

> "And the kings of the earth, and the great men, and the rich men, and the mighty men, and every *bondman*, and every *freeman*," etc.

will be there; clearly implying that slavery will exist, and that the relations of *master* and *slave* will be recognized, to the end of time!

These sacred truths stand in the face of all our

Abolition priests, to teach them the two following moral lessons:

First. — That all the finer feelings of humanity were cherished in the bosoms of slave-owners — and that devout slave-owners received no rebuke from the lips of the Redeemer for holding their slaves in bondage; yet, according to Abolition Christianity, they were guilty of "*the accursed sin of slavery.*"

Second. — That the bonds of the slave may provoke the wrath of the Abolitionist, but not of the Redeemer — who smiles alike on the devout master and the pious slave, having prepared for each a place in Heaven!

Abraham, called the father of the faithful, and the friend of God and man, was a large slave-holder, and, upon his death bed, bequeathed his slaves unto his son Isaac; and yet, the angel of God stood by the couch of the dying patriarch, cheering his expiring moments with the certain, but then anticipated joys of paradise!

And Paul! the inspired preacher, whose spirit was caught up to the third Heaven, and heard things it was not lawful to utter — yes, Paul! who endured stripes and imprisonment, who was stoned and beaten with rods, who was ofttimes in perils, on the waters, in the wilderness, among robbers, among false brethren, who endured weariness and painfulness, and hunger, and thirst, and cold, and weakness — Paul! who received just such a *salary* as this for preaching the gospel to the slaves and slave-holders in Rome, had no heart to pity the bonds of *Onesimus!* On the contrary, he chided him for absconding from his master, and bid him ask pardon of his God for going off upon "an underground railroad!" This is not all that Paul was guilty of—after arresting *Onesimus*, and returning him to his rich master, he accosted that master as *his dearly beloved brother!*

It will not be charged that Paul had *fallen from grace*, and therefore became the advocate of slavery. He was translated to the third Heaven *before* he taught the masters and slaves of Rome their moral obligations, but *after* this, he died a most triumphant death, and declared that he had fought the good fight, and *kept* the faith, as well in reference to slavery as other vital questions.

Moses received his divine authority on the Mount, *before* he wrote the law of bondage for the poor in Israel. And upon the precepts of the Patriarchs and Apostles, we rest our hopes for the present and eternal felicity of the masters and slaves of the South.

But, a strange star has appeared in the North, ominous of a more merciful dispensation to the slave than that which appeared in Bethlehem of Judea! And, twinkling over the dwellings of that holy band of Priests, who denounced the Fugative Slave-Bill of congress in terms of rebellious indignation in the house of God;—and applying *forty parson power* to the present Chief Magistrate, touching the Kansas question, a voice is now to be heard in the New England heavens, saying, "Lo! these—these holy priests are the friends of the colored race, and not the Saviour and his Apostles!"

But I am to be told, for this is the argument of Abolitionism, that "*American Slavery*" differs in *form* and *principle* from that of the chosen people of God, as set forth in the Bible. On behalf of the South, I accept the Bible terms as the definition of our slavery, and its precepts as the guide of our conduct.

We desire nothing more — we will not be satisfied with anything less. To be candid, the South has fashioned her form of slavery after that in the Bible. Even the right to "buffet," which is esteemed so shocking to Abolitionists, finds its express license in the gospel. We are there taught to take it patiently, when, as servants, we are "*buffeted for our faults.*" 1 Peter, ii. 20. Nay, what is stronger, God directs the Hebrews to "*bore holes in the ears of their brothers,*" to *mark* them, when, under certain circumstances, they become *perpetual slaves.* The master is told, in the Mosaic law of bondage, to confine his slaves to the door-post, and there to bore his ears through with an *awl,* as the mark of *perpetual slavery.* Exodus, xxi. 6. We have never gone this far at the South; though, in all material respects, we have fashioned our system after that laid down in the Bible.

American slavery is not only not sinful, but especially commanded by God through Moses, and approved through the Apostles by Christ. And I might conclude its defence by asserting that what God ordains, and Christ sanctifies, should command the respect and toleration of even Northern Abolitionists. But I will remark, while on this subject, that the *selling* of bondmen, by and among the Hebrews, was authorized by the law of Moses, and the practice was in vogue before the giving of the law. In the *new* law given from Sinai, the practice of selling *white brethren,* Hebrews, was forbidden, but they were allowed to make merchandise of the Canaanites, the *negro descendants of Ham,* then the aborigines of old Canaan. The Hebrews were allowed to sell one another at home, but not to sell each other to *strangers;* but *heathen negroes,* they were allowed to buy and sell — to traffic in them as articles of trade and commerce, driving them to the best slave markets they could find. See Exodus, xxi. 7; and Leviticus, xxv. 42.

But to make the fact still more clear, namely, that the Hebrews did deal in slaves of the *negro race,* see the Book of JOEL, 3d chapter, where we learn that the people of Tyre and Sidonia sold their little ones at drinking-houses for *wine*—separating infants from their mothers. I claim that the statutes of the Southern States are more *lenient* than the laws of Moses, because they protect the slaves against these *Israelitish* cruelties. See Bouvier's Law Dictionary, under the head of "Cruelty to Slaves." I quote from that book: "By the civil code of Louisiana, Act 192, it is enacted, that when a master shall be convicted of cruel treatment to his slave, the judge may pronounce, *beside* the penalty established for such cases, that the slave shall be sold at public auction, in order to place him out of the reach of the power of his master who has abused him." I quote from the New York Herald, March 15, 1856, a statement I know to be true: — "A man named *Hunter* has been fined $1000, and forfeited six slaves, at New Orleans, for selling them in such a manner as to separate *mother* and *child,* contrary to the laws of Louisiana."

Thus it will be seen, that we have laws to protect slaves in the South, laws to punish cruelty, and they are enforced. And though I am not expected to quote "line upon line, and precept upon precept, here a little, and there a little," I will take occasion to say, once for all, that similar laws exist in all the Slave States!

As to the law of Moses authorizing the slave traffic, it was in force in America, and carried on chiefly by Northern men, until Congress passed a law in 1807, which took effect January 1st, 1808, declaring it to be *piracy*, and punishing it with fine and imprisonment. Twenty years previously, whilst the Constitution of our country was being formed, a committee, a majority of whom were from *Slave States*, reported a section authorizing Congress to abolish the trade after the year 1800; but this was zealously opposed by the Northern States, and the period was extended until 1808; thus giving eight additional years to the "inhuman traffic," by the votes of *New Hampshire*, *Massachusetts*, and *Connecticut*, while the votes of the South, including *Virginia*, were against such extension. Thus the trade was continued eight years longer than it should have been, by the votes of men from *New England*, who considered it their duty to guard the commercial interests of their *pious constituents!* And what were legitimate articles of commerce in those days, with which ships sailing from New England ports bought Africans in their own country? I answer, gunpowder, guns, trinkets, beads, looking-glasses, tobacco, segars, and New England *rum*. Slaves, in those days, and at different times, were advertised to be exchanged for these articles, in the *Boston* papers!

But I am to be told that among the peculiarities of "American Slavery" are these: slaves are placed upon the block at the South, and sold to the highest bidder—that they are abused in "slave-pens, in cotton-fields, among cotton-gins, and in the rice swamps of the South." And I am to be told that abuse of power and authority, such as may be seen at the auction-blocks and whipping-posts of the South, is a part and parcel of our system of slavery, and *inseparable* from it. I deny the truth of this assertion. Power is not always abused. All masters do not abuse their slaves —a small proportion do, and therefore abuse is *separable* from our system of slavery. In the *Creole* settlements of Louisiana, there are a few slave-owners who are cruel, but these are neither *Protestants*, nor *native* Americans. In our cotton-growing States, our hardest task-masters are *Northern* men, by birth and education! Bad men abuse negroes; good men do not. And in all cases, the abuse arises from the character and disposition of the master, and not from the system.

If the principle were a correct one, that it is proper to pronounce and treat as *sinful*, everything that has been abused, we should soon undermine the foundation upon which society rests, and destroy the harmony of every relation that God has instituted. The relation of our lawgivers and judges has been abused. The marriage relation has been abused. The blessed Bible has been abused. The Sabbath has been abused. The truths of Christianity have been abused. And nowhere in this country have these things been more shamefully abused, than north of Mason and Dixon's Line! Shall we then pronounce all these sacred relations and institutions sinful, and treat them as such? We *ought not*, and we *will not;* therefore, we *should not*, on the ground of its abuse by a few men, pronounce and treat as sinful, the relation and position of a slaveholder in the South!

A correct idea of the real treatment of slaves in the South, may be gathered from the "Advice, Orders, and Instructions" of our large slave-owners. I will read you some extracts from a small pamphlet, of fifteen pages, the title-page of which runs thus:

"*Advice, Orders, and Instructions for the Management, Government, and Guidance of the General Agent, Overseers, and Employees, on the Plantations of* JOSEPH A. S. ACKLEN, *situate in the Parish of West Feliciana, in the State of Louisiana, opposite the mouth of Red River.*"

MR. ACKLEN is a wealthy planter, and owns several plantations, which are well stocked with negroes, and to each overseer he gives a copy of this pamphlet, and requires him to follow its teachings, to the letter. Hear what is said:

"Punishment must never be cruel or abusive, for it is absolutely mean and unmanly to whip a negro from mere passion and malice, and any man who can do so, is utterly unfit to have control of negroes."

"My negroes are all permitted to come to me or my agent with their complaints, and in no instance *shall* they be punished for so doing; and in my absence, I enjoin it upon my agent to attend to their complaints, and examine them, and if they have been cruelly or inhumanly treated, the overseer *must be at once discharged.*"

"Feel, and show that you feel, a kind and considerate regard for the negroes under your control. Never cruelly punish them, nor overwork them, or otherwise abuse them, but seek to render their situation as comfortable and contented as possible: see that their necessities be supplied; that their food and clothing be good and sufficient; their houses comfortable; and be kind and attentive to them in sickness and in old age.

"See that the negroes are regularly fed, and that their

food is wholesome, nutritious and well cooked, and that they keep themselves clean. At least once in every week, visit each of their houses, and see that they have been swept out and cleaned; examine their bedding, &c., and see that they have been well aired, their clothes mended, and everything attended to which conduces to their comfort and happiness.

"If any of the negroes have been reported sick, without delay see what ails them, and that proper medicine and attendance are given.

"The regularly appointed minister for my places must preach on Sundays during daylight.

"Christianity, humanity and order improve and elevate all, and injure none; whilst infidelity, selfishness and disorder curse some, delude others, and degrade all. I want all my people encouraged to cultivate religious feelings and morality, and punished for inhumanity to their children or stock, for profanity, lying or thieving."

This is not an *isolated* case by any means, but these and similar regulations govern all the large slave plantations in the South. Do they not compare favorably with the treatment of white slaves at the North? I think so. Nor is it at all strange that most of our fugitive slaves, after a short residence in a free State, desire to return to bondage again! Hear the following items, which are only so many out of hundreds of similar cases, constantly occurring:

"RETURNED TO SLAVERY.—The Hartford (Connecticut) Times gives an account of Caroline Banks and her children, and Mary Francis, slaves lately liberated by their mistress, (Mrs. Sarah Branch, of Chesterfield, Va.,) who have voluntarily returned to bondage, after trying to support themselves in Boston as free people. They declared that they have toiled constantly and could scarcely gain a subsistence, and wanted a master to protect them."—*South Carolinian.*

"A VOLUNTARY SLAVE.—Instances of this kind are becoming more and more numerous every day.—We clip from the *Frontier (Texas) News* of the 3d July, 1858.

"While in attendance on the District Court, in Tarrant county, one day of the previous week, I witnessed the ceremonies, on the occasion of a free negro voluntarily going into slavery. He came into court cheerfully, and there stated in answer to questions propounded by the court, that he knew the consequence of the act—that he had selected as his master W. M. Robinson, without any compulsion or persuasion, but of his own free will and accord. Two gentlemen came in and stated under oath that they had signed his petition at his request, and that the gentleman he had selected as his master, was a good citizen and an honorable man, &c. Jerry is a fine looking negro, some forty years of age, and appears to be smart."

"PREFER SLAVERY.—A negro man, who had been emancipated by his master's will, voluntarily re-entered servitude on Monday last, preferring the condition of a slave to that of removal to a free State. He selected Mr. Huckstep as his future master. His value was assessed at $650, one-half of which amount Mr. Huckstep has to pay into the State treasury."—*Charlottsville (Va.) Advocate.*

"PETITION FOR VOLUNTARY ENSLAVEMENT,

"IN CHANCERY AT ROGERSVILLE, TENNESSEE.

"*Ben, a man of color, and William Miller, Esq.*

"NOTICE is hereby given that Ben, a man of color, has this day filed his Petition in our said Court, asking to become the slave of the said Miller, under an act of the General Assembly of said State, passed the 8th day of March, 1858.

"R. C. FAIN, C. & M."

"*May* 29*th*, 1858."

I am personally acquainted with the parties in the last of the several cases here named, as well as with the clerk and master in chancery—they reside about 75 miles from where I do. I reside in East Tennessee, a section of the State comprising 30 counties—I have resided there for 30 years, and 20 years of that time I have been the editor of a public journal, having quite a large circulation. I only name this fact to show that I have some little acquaintance there. I feel warranted in the assertion that *one-half* of all the negro slaves in East Tennessee, would refuse their freedom to-day, if tendered to them, no matter under what circumstances. And fully *two-thirds* would refuse to be set at liberty, if required to leave the State!

Now, I hold this truth to be self-evident, that whatever improves the moral, mental and physical condition of a people, is a blessing to them, and ought to be "perpetuated." That slavery *has* improved the moral mental, and physical condition of the negroes enslaved, must be evident to every one who compares the condition of the southern slaves with the free negroes of the North, and of the West India Islands, to say nothing of the natives of Africa. Nay, more, slavery, only, can elevate the negro race from their state of pristine barbarism; the continuation of slavery is absolutely necessary to prevent the civilized negroes of the South from relapsing into their old savage state, in which the slaveholders at first found them.

The negroes of Africa are among the most degraded of the colored race. They subsist principally upon the spontaneous productions of the forest. They have no knowledge of agriculture, architecture, the mechanic arts, or any of those arts and sciences which tend to elevate and expand the intellect, and secure the rational enjoyments of life. The light of Divine truth has never pierced their benighted minds; the feeble operation of their reason has not even revealed to them a glimmering of the existence of a God; and worshipping stones, insects, and reptiles, their moral character is in harmony with the grovelling objects of their adoration. Fierce and cruel, cowardly and treacherous, ignorant and lascivious — they are engaged in constant wars, burning their enemies at the stake, and feeding on their flesh — whole tribes in abject slavery — it is not to be wondered at that intelligent travellers have been led to class them as a superior species of the monkey tribe!

Turn from this loathsome picture of brutalized humanity, to the sunny plains of the South, the land of the olive and the vine, where the great ruler of the universe has covered the earth with tropical fruits, and what do we see? We behold hundreds of thousands of industrious, civilized laborers, clothed in the garb of civilization, eating the bread of contentment, produced by their own labor, under the supervision of *Caucasian* intelligence and *Christian* benevolence, and increasing in numbers with a rapidity, which clearly indicates that their physical condition is superior to that of any other servile laborers on earth!

Revelation has risen, full-orbed, and shines in a burst of glory on the benighted minds of our Southern slaves, chasing away the gloom of superstition. Scarcely a Sabbath rolls round, but hundreds of thousands of Southern slaves, listen to the glad tidings of the Gospel, and hundreds of thousands of them have attached themselves to the Church of Christ. There are as many slaves within the fold of the Church in the South, in proportion to the population, as there are white persons, if not more!

Connected with the Methodists, are......	200,000
Missionary and Hard-Shell Baptists......	170,000
Old and New School Presbyterians.......	18,000
Cumberland Presbyterians.................	20,000
Episcopalians	7,000
All other sects combined....................	26,000
Methodists in Virginia and Maryland, included in the Northern Methodist Church	25,000
Total Colored members in the South.....	466,000

When in Mobile last winter, I assisted the venerable BISHOP KAVANAGH in the Sabbath services, at *one* of the several African churches in that city. It was a large brick church — not fine, but substantial, and seated 1500 persons. It cost $7000 and $6000 of that was contributed by the slaves themselves, who have a membership in that congregation of 700. They were well dressed, and spiritual in their devotions, turning to the pages in their Hymn Books when announced from the pulpit. I there saw pious slaves rejoicing around the altar with their wealthy masters, and the good Bishop! I have seen the same in Savannah, Macon, Memphis, Nashville, Charleston, Richmond, Huntsville, and in the city where I reside; and in most of these I have preached to the slaves. And if, at any time, I have found fault with the colored congregations in the South, it has been because of their extravagance in dress, and the wearing of an excess of *jewellery*, and of the fluttering gew-gaws worn by your fine ladies in Philadelphia!

Do the Anti-Slavery clergy of the North — does my Reverend Abolition competitor — see nothing in all this, for which to thank God? Millions of dollars have been spent, and hundreds of valuable lives sacrificed in the attempt to evangelize the negroes of Africa, and yet *slavery*—the abhorred, cursed, and reviled institution of slavery—has brought five times more negroes into the fold of the Church than all the missionary operations of the world combined. Slavery has tamed, civilized, *Christianized*, if you please, the brutal negroes brought to our shores, by New England *kidnappers;* it has elevated them physically, mentally; morally, and therefore it has proven a blessing to them, and ought to be "*perpetuated.*"

The sinless spirits that surround God's throne to-day, who are transported with all the ecstasy of an overwhelming affection, and bend themselves in rapturous adoration at the shrine of infinite and unspotted holiness; and behold with heavenly fascination the moral beauty of slavery, which even throws a softening lustre over the awfulness of the Godhead; those pure and holy spirits, whose sinless existence lies in the knowledge and admiration of Deity; and who see sin in all its malignity, and salvation in all its mysterious greatness, look down with delight upon what slavery is doing for the African race! Oh! with what desire do they ponder on God's ways, when, amidst the urgency of all demands, which look so high and indispensable, they see the unfolding of the attribute of mercy, and the Supreme Lawgiver bending upon the abject African race an eye of tenderness, and in his profound and unsearchable wisdom, devising for them the institution of slavery, as a plan of restoration; the everlasting Son, moving from his dwelling-place in heaven, to carry it forward through all the difficulties by which it is encompassed; and by the virtue of his mysterious sacrifice, magnifying the glory of every other perfection; making mercy triumph over them all, and throwing open a way by which the polluted African (with the whole lustre of the divine character untarnished) may be re-admitted into fellowship with God, and be again brought back within the circle of his loyal and affectionate family. Who would have thought it! The wonder-working God, who has strewed the field of immensity with so many worlds, and who would shatter them to atoms, before his truth or holiness should undergo the least suspicion of a stain; comes down to dwell with man, and by his wisdom, with the fragments of a different chaos, (the wreck of rebellion) brings light, life, harmony, and salvation, to the African race, through the mild and benignant institution of slavery! O Lord God! thou art great in counsel! Thou art the wonderful Counsellor!

But I go further. While I hold, and I think I have proven, that the condition of Southern negroes has been vastly improved by slavery; I also assert, without fear of successful contradiction, that slavery, only, could have worked that improvement, and that the preservation of the relation of master and slave is essential to the continued improvement and future welfare of the negro race of the South. I assert that "American Slavery" is a blessing; a blessing to the master, a blessing to the non-slave-holders of the South, a blessing to the civilized white race in general, and a blessing to the negro slaves in particular.

To prove this I bring forward the testimony of

Abolitionists *against* slavery. In their zeal to cast odium on slavery, the Abolitionists prove everything in favor of the "peculiar institution;" for they prove that the slaves of America are the only negroes to be found who are really contented, comfortable and happy. The *American Missionary Association*, in their seventh Annual Report, for 1853, at page 49, says:

"The number of missionaries and teachers in Canada, with which the year commenced, has been greatly reduced. Early in the year, Mr. Kirkland wrote to the Committee, that the opposition to white missionaries, manifested by the colored people of Canada, had so greatly increased, by the interested misrepresentations of ignorant colored men, pretending to be ministers of the Gospel, that he thought his own and his wife's labors, and the funds of the Association, could be better employed elsewhere."

Next in order, I call your attention to the *Annual Report of the American and Foreign Anti-Slavery Society*, for 1853, which discourses thus:

"The friends of emancipation in the United States have been disappointed in some respects at the results in the West Indies, because they expected too much. A nation of slaves cannot at once be converted into a nation of intelligent, industrious, and moral freemen. — It is not too much, even now, to say of the people of Jamaica, their condition is exceedingly degraded, their morals wofully corrupt. But this must by no means be understood to be of universal application. With respect to those who have been brought under a healthful educational and religious influence, *it is not true.* But as respects the great mass, whose humanity has been ground out of them by cruel oppression — whom no good Samaritan hand has yet reached—how could it be otherwise? We wish to turn the tables; to supplant oppression by righteousness, insult by compassion and brotherly-kindness, hatred and contempt by love and winning meekness, till we allure these wretched ones to the hope and enjoyment of manhood and virtue. — The means of education and religious instruction are better enjoyed, although but little appreciated and improved by the great mass of the people. It is also true, that the moral sense of the people is becoming somewhat enlightened. But while this is true, yet their moral condition is very far from being what it ought to be. It is exceedingly dark and distressing. Licentiousness prevails to a most alarming extent among the people. The almost universal prevalence of intemperance is another prolific source of the moral darkness and degradation of the people. The great mass, among all classes of the inhabitants, from the Governoı in his palace to the peasant in his hut — from the Bishop in his gown to the beggar in his rags — are all slaves to their cups."

To strengthen the charges made by American Abolitionists, I add the following from the London *Times*, of the same date. In speaking of the results of emancipation in Jamaica, it says:

"The negro has not acquired with his freedom any habits of industry or morality. His independence is but little better than that of an uncaptured brute. Having accepted few of the restraints of civilization, he is amenable to few of its necessities; and the wants of his nature are so easily satisfied, that at the current rate of wages, he is called upon for nothing but fitful or desultory exertion. The blacks, therefore, instead of becoming intelligent husbandmen, have become vagrants and squatters, and it is now apprehended that with the failure of cultivation in the island will come the failure of its resources for instructing or controlling its population. So imminent does this consummation appear, that memorials have been signed by classes of colonial society hitherto standing aloof from politics, and not only the bench and the bar, but the bishop, clergy, and ministers of all denominations in the island, without exceptions, have recorded their conviction, that, in the absence of timely relief, the religious and educational institutions of the island must be abandoned, and the masses of the population retrograde to barbarism."

MR. BIGLOW, editor of the New York *Evening Post*, a few years ago spent the winter in Jamaica, and in noticing the decline in the Agriculture of the Island, and the quantity of lands thrown out of cultivation, he says:

"This decline has been going on from year to year, daily becoming more alarming, until at length the island has reached what would appear to be the last profound of distress and misery, when thousands of people do not know, when they rise in the morning, whence or in what manner they are to procure bread for the day."

GOVERNOR WOOD, of Ohio, on his way to Valparaiso, in 1853, thus describes what he witnessed at Kingston, Jamaica, while the steamer remained in that port:

"We saw many plantations, the buildings dilapidated — fields of sugar-cane half-worked and apparently poor, and nothing but that which will grow without the labor of man, appeared luxuriant and flourishing. The island itself is of great fertility, one of the best of the Antilles; but all the large estates upon it are now fast going to ruin. In the harbor were not a dozen ships of all nations — no business was doing, and everything you heard spoken was in the language of complaint. Since the blacks have been liberated they have become indolent, insolent, degraded, and dishonest. They are a rude, beastly set of vagabonds, lying naked about the streets, as filthy as the Hottentots, and, I believe, worse."

BISHOP KIP, of the Episcopal Church, on his way to California, in 1853, bears this testimony as to what he witnessed at the same port, while the steamer stopped to take in coal:

"The streets are crowded with the most wretched-looking negroes to be seen on the face of the earth. Lazy, shiftless and diseased, they will not work, since the manumission act has freed them. Even coaling the steamer is done by women. About a hundred march on board in a line with tubs on their heads (tubs and coal together weighing about 90 pounds), and with a wild song empty them into the hold. The men work a day, and then live on it a week. The depth of degradation to which the negro population has sunk, is, we are told, indescribable."

But here is a portion of a letter from *Gerritt Smith* to Gov. HUNT of New York, in 1852. My friend *Mr. Pryne* assisted, but the other day, in a "Liberty Party" Convention at Syracuse, in nominating Mr. Smith for Governor. Speaking of his ineffectual labors in trying to prevail on the free colored people to betake themselves to mechanical and agricultural pursuits, he says:

"Suppose, moreover, that, during all these fifteen years, they had been quitting the cities, *where the mass of them rot both physically and morally*, and had gone into the country to become farmers and mechanics — suppose, I say, all this —and who would have the hardihood to affirm that the Colonization Society lives upon the malignity of the whites—but it is true that it lives upon *voluntary degradation of the blacks.* I do not say that the colored people are more debased than white people would be if persecuted, oppressed, and outraged as are the colored people. But I do say that they are debased, deeply debased; and that to recover themselves they must become heroes, self-denying heroes, capable of achieving a great moral victory — a two-fold victory — a victory over themselves and a victory over their enemies."

So says Gerritt Smith, Mr. Pryne's Liberty candidate for Governor of New York! So says the great apostle of Northern Abolitionism, to whom my competitor expects to be consigned after death, labelled "*right side up with care!*"

I conclude my testimony on this point with an extract from the speech in the Canadian Parliament, but recently, by COL. PRINCE, an Englishman educated in all the Anti-Slavery prejudices peculiar to the English school. I copy from the New York *Day-Book*, foı July 17, 1858:

"Hon. Col. Prince said he was wishful to move a rider to the measure. The black people who infested the land were the greatest curse to the Province. The lives of the people of the West were made wretched by the inundation of these animals; and many of the largest farmers of the county of Kent had been compelled to leave their beautiful farms, because of the pestilential, swarthy swarms. What were these wretches fit for? Nothing. They cooked our victuals and shampooned us; but who would not rather that these duties should be performed by white men? The blacks were a worthless, useless, thriftless set of beings. They were too indolent, lazy, and ignorant to work, too proud to be taught; and not only that, if the criminal calendars of the country were examined, it would be found that they were a majority of the criminals. They were so detestable, that unless some method was adopted preventing their influx into this country by the 'underground railroad,' the people of the West would be obliged to drive them out by open violence. The bill before the House imposed a capitation tax upon the emigrants from Europe; and the object of this motion was to levy a similar tax upon blacks who came hither from the States. He now moved, seconded by Mr. Patton, that a capitation tax of 5s. for adults, and 3s. 6d. for children, above one year and under fourteen years of age, be levied on persons of color emigrating to Canada from any foreign country. Ought not the western men to be protected from the rascalities and villanies of the black wretches? He found these men with fire, and food, and lodging, when they were in need; and he would be bound to say that the black men of the county of Essex would speak well of him in this respect. But he could not admit them as being equal to white men; and, after a long and close observation of human nature, he had come to the conclusion that the black man was born to and intended for slavery, and that he was fit for nothing else. (*Sensation.*) Hon. gentlemen might try to groan him down, but he was not to be moved by mawkish sentiment; and he was persuaded that they might as well try to change the spots of the leopard, as to make the black a good citizen. He had told black men so; and the lazy rascals shrugged their shoulders, and wished they had never ran away from their 'good old massa' in Kentucky. If there was anything unchristian in what he proposed, he could not see it, and he feared that he was not born a Christian."

Before I take my seat, I will notice, though briefly, the singular speech of the gentleman last evening! He spoke some three-quarters of an hour after I had concluded my speech of one hour and a quarter, and abruptly closed, by saying that *I* had advanced no arguments for him to answer! I should be sorry to think that the impartial and intelligent portion of the audience were of the same opinion. When I beheld upon his table, as I did, his array of pamphlets, bound books, and other Abolition documents, I really looked for a reply as ponderous as the famous Report of Lord North to the British House of Commons!

The gentleman set out by saying that he would make an announcement that would even startle the Free Soilers and Black Republicans of Philadelphia! He was for driving slavery from the Slave States—the Union should rock as long as it rested upon the bosoms of four millions of slaves; that, until it was abolished, Southern masters would have to sleep with pistols under their pillows! This did startle even the Free Soilers and Republicans of Philadelphia! And I am proud to know that such incendiary—nay, such infinitely infernal—sentiments, meet with the indignant frowns, scorn, and contempt of all virtuous, honorable, and conservative men in Philadelphia. I know the good people of Philadelphia; I know them to be a conservative people, going to no extremes, either with Pro-Slavery men or Abolitionists. I shall so represent them in the South. I will point our people, with pleasure, to the period, not many years ago, when, in the immediate vicinity of this magnificent hall, they assembled and burned to ashes a building desecrated by Abolition meetings, from which *buck negroes* walked home with white women!

But we must sleep, in the South, with pistols under our pillows! Yes, this is the spirit, and these are the purposes, of that class of Abolitionists of which this gentleman has assumed to be a leader. If ever our blood is shed in the South, it will be by our negroes, whose Southern raising and instincts have imparted to them the chivalry of the South. If none but *blue-bellied* Yankees and unmitigated Northern Abolitionists come down upon us, we shall sleep with nothing more terrific under our pillows than *spike-gimblets!* If, however, at any time, an army of Abolitionists from the North shall conclude to make a descent upon the slaveholders of the South, and this gentleman accompanies the army, I will thank him to let me know which regiment he is in. And "when Greek meets Greek, then comes the tug of war."

This determination on the part of Abolitionists either to crush slavery where it is, or to dissolve the Union, is becoming general. The following card, signed by five of this gentleman's associates and "boon companions," shows their spirit, and their utter disregard of all laws, human and divine:

"Whereas, it must be obvious to all, that the American Union is constantly becoming more and more divided, by slavery, into two distinct and antagonistic nations, between whom harmony is impossible, and even ordinary intercourse is becoming dangerous;

"And whereas Slavery has now gained entire control over the three branches of our National Government, Executive, Judiciary, and Legislative; has so interpreted the Constitution as to deny the right of Congress to establish freedom even in the territories; and by the same process has removed all legal protection from a large portion of the people of the Free States; and has inflicted, at many times and places, outrages far greater than those our fathers rose in arms to repel;

"And whereas there seems no probability that the future will, in these respects, be different from the past, under existing State relations:

"The undersigned respectfully invite their fellow citizens of the Free States, to meet in Convention, at ——, in October, 1857, to consider the practicability, probability, and expediency of a separation between the Free and Slave States, and to take such other measures as the condition of the times may require.

"THOS. W. HIGGINSON,
WENDELL PHILLIPS,
F. W. BIRD,
DANIEL MANN,
WM. L. GARRISON."

But the gentleman complained of my abuse—said I uttered hard things against Northern men and Northern society. Ye gods and little fishes! Only think of *Abram Pryne*, the bitter and unrelenting editor of the *McGrawville Reformer*, whose columns, day in and day out, afford such an intemperance of bad language, and such an exhibition of abusive words, towards the entire South, as must be offensive to God, and all decent and conservative men, complaining of hard words applied to Northern men and Northern society!

The dictionaries of "Billingsgate" may be searched in vain to find language more unbecoming a decent press, not to say one conducted by a minister of Him, who, when He was reviled, reviled not again! No longer ago than last evening, this gentleman more than once applied the term of "*ruffian*" to slaveholders, and in his mad ravings, under the excitement of the occasion, he descended to the use of such foul denunciations, that from that, or some other cause, a score of gentlemen left the hall at one time! I have listened to no parallel to his denunciations, in the ribald partisan harangues of political demagogues! And yet the gentleman complains that I use hard words toward the Abolition villifiers of the South, and the vile conspirators against this glorious Union!

Here is an article from the New York *Independent*, of November, 1856, one of the gentleman's Abolition exchanges. I have no doubt that he copied it with approbation; and now does not blush to endorse it, foul and false as it is in every line:

"The mass of the population of the Atlantic coast of the slave region of the South, are descended from the transported convicts and outcasts of Great Britain. For a century previous to the Revolution, thousands of those offscourings of the jails and hulks of England were poured out on the shores of Maryland, Virginia, the Carolinas, and Georgia,—*and nowhere else!* Those were THE PENAL COLONIES OF GREAT BRITAIN. Their legislative history proves it. And Captain James Cook was sent on his second voyage of discovery to seek a new country which might serve as a substitute for those lost convict settlements.

"O glorious chivalry and hereditary aristocracy of the South! Peerless first families of Virginia and Carolina. 'Look unto the rock whence ye were hewn, and to the hole of the pit whence ye were digged.' Progeny of the highwaymen, and horse-thieves, and sheep-stealers, and pickpockets of Old England! 'Go, vilest of the vile,' out of all union with communities of decent origin, and following your true moral and natural affinities, seek your real kindred and political fraternities with those whose ancestors were turned from the ocean-path which yours took, and founded their 'chivalrous' colonies in New South Wales and Van Dieman's Land. Go to Botany Bay, with your hereditary lawlessness, violence, and murderous, thievish propensities, and stain no longer the character of that true and noble-descended *free* American people who have too long endured the loathsome connection with you."

But again, the *Age of Reason and Freedom*, an Abolition paper of the *Parson Pryne school*, published at the Berlin Heights, Free Love Institution, near Sandusky, Ohio, after admitting that the Bible favors the institution of Slavery, adds:

"My heart's blood curdles at the thought. You may search all heathendom, from the blackest half-human of Ethiopia down to the most refined Caucasian, and you cannot find one *so monstrous, so inhuman,* and *so infernal.* You may say this is not a true representation of God. It is the God for whose cause more human blood has been spilt than for all other causes combined — the God of the Bible — the God my brother cursed. It is the God of the religion that banished Roger Williams from the commonwealth because he believed in extending civil rights outside of their own church. * * * That sacrificed the life of my school-fellow, Richard Dillingham, in the Nashville Penitentiary, and in the Queen City caused a mother to murder her own child. The God of the religion that upholds the oppression and robbery of the poor on the one hand, and the extravagance and vice of the rich on the other."

The gentleman said, in so many words, that there never could be a slave *legally* held in bondage on this Continent—that the King's Bench decreed *three years before* the Constitution of the United States was framed, that slavery should not exist in these colonies! Then the decrees of the King's Bench should be more binding on the citizens of the United States than their own Constitution, and the laws enacted under it. What an argument for a man of respectable pretensions to make! It was because of the oppressive decrees of the King's Bench, if the gentleman please,—because of the oppressive taxes imposed upon these colonies, that they rebelled, and declared the war of the Revolution. Verily, if the decrees of the King's Bench, passed before our independence was declared, relating to slavery, are still of binding force here, they are equally binding in reference to taxes. The gentleman must be a *Royalist*, and if so, he had better repair to England.

His argument touching the Constitution, and the right of States to enact laws favoring slavery, was as destitute of reason as any thing could be. It was the stale material of the Abolitionists, often confuted, and as often re-hashed by abler hands than Mr. Pryne. Its shallow commonplace phraseology, was relieved by the bitterness and malignity of the spirit he displayed.

The gentleman commenced his speech, and then concluded it, in a whining tone, and in suppliant language, complaining that he was not distinguished — that his name and fame had not been heralded in advance of his arrival! These were items that the audience were aware of, without his publishing it!

And how did he meet my charge against the people of New England for stealing negroes from the coast of Africa, and selling them into perpetual bondage, for the sake of gain? Why, gentlemen, he boasted that they had the *enterprise* to steal, and the South had not! How revolting is such a boast! What a monstrosity for a minister of our Holy Religion, to boast that he has descended from, and is associated with a people who have the energy and will to live by plunder and piracy!

Finally, I understood the gentleman to deny in most emphatic terms, that Abraham ever owned slaves, or held his fellow men in bondage, and to call for the proof! Does the gentleman suppose that I will consume my time in looking out, and reciting the proof of what every Sunday-School scholar in the land knows? Is he a teacher in Israel, and thus ignorant of the teachings of God's word? If he will read the Old Testament Scriptures, he will there learn that Abraham, called the father of the faithful, was a large slave-holder—that upon his death bed, like a Southern planter, he executed his last will and testament, bequeathing his numerous slaves unto his son Isaac—that the angel of God stood by his dying couch, approved the disposition he made of his *slave property*, and cheered the good old slave-holder, in his expiring moments, with the certain, but then anticipated joys of paradise! And if their custom were, in those days, to record wills in Probate Courts, I have no doubt but this angel of the living God, was the subscribing witness!

Intending to give the gentleman a thorough course of instructions during this week, upon the great and exciting topic of American slavery, I propose to give them to him in *broken doses*, and hence I yield him the stand, that he may make such defence as he feels prepared for!

"OUGHT AMERICAN SLAVERY TO BE PERPETUATED?"

NEGATIVE, II. — BY ABRAM PRYNE.

LADIES AND GENTLEMEN:—I promise you that I shall not, in my speech of this evening, or on any evening during this debate, go beyond an hour by a second; and I regret that the length of my opponent's speech unfortunately crowds me so much at the end of this discussion, that I am obliged to beg your patience in giving me a fair hearing, as I have plead for your patience towards him. I shall now proceed directly to my argument.

The first question that I have to raise here is, Does God sanction American slavery? Is God to be regarded as the supporter and upholder of American slavery? Let us, for one moment, measure the matchless magnitude of this question, and see what it involves. What a question to ask in the light of the Divine Government — whether God sanctions slavery! It is equivalent to asking whether God sanctions the worst theft that has ever desolated the world. If, as was so conclusively argued last night, American slavery had its beginning and its continued existence in theft, then you cannot prove that God sanctions slavery unless you prove him to be a thief. He who said, "Thou shalt not steal," is he to be regarded as the abettor of the mightiest robber-foray ever undertaken against the human race? He who threw the guard of his own royal prohibition of theft around every article of property which man can acquire, did he leave humanity unprotected from man-thieves, by the bulwarks of his law? Nay, more, did he make a special provision for the stealing of men. Who dares look into the Bible for proof that he is such a God?

Again, it involves the question whether God is the supporter of the disruption of the marriage relation, the breaking up of the marriage ties and of wholesale adultery. The gentleman on the other side has kindly vouchsafed some information, all new to me, about the Five Points in New York. He has also told us that there are Five Points in the South; and that was not new to me, for I knew before that there was a miniature Five Points on each plantation in the South. Now, gentlemen, to prove to you that slavery does thus break up the marriage relation, let me read a single authority:

"Slaves were not entitled to the conditions of matrimony, and therefore they had no relief in cases of adultery; nor were they the proper objects of cognation or affinity, but of *quasi-cognation* only." — (*Dr. Taylor's "Elements of the Civil Law," p.* 429.)

God, to be a slave-holder, must sanction that; and who dare blaspheme Him by making such a declaration?

Again: does God sanction the violation of the parental relation? For slavery's law allows the master to separate father and child, if he will. God, who instituted this relation, must be proved to sanction its continued and perpetual disruption, if he sanctions slavery. Here is the testimony of the Savannah River Baptist Association on this point:

"In 1835, the following query relating to slaves was propounded to the Savannah River Baptist Association of ministers: Whether, in case of involuntary separation of such a character as to preclude all future intercourse, the parties may be allowed to marry again?

"ANSWER.—That such separation, among persons situated as our slaves are, is, civilly, a separation by death, and they believe that, in the sight of God, it would be so viewed. To forbid second marriages in such cases, would be to expose the parties not only to greater hardships and stronger temptations, but to *church censure* for acting in *obedience to their masters*, who cannot be expected to acquiesce in a regulation at variance with justice to the slaves, and to the spirit of that command which regulates marriage between Christians. *The slaves are not free agents*, and a dissolution by death is not more entirely without their consent and beyond their control than by such separation."

Again: do God and the Bible sanction robbing the laborer of his hire? Hear me answer in the language of James:

"Behold, the hire of the laborers who have reaped down your fields, which is of you kept back by fraud, crieth: and the cries of them which have reaped are entered into the ears of the Lord of Saboath."

What say you, workingmen of Philadelphia, does God sanction the wholesale robbery of the laborer of his wages?

But I pass to another question: does God sanction the stealing of men, women and children? Hear me answer in the language of the Bible: "He that stealeth a man or telleth him, or if he be found in his hands, shall surely be put to death," (and every one that takes the man from his own God-appointed ownership steals him,) "and he that selleth him," and, to cap the climax, to cover the whole ground of slavery, he that holdeth him in his hands, the Bible says, shall be put to death. Of course the children of slaves are born with the right to freedom, and he that enslaves them as really steals them as if he brought them in chains from the coast of Africa.

Let me say that the nature and relation of man forbid that God should sanction the institution of slavery. The Bible tells us that God created man in his own image, breathed into him immortality, threw around him the drapery of his own form; and slavery claims the right to hang chains upon the form of God, to load down with fetters the human soul, around which God threw the mantle of his own beautiful divinity in the form in which he enshrined it. Oh! tell me not of impiety of any other kind in the presence of that overpowering impiety which would load the form of God himself with chains, and claim to derive from God the right to do it.

Does not the Divine image which man bears give us some impression with reference to God's own regard for the sacredness of his rights? Does not the fact that God clothed man in His own form, condemn and convict him who, with ruthless hand, would degrade the soul of man, and enslave him? Has not the guarantee of God's own form been thrown around the soul to secure its freedom? Will you hang chains on God? Will you bind shackles upon the form which He wears?

I proceed now more directly to the textual argument which is involved in this question, though I shall not be able to follow my friend throughout. He started with the statement that it was the business of the negative to follow the argument of the affirmative. I beg leave to put in a condition — that the affirmative shall produce an argument capable of being followed. Where that happens to be lacking, I, of course, shall be unable to follow it. Who can follow a pound of feathers before a gale of wind. While following the arrangement that I had made before I listened to his speech, I shall proceed a little out of his order, but will reach every point that he has touched.

In the first place he hints at the curse said to have been pronounced by Noah on the descendants of Ham; and this curse we are to accept as a reason why the black man should be enslaved. Noah's curse, let me say, was pronounced on Canaan; and there is no more proof that Canaan was a black man than that the whitest man before me is a black man.

But, not to dwell on that, what is the strength and force of Noah's curse? The whole story is told in the verse which I will read:

> "And Noah awoke from his wine and knew what his sons had done unto him, and he said, Cursed be Canaan; a servant of servants shall he be unto his brethren."

What a terrible gap must be filled up to reach the inference that this curse of drunken Noah, just waking up from the effect of his over-dose of wine, carries with it the sanction of God! Who says that *God* cursed Canaan? The Bible makes no such statement; it merely tells us of Noah, that on suddenly rising after a drunken fit, and supposing that his grandson had mistreated him, he, as drunken men are apt to do —

> "Unpacked his heart with words,
> And fell to cursing, like a very drab."*

* A scullion.

But who can give us, from the Bible or from any other source, the shadow of evidence that God ever sanctioned that curse? I call on my opponent for the proof.

God is not to be held responsible for the angry words of a patriarch in his wine, nor for all the deeds of the patriarchs. The Bible states facts—but by no means holds God responsible for the existence of many of its facts. Nothing can claim his sanction unless that sanction is plainly recorded.

Even if there was some force in Noah's curse, it was fulfilled in the case of the Canaanites. But not stopping to urge that argument, let me ask who made the South the executors of Noah, to carry out his curse? When did they take out letters testamentary on Noah's estate? Canaan was to be a servant of servants. Are the slaveholders servants? Even did I admit (which I do not) that Noah's curse had some force in enslaving somebody to the Jews, what a jump of logic to conclude thence that Southern men have a right to enslave the negroes!

And now I come to the case of Abraham. We are told that Abraham was a slaveholder. Gentlemen, I meet that declaration with a plump denial; and I shall satisfy you in a moment that I do so on the best ground of argument.

In the first place, Abraham's head servant was his lieutenant in war, who, as the leader of 118 armed men, went forth on a foray against the surrounding nations. When gentlemen will arm their slaves, and lead them out into an unpopulous country, and bring them back again safely, none rebelling, though there be 118 slaves to one white man who is in command — then they may begin to argue some analogy between their system and the Abrahamic.

Again, I prove to you that Abraham's servants were not slaves, from the fact that Abraham's head servant was declared by Abraham to be his heir — the natural and lawful heir of his whole property. The slave laws of the South affirm that a slave can own nothing, hold nothing; that he cannot be the party to a contract, or have any tenure of property.

Here was a man who did own and did hold property — who was heir-in-law of Abraham, the richest man of his day; yet we are asked to believe that the system of servitude then prevailing is analogous to the system of slavery now existing in the South, which declares a slave to be goods and chattles personal, to all intents, purposes, and constructions whatsoever — unable to own anything, hold anything, or be a party to a contract. Furnish arms to your slaves at the South; put property in their hands; give them some position that was occupied by Abraham's feudal retainers (if I may borrow the language of the middle ages): and you will see how long you will be able to hold them as slaves. Fulfil one out of six of the conditions of that Abrahamic system of servitude, and you break down a dyke, whose removal would cause the dark waters of slavery at the South to rush out with such a flood that no man could stem its tide.

Again: Abraham's head servant went with his son to get a wife. Abraham trusted him to go on a long journey, upon a mission that was dearest to his own heart. Travelling day after day, with a retinue of camels and companies of men and women, through a wild country, into which he could readily have fled — I ask you, if he had been a slave — subject to the lash — goods and chattels personal — who does not believe that he would have run away? The truth is, that Abraham was a prince, and his followers and military retainers, who tilled his land, and attended his flocks, were, in the language of the East, called his servants. This was the relation between him and them, and it did not at all involve the chattel principle which is the soul of American slavery.

The word "servant" in the Old Testament no more necessarily means "slave" than it does in the language of New England or the city of Philadelphia. It is a common term; and I offer as my authority one of Philadelphia's noblest sons, who, having carefully given his vast learning to the investigation of this question, has announced his conclusion that the word "servant," as applied to persons in the Bible, determines nothing with reference to the tenure by which they were held, and would apply to a New England servant as well as to any other. I speak of the testimony of Albert Barnes, who states his conclusion in these words:

"From this examination of the terms used to denote servitude among the Hebrews, it follows that nothing can be inferred from the mere use of the word in regard to the *kind* of servitude which existed in the days of the patriarchs."— *Barnes on Slavery.*

Again, Mr. Barnes says:

"The Hebrew words, *ebĕdh*, *ăbōdhâ*, and *ăbŭddâ*, rendered commonly *servant*, *service*, and *servants*, (Job i. 3,) are derived from *âbădh*, meaning *to labor, to work, to do work.* It occurs in the Hebrew Scriptures some hundreds of times in various forms of the word, and is never rendered *slaves,* but commonly *servants,* and *serve.*

But I have another question to ask: Did everything done by the patriarchs receive the approbation of God? Not at all; and the fact that a system of servitude obtained among the patriarchs cannot prove that it had the Divine approbation, unless you can show that it is sustained and sanctioned by the letter of the Bible. The mere fact of its existence proves nothing; for all these patriarchs were guilty of wrong-doings. Jacob filched from his brother Esau his birthright by a trick; Abraham denied his own wife, and, by the denial, subjected her to the danger of prostitution; and even Noah, as we have already seen, got drunk. The Bible states these facts without comment, just as it states the fact that these patriarchs held servants; and by the bare statement of the fact, it sanctions one as much as the other..

In the next place, I deny any analogy between this system of servitude and American slavery; because, in the whole Jewish economy, no man ever sold a servant. I defy my opponent to find an instance, from the beginning to the end of the Bible, where a Jew is ever said to have sold a servant after he came into his possession. Therefore, those servants were not subject to the laws of property, as are the slaves of the South at this day. Had they been "goods and chattels personal," we should have had some record of their sale by their master. But no such record can be found; and the inference is irresistible that they were not property. Again, you will remember that passage of the Bible which reads:

"Thou shalt not deliver unto his master the servant which is escaped from his master unto thee."

Thus we see an "underground railroad" had come to the surface all over Judea. Every servant that felt oppressed had the Divine sanction to flee anywhere he pleased, and, by the prohibition of God, no man should send him back to his master, but all were commanded to allow him to remain unmolested. Proclaim that law to the bondmen who tremble at the crack of your whip; let the declaration go forth as the law of the South that no fugitive act exists, that every slave who can make good his escape shall be free; and in a fortnight, the population across the lakes in Canada will receive such an accession, and the South become so nearly depopulated, that gentlemen who now live by squeezing out of the poor oppressed negroes the coats they wear, and the dinners they eat, and the jewelery they flourish in Northern cities, will be compelled to work for a living.

But whatever may have been the system of servitude that obtained among the Jews, (and I still insist that it was as far removed from the chattel-principle, the dark feature of American slavery, as is the relation between a New England servant-girl and her mistress)—whatever may have been the system that obtained, every forty-nine years it was abolished by the jubilee. Every forty-nine years, liberty was "proclaimed throughout the land, to all the inhabitants thereof."

Every forty-nine years, one grand, universal, abolition jubilee swept over the whole land of Judea. The gentleman on the other side tells us that his system in the South is modelled after the Mosaic. Is it not time, after two hundred years of slavery, to have four jubilees at once. Stick to the letter of the Bible on this point if you will; make your system conform in this particular to that which obtained in Judea, and slavery will be swept down, and pass away as the fog before a summer's morning.

I do not stop to-night to enter largely into the argument with reference to the teachings of the New Testament; nor have, thus far, more than glanced at the argument of the Old Testament. But I must be allowed to say that all the precepts of the New Testament are against slavery; and American slavery is so terribly inimical to the whole Bible, that the South is thrown into an agony of fear the moment a half dozen poor, ragged slaves gather in the basement of some church, in order to be taught the language of the New Testament. Sir, if the Bible so strongly sanctions slavery, why do you not, like sensible men, teach it to your slaves? Why not teach every slave to read it, that he may have the full benefit of feeling that he is under the influence of a Divine God-appointed system? "Search the Scriptures?" is the command of God; but slavery says to the slaves, "If you dare attempt to look into the Scriptures — if you gather together to gain Scriptural instruction — we will send our creatures to disperse you under the crack of the lash. You shall not be permitted to learn to read the Bible."

Why, if slavery and the Bible are so entirely in affinity, if each so admirably supports the other, how foolish are these gentlemen of the South that they do not teach every slave to read the Scriptures! God reveals his will to man in the Bible. Slavery says to four millions of her boasted Christians of the South, "If you learn to read that Bible, I will score your backs with the lash until the skin shall peel off," and yet attempts to prove that that same Bible which God revealed for all men sanctions that oppression which prevents them from reading it.

I notice to-night only a few of the passages which the gentleman has quoted in his speech. I would, at this point, merely say, in a general way, that just in proportion as you make an impression that slavery is sustained by the Bible, you bring the Bible into scorn and contempt. I say that the slave who believes that the Bible supports slavery, ought to hate it. I say that, if the slave believes that the religion taught him at the South makes him a slave, he ought to trample it under his feet. Such enlightenment, such philosophy, such Christianity, are so far from being a blessing to him, that the heaviest curse the dark spirit of slavery has ever inflicted upon the soul of the slave, is the religion of the South under which she professes to hold him in bonds.

My opponent said, in his speech of last night:

> "When Christ was doomed by a cruel Roman law to its most ignominious condemnation, he did not so much as resist it."

What would he have us infer — that, therefore, the cruel Roman law which hung him upon the cross was right? Is that the inference? Does he intend to argue that, because I go for the repeal of these cruel laws against the slave, I am violating the example of Christ? Does it follow that the slaveholders' laws of the South are right, because Christ did not resist laws equally tyrannous? By no means. For Christ did not resist his own crucifixion; and if nothing but what Christ resisted is wrong, then Christ's crucifixion was not wrong!

The gentleman on the other side tells us that Jesus never denounced slavery. Has he never read the words: "Undo the heavy burdens?" A crushing burden is laid on the back of the poor slave at birth, which he carries all the days of his life, until he sinks under it into his grave. Our Revolutionary fathers rebelled against a burden which, compared with slavery, is as a man's little finger to his loins; and if their rebellion was for a moment justifiable, then the slave would be doubly justified in asserting his freedom with arms in his hands. In the name of God and humanity, what is heavier than the burden of slavery? Has he never read the words: "Break every yoke, and let the oppressed go free?" When every yoke shall be broken, I take it, the horrid yoke of American slavery will be broken. I call upon those gentlemen who hold this theory, to convince me that they believe the Bible, by carrying out this palpable and incontrovertible passage, by setting forth to "break every yoke and let the oppressed go free."

Again: the prophet Isaiah, in describing the purpose of Christ's mission to the world, uses this beautiful language:

"The Spirit of the Lord God *is* upon me; because the Lord hath anointed me to preach good tidings unto the meek; he hath sent me to bind up the broken-hearted, to proclaim liberty to the captives, and the opening of the prison to *them that are* bound: To proclaim the acceptable year of the Lord, and the day of vengeance of our God; to comfort all that mourn."

Thus is Christ revealed as a universal emancipator. Shall I be told again that Christ has never said a word against slavery? If I should be, you will agree with me that I am not bound to believe it.

Has he never read: "All things whatsoever ye would that men should do to you, do ye even so unto them?" And would he that men should doom him to a life of bondage; that they should sell his wife on the auction-block, and his daughters to a slave-trader? Would he have the light of knowledge shut out from his soul, and the Bible denied to his children? Why, then, do this to others, and still claim to be a servant, nay, a minister, of Christ?

My friend has told us, both last night and to-night, that Abolitionists themselves have complained of the colored people; and he mentions Gerritt Smith as one who has done so. He has; but there is something of which he is at this very time complaining more loudly, making his own deep-toned voice reverberate over the hills of New York State. He is proclaiming the wickedness of the South, which, while it has for ages crushed the slave under its heel, is now astonished that he does not rise into the dignity of an intellectual man at one leap. He knows, as we all do, that the vices of the slave have been learned on the plantation, and that no people can be expected to rise in a moment from the effects of such a horrid education. The South denies all means of intellectual culture to the slave; flogs him for learning to read; abuses him for every struggling effort of his mind to gain culture; and then, after having put out the light of intellect from his soul, is astonished that he is intellectually weak, and gives such weakness as the cowardly reason for continuing to abuse him.

But if gentlemen think that the fugitive slaves of this country are men lacking in intellect, I can only say, that had my opponent accepted the offer of Frederick Douglass to meet him in this debate, he would have gone back to Knoxville, Tennessee, with his notions of the want of intellect of the African all upset.

And you will excuse me for saying, in this connection, that had he met another colored man whom I can mention — darker than Frederick Douglass, who is a mulatto — a real African of the olden type, six feet two inches in his shoes, and weighing over two hundred pounds, he would have thought himself in a Chinese museum of wit, sarcasm, and logic, where pyrotechnics were flashing around him from the brain of Samuel R. Ward.

I only regret that I have not his power of argument, of diction, and of rhetoric, with which to meet my friend to-night.

In regard to Gerritt Smith's complaining of the colored people, has he not shown his genuine kindness of heart towards them, his love for them, by telling them their faults; while he is, in his efforts to assist them, distributing among them, with princely liberality, his own fortune. And the best thing to be said yet of Gerritt Smith's good deeds in that direction, is, that he is to-day on the stump in my own glorious Empire State as a candidate for Governor, under the pledge that if he should be elected, and an effort should be made to take a fugitive slave from the State of New York, he will call out the whole military force of the State to resist it. Such lukewarm friends of the African as that, may God multiply! And, gentlemen, let me say that, when this debate shall have been concluded, I shall, with pleasure, hasten home to my native State, to take the stump for Mr. Smith.

And now let me refer to another point in the argument of my opponent. We have had brought to our notice the case of Paul's apprehension of Onesimus; and it has been urged that Onesimus was a fugitive slave, and Paul a slave-catcher. Let us see what was the language which Paul used in writing to Philemon:

"Receive him not now as a servant."

Then Paul did not send him back as a servant, but as a freeman.

"Receive him not as a servant, but above a servant, a brother beloved, specially to me, but how much more unto thee, both in the flesh and in the Lord? If thou count me, therefore, a partner, *receive him as myself.*"

I suppose my friend will not contend that Paul wished Philemon to receive *him* with the cat-o'-nine-tails. I suppose that he will not agree that Paul wished Philemon to place him in the stocks, and put him on bread and water, and baste his back, and anoint it with brine and pepper. He will not argue that this is what Paul meant by his injunction that Onesimus should be received as a brother—"not now a servant, but above a servant, a brother beloved." So it seems Paul was an emancipationist; that he set Onesimus free, and sent him back, with the apostolic command to his master that he should let him remain free. This is your boasted argument from Paul's letter to Philemon. Practice Paul's teaching here, and I am content. I would be willing to send all the fugitives in Canada back in the same way Paul sent back Onesimus, with an order for free papers and a brother's inheritance in the estate, provided you would guarantee that the slaveholders would receive them, "not as servants, but as brothers beloved."

I would refer, also, to the case of Ziba, the servant of Saul. He, we are told, had twenty servants himself. He therefore held property, and could not be a slave; for, according to the slave law of the South, no slave can hold property. He was the servant of Saul in the sense in which all the retainers of captains are called their servants. They were mere feudal military retainers. In this sense the word "servant" is applied to them; and that is all the force that it has in all these cases.

Paul is quoted again as saying

> "Art thou called *being* a servant? care not for it: but if thou mayest be made free, use *it* rather."

That is to say, If you are a slave and the cars of the underground railroad come along, jump on and get your freedom if you can. If you are a servant, bear it patiently while you must, but the moment an opportunity occurs for you to escape, make the best of it, and get away as soon as you can.

Of course Paul advised servants to be obedient and get along as smoothly as they could while compelled to remain in that position. I would give the same advice, would say show no impatience, no restlessness, let your master think you are passive and content, while your condition is inevitable, but "If thou mayest be free use it rather," and when the train arrives on the underground railroad take a through ticket.

We are referred to passages exhorting the slaves to patience and forbearance; and in regard to these, you will mark this, that they all condole with him as suffering a very hard lot, telling him to bear it in the name of God and Christ. They tell him that to bear buffeting is creditable to him. But they all plead that he is not in his right condition, and urge him to bear it until he shall have an opportunity to get away. Such passages as these the pro-slavery side of the argument may make the most of.

The argument is urged that as Jesus did not denounce slavery by name, it follows that he did not regard it as a crime. This argument is based upon the assumption that everything that Christ did not denounce in set terms is innocent. It will take but a moment to show the glaring fallacy of this proposition. But one sermon of Jesus has come down to us, and the report of that is by no means full. That sermon was addressed to non-slave-holding Jews, and not especially to slave-holding Romans, and of course that single sermon could not go minutely into the various questions of civil rights, social conditions, and political economy, which have since agitated the world. But he did lay down broad and deep, great first principles, which when carried out would overturn every form of oppression. He did not denounce the cruelties and brutalities of the gladiatorial shows of the Roman Amphitheater, by name, nor did he directly discuss the wickedness of the Roman government in detail, but does it therefore follow that he sanctioned all these? His short ministry of only three years, shut him up to the necessity of dealing in first principles, leaving the future to develop and apply them to all phases of the after life of man, and these first principles are at all points at enmity with American slavery.

Here are a few passages from the Bible which show its teachings on human rights:

"Thou shalt love thy neighbor as thyself."

"Let the oppressed go free."

"Proclaim liberty throughout the land to all the *inhabitants* thereof."

"Thou shalt not respect the persons of the poor nor honor the persons of the mighty, but in righteousness shalt thou judge thy neighbor."

"Envy not thou the oppressor, and choose none of his ways.

"Do justice to the afflicted and needy, rid them out of the hands of the wicked."

"Execute judgment and justice; take away your exaltations from my people saith the Lord."

"He that oppresseth the poor reproacheth his maker."

"I will be a swift witness against the adulterer, and against false swearers, and against those that oppress the hireling in his wages, the widow and the fatherless, and that turn aside the stranger from his right, and fear not me, saith the Lord of Hosts.

"He that stealeth a man, and selleth him, or if he be found in his hand, he shall surely be put to death."

"Whoso stoppeth his ears at the cry of the poor, he also shall cry, but shall not be heard."

"Therefore thus saith the Lord; ye have not hearkened unto me, in proclaiming liberty, every one to his brother, and every man to his neighbor: behold, I proclaim a liberty for you, saith the Lord, to the sword, to the pestilence, and to the famine; and I will make you to be removed into all the kingdoms of the earth."

"Call no man master, neither be ye called masters."

"All things whatsoever ye would that men should do to you do ye even so to them."

"Be kindly affectionate one to another with brotherly love; in honor preferring one another."

"Do good to all men, as ye have opportunity."

"Stand fast therefore in the liberty wherewith Christ hath made you free, and be not entangled again with the yoke of bondage."

"If thou mayest be made free, use it rather."

"The laborer is worthy of his hire."

"Where the Spirit of the Lord is, there is liberty."

The *Baltimore Sun* while criticising the work of some clerical flunky who published a Bible defence of slavery a few years ago, excoriates him as follows:

"Bible defence of slavery! There is no such thing as a Bible defence of slavery at the present day. Slavery in the United States is a social institution, originating in the convenience and cupidity of our ancestors, existing by State laws, and recognized to a certain extent—for the recovery of slave property—by the Constitution. And nobody would pretend that, if it were inexpedient and unprofitable for any man or any State to continue to hold slaves, they would be bound to do so on the ground of a "Bible defence" of it. Slavery is recorded in the Bible, and approved, with many degrading characteristics. War is recorded in the Bible, and approved, under what seems to us the extreme of cruelty. But are slavery and war to *endure* for ever because we find them in the Bible? or are they to *cease* at once and for ever because the Bible inculcates peace and brotherhood?"

My opponent, as you remember, last night denounced the slave trade in language such as I could not command myself. To-night he tells us the slave trade is sanctioned by God and the Bible. Which end of his argument shall I take — the argument of last night or the argument of to-night? But I have driven him, as I knew I should, to plant his feet on the slave-trade as the only means of logically supporting slavery itself. He has amended his logic, though his premises are false.

We have been told again to-night that all the oriental nations were slave-holding nations. Let us for one moment dig up from the past their history, and see how God himself shows his sanction or disapprobation of slavery. Egypt held slaves; for 430 years the Jews were slaves in Egypt. But escaping, they all took the underground railroad which led through the Red Sea. Their oppressors followed on a grand national slave hunt, but God himself being against them, the waves of the sea swallowed them up. Pharaoh and his entire host were swept away by the besom of destruction in the attempt to get back their fugitive slaves. God sanctions slavery, does he? and yet he causes the sea to swallow up an army of hundreds of thousands who are attempting to regain possession of their fugitive slaves!

Again: throughout the history of the Jews, God is continually pointing back to the days of Egyptian slavery, to warn the Jews against oppression, saying to them in effect, "Do not forget that you were slaves in Egypt; do not forget the wrongs under which you suffered; do not forget the horrors of that system, and do not inflict them upon others." And if we wish to follow the history of Egypt and see what effect slavery had in perpetuating her existence and her glory, let the dust that is gathered more than sixty feet deep at the foot of the Pyramids since art and glory left the land of Egypt tell us what effect such institutions have had upon her existence and her glory. The desolations of Egypt to-day proclaim aloud to the world God's standing disapprobation of the cruelty of Egyptian oppression. Take the case of Babylon, if you please. The Bible declares that Babylon was destroyed for her oppression, because she dealt in slaves and the souls of men. Again: all men at all conversant with her history know that Rome was destroyed because of the very same corruptions which are now eating in upon the vitality of our own nation. Rome was ultimately ruined by the inroads of her system of slavery.

Thus, any man familiar with the history of nations sees at a glance that the grand leveller of all national greatness and glory has been the corruptions engendered by oppression among nations holding slaves.

With reference to the cruelty practised upon Southern plantations, I have said nothing. I do not come here to ask that slavery shall be abolished because the masters of the South whip their slaves cruelly—because they dress them in such a manner as not to protect them from the cold — because they hunt them with blood-hounds — or because of any of the horrid inflictions upon their persons which characterize the entire field of Southern society. I come to ask that slavery shall be abolished, because the very condition itself, in its best and happiest form, is such an outrage against God and humanity that it ought not to exist on earth.

Dress your slave in silks, feed him upon the choicest viands of the land, wait upon him yourself at your own table, give him all the luxuries with which you can surround him, yet still insist that he shall be your slave, and I will still demand his freedom with a voice as earnest as though he were suffering from the most terrible inflictions of cruelty. While I know that slavery is cruel — while I feel the deepest indignation at the wrong and outrage which it heaps upon the slave,—yet apart from all this, the condition of slavery is in itself the deepest and most damning wrong, and the mere incidents are not to be brought in question in an argument of this sort.

My opponent has given us a long extract from some man's plantation rules, wherein he tells his overseers that they must listen to the complaints of the slave. Would my friend regard it as a peculiar kindness that some man should take him and make him a slave, and then, out of regard for him, should command somebody to listen to his complaints?

Perhaps it will be replied that slavery should not lay its hand upon the white man. The color of the cuticle, I take it, does not measure the worth of humanity; and as you and I would not ask for some man to complain to, but would demand before God and the law, the right to protect our own rights, and shield ourselves under the government, so I ask the same for the slave.

These plantation rules provide that the slave's bedding shall be examined. The bed that Frederick Douglass had, when in slavery, would not, according to his description, have taken a very long examination. It was an old bag, into which he used to crawl head foremost. That was his bed for the winter — all that he had. The bedding to be examined would, I apprehend, generally be found to be the soft side of a plank, or the hard ground. Though some gentlemen may provide better for their slaves, yet I know that on the sugar and cotton plantations this is the general character of the bedding.

Again: it is affirmed that American slavery ought to be perpetuated because it improves the morals of the slave. The slaves, it is said, become members of Southern churches, and are made religious men. Let me say that the fact that the slave is not morally beneath the heathen does not show that slavery improves his morals; it only shows that he has native moral instincts sufficient to enable him, *even in spite of slavery*, to get from the glimmering light of surrounding civilization some ideas of morals beyond those of the heathen.

Improve a man's morals by whipping him for reading the Bible? Improve a man's morals by sending policemen to break up his sabbath-schools? Improve a man's morals by chaining him to a cart while his master has gone to the communion-table? Improve a man's morals and regard for the Bible by telling him that the Bible sanctions his being whipped and driven all his life in the cotton-field without pay? Gentlemen, this mode of improving morals certainly obtains nowhere but in the South; and I take it that Southern morals may yet be improved a long way before the Millenium will dawn.

We have it affirmed that it is only by slavery that the character of the slave can be elevated. Yet we are told that, after two hundred years of slavery, he is so immoral and thriftless that he cannot take care of himself. I ask that we may determine this question by determining what would be the result of two hundred years of freedom. If, at the close of that period, we shall have failed to elevate his character, then we will be converted to the doctrine that slavery is the condition most conducive to his moral improvement; and the missionary work of my friend may then go on at the North.

We have been told that three-fourths of the slaves in Tennessee would refuse their liberty if offered to them. Oh! I would like to see the experiment tried! When the Legislature of Tennessee shall have offered to them their liberty, and they shall have refused, then, and not till then, can this statement be received. If the slave owners of the South are as sure that their slaves would refuse the boon of liberty, why do they meet with such terrible malignity all Abolitionists who may tell their slaves that there is a chance for freedom?

Let me now, in closing these remarks, announce that I shall to-morrow night consider the question of slavery in its relation to commerce, to art, to the advance of intelligence, to the development of national greatness; and I hope to show that slavery is the great incubus resting upon the material growth and progress of our country. I hope to prove that not only the welfare of the slave, but the interests of the white man, the prosperity of the whole nation, as well as the command of God, the dictates of humanity and the claims of justice, demand that American slavery shall be abolished.

STATEMENT

Read to the audience, Thursday, Sept. 9th, 1858.

REV. MR. PRYNE and myself stipulated by letter, that in this discussion I was to lead—that I was at no time to exceed *one hour and thirty minutes* in the delivery of a speech. We further stipulated that our friends present, meaning those adhering to our views, should not interrupt either him or myself. I have not yet occupied *one hour and thirty minutes* in either address delivered, nor will I do so this evening; but last evening I was interrupted with repeated cries of "time expired," and not even allowed time to conclude my entire address. This annoyance came from ruffians and insolent free negroes.

I ask no favors—no quarters—no sympathy from Abolitionists—and I expect none; but I demand *justice*, and a compliance with our written contract, which has been read before this audience. The South has been well represented in this Hall, the two evenings past, and she is well represented here this evening, although three or four to one, of the entire audience are against us in their feelings and sentiments; but the friends of the South have not interrupted Mr. Pryne, and will not do so, whether he shall close within the limits of our agreement, or go beyond them. Southern men, unlike Abolitionists, are men of good breeding!

If *persons*—I will not say *gentlemen*, friendly to the cause of Abolition—are sick of this discussion, and of the facts and figures I am laying before them, and wish to break it up, let them say so, through their reverend spokesman, and we will discontinue it quietly, and disperse as becomes gentlemen. Otherwise, we will continue it, and adhere to the written agreement between the speakers.

Respectfully, &c.,

W. G. Brownlow.

"OUGHT AMERICAN SLAVERY TO BE PERPETUATED?"

AFFIRMATIVE, III.—BY W. G. BROWNLOW.

SUCH points in the last rejoinder of MR. PRYNE, as I may deem important to notice, I will pay my respects to before I take my seat.

The *New York Daily Times*, for the 8th of March, gives to the world some interesting statistics, drawn from the Annual Report of the Penitentiary of Louisiana. These statistics, the Anti-Slavery editor of that widely-circulated Journal makes a text for a column of bitter and sweeping denunciations, and false and infamous allegations against the morality, and social condition of the Southern States generally. I am a constant reader of the newspapers and magazines, both North and South, and of the controversies growing out of the Slavery question; and I must be allowed to say, that I have rarely read any production more unsparingly false and abusive, than that article. It concedes that the constitutions and laws of the Southern States, generally, "are framed in a spirit of enlightenment and humanity," such as have the appearance of coming from "a sober and God-fearing people," but then it goes on to describe the people that framed these constitutions, and enacted these laws; and what is more wicked and infamous than all, it gives the subjects upon whom these laws are executed, *convicts in State Prisons, as apt illustrations of Southern society generally!* It speaks of the better classes of society in the South, as a set of men under the sway of brutal and tiger-like passions, ferociously killing, shooting, stabbing, wounding, and mutilating each other, without any plausible pretext, and without feeling any responsibility to either God or man! The editor even says that these offences are of daily occurrence, and that they take place in all the States, and show the leading *traits* of character among Southern men! I will give the precise words of the *Times* on this point, in its sweeping charges against the South. It says of our homicides and fights,—"daily homicides, mutilations and fights, which take place in *all parts* of the country," and speaks of "the unbridled and implacable ferocity displayed by *every white man* who happens to get into a dispute with his neighbor."

What an indiscriminate attack upon the Southern people! And how common these attacks are at the North! How gross and palpable their calumny! And the occasion for this tirade, the *Times* has drawn from the criminal statistics of Louisiana, which it says grows out of the "little regard in the South for personal liberty;" meaning that the Southern people hold African slaves in bondage!

I was in New Orleans more than once, during the past spring and winter,—I saw and conversed with dif ferent members of the Louisiana Legislature, which adjourned while I was last in that city. I then and there procured the official records of the Louisiana penitentiary, and they do not justify the statements of the *Times*. If these records prove anything, they establish the criminal degradation of Northern society, and the superiority of Southerners in the scale of civilization.

True, the records show that a large proportion of the offences for which men have been sent to the penitentiary in Louisiana, are the class of crimes the *Times* has specified, to wit: murders, manslaughter, poisonings, assaults with intent to kill, house-burning, forgeries and thefts; — but these are not "the special crimes of the South," nor are they the "monster evils" of Louisiana, as falsely alleged.

Now, that these crimes have been committed in Louisiana, I admit, and that the persons thus offending have been sentenced to the penitentiary by Louisiana jurors and judges, under the wholesome operation of Louisiana laws, is equally true. But *who* committed them? And *where* did these offenders come from? They were not natives, or persons trained up in the South. An analysis of the penitentary records will show that these criminals, paraded before the world, by this Anti-Slavery New York editor, as illustrative of Southern morals, are natives of foreign lands, and of the Abolition States of this Union. The proportion of them from all the Southern States is very small; an essential item, which the editor seems altogether to have overlooked. The largest number consists of *foreigners*, of various nations; the next largest that of natives of the Northern and North-Western States — of whom, *Brother Pryne*, your own beloved New York furnishes the greatest number of any one State, North or South!

The number of convicts in the penitentiary of Louisiana, is 244, white men and women. The authorities of the State had the census of the birth-place of every convict taken, during the past year, with the following result, which I beg leave to repeat, that the Abolitionists who hear me may see where the criminals are reared up and educated:

"Of the 109 who were American born, 59 were natives of Free States, and 46 of Slave States, so that the Free States had a large majority of the model criminals.

"Of the whole number of convicts, *less than one-fifth* were natives of Southern States. Four out of every five were born, and most of them trained up, under other influences.

"Of the whole number of 244, only *nine* were natives of Louisiana, about *four* per cent. of the whole mass—while New York alone—we ask the *Times* to note this interesting piece of information—New York alone contributed 22, or about 9 per cent. of the whole criminal body—the selected examples of the characteristic crimes of the South.

"The following is a more detailed list of the nativities of these criminals:

"*Northern States.*—New York, 22; Pennsylvania, 9; Ohio, 9; Illinois, 5; Massachusetts, 3; Connecticut, 3; Indiana, 3; New Jersey, 2; New Hampshire, 1; Rhode Island, 1; Maine, 1—59.

"*Southern States.*—Louisiana, 9; Virginia, 6; Missouri, 6; Maryland, 5; North Carolina, 3; South Carolina, 3; Georgia, 3; Alabama, 3; Mississippi, 3; Kentucky, 2; Arkansas, 1; District of Columbia, 2—46."

Now, the great Empire State, from which my worthy competitor hails, and which cast her Presidential vote for "Fremont and Dayton"—I intend no disrespect to the gentleman—New York furnishes *two* convicts to the penitentiary of the far distant State of Louisiana, for every *one* who is a native of the State; while Pennsylvania and Ohio, two anti-slavery States, furnish each a number equal to the Louisiana contribution. Pious, puritanical Massachusetts, of the extreme North, has as many representatives in the Louisiana penitentiary, as the *adjoining* State of Mississippi, and *three* for every *one* furnished by the adjoining State of Arkansas, where stabbing men with "Arkansas toothpicks" is so common! Connecticut, educated, conscientious, and pious Connecticut—famous for her love of *freedom*, *wooden-clocks*, *wooden-hams*, *wooden-nutmegs*, *wooden-shad*, and *cow-heel flints*, furnishes as many as Georgia, whose citizens are an unmitigated tribe of slave-drivers!

Of the 347 convicts, of all classes, who now crowd the cells of the Louisiana State Prison, 145 are from the parishes of Orleans and Jefferson, contiguous parishes on the river, where the foreign and Free-State immigrants congregate. The river parishes, at all times open to the incursions of rogues from abroad, as high up as the Mississippi and Arkansas lines, contributed 50, showing that the interior of the State, remote from the highways, furnished only 62 of all classes. Of these only *nine* are natives of Louisiana; not even a convict for each parish; while there are *twelve* interior parishes from which there is not a single convict, native or imported, immigrant or rover!

Northern papers and politicians, as well as clergymen, make the crimes that are committed at the South a matter of fault-finding with the "the peculiar institution," and charge these evils to the demoralizing effects of negro slavery. Northern men are so accustomed to look abroad for news, and are so familiar with crime at their own doors, that the statistical reports of crime in the South make up interesting items of news, and afford occasions for elaborate criticisms on Southern society. Facts, however, are decidedly against their theories, and show the comparative tone of bad morals in the North to be much more and worse than in the South. Whoever will make a comparison of the statistics of crimes, in the non-slaveholding States, with States in the South, will find that there is a large balance for good in favor of the South.

To illustrate, briefly, this point, Louisiana has nearly *double* the population of Connecticut, yet, by the census of 1850, as many as 545 natives of the United States were convicted of crime in Connecticut, against 197 in Louisiana!

Virginia has one-third more population than Massachusetts, yet, by the same census, there were in the penitentiary of Massachusetts 270 natives of the United States, and all of New England except a few free negroes, against 160 in Virginia, half of whom were from *Free States!*

The State of Massachusetts last year had 24,905 paupers, who were supported by a direct tax, or relieved by public charity, at the enormous expense of $ 521,254! The number of indigent children in Massachusetts, last year, was 1188, supported at the public charge.

But I am not done with the penitentiary statistics of the country. Anti-Slavery men have made this issue, and I intend to make them sick of the *details.* And now for the supply of criminals in the penitentiary of Virginia. On the 12th of last March, the Virginia State Prison contained more prisoners than ever before inhabited its gloomy cells. The cells were closely filled, there being from two to four in each, and still they were coming!

The number of white persons, male and female, was	240
Free Negroes	97
Slaves to be transported	4
Total number of convicts	341

A gentleman writing to me in April, in answer to my inquiries, and from the city of Richmond, said:

"There are only about *one-third* of our convicts natives of Virginia; the rest are foreigners and natives of other States. According to population, New York is equally represented with Virginia!"

The Report of the President and Directors of the Maryland penitentiary, for January, 1858, shows that there were 415 prisoners; natives of the United States, 332; white natives of Maryland, 100. The other white natives hail from Pennsylvania, New York, Massachusetts, Delaware, New Jersey, Connecticut, and the District of Columbia. Pennsylvania has the largest representation of any Free State, namely, TWENTY-ONE.

The Report of the Officers of the Mississippi penitentiary, for 1857, shows that 105 convicts were in the cells. Of these, *sixteen* were natives of Mississippi, and *seventeen* were from the States of Pennsylvania, New York, New Jersey, Ohio, Indiana and Wisconsin; the North being able to out-poll Mississippi *one* vote in her own penitentiary!

The "Report of the State Prison Inspectors" of Alabama, for 1857, shows that there were 219 prisoners confined, and *thirty-one* of these were natives of Alabama. The same number hail from New York, Maine,

Illinois, Pennsylvania, Connecticut, Massachusetts, Ohio, New Jersey, and Rhode Island; *New York* having a delegation of *thirteen!* Thus Alabama and the Free States are *tied* in her own penitentiary!

Reverse this picture — go into your Northern penitentiaries, and while you have *double* the number of convicts that we have in the Southern States, you will rarely find a native of any Southern State, unless it be a villanous negro the Abolitionists have stolen from us, and then sent to prison to get rid of him!

But, I must be indulged while I refer to the statistics of crime in Ohio, a State occupying a high position in the scale of freedom. I have inspected the last Annual Report of the Ohio penitentiary, and a painfully interesting document it is!

> "The whole number received during *one* year, and that year ending November 1, 1857, was 244; white males, 205; colored males, 20; white females, 5; colored females, 1; white male United States prisoners, 13; making the nett receipts for one year, of white and colored, 257! These additions left 608 convicts in the penitentiary on the first of November."

Where did all these come from? where were they born? I will give you the leading items of the Report:

> "Africa, 2; England, 8; France, 3; Germany, 19; Ireland, 27; *New York*, 37; Pennsylvania, 23; Ohio, 74. What were their crimes? Grand Larceny, 56; Burglary, 44; Burglary and Larceny, 17; Horse-stealing, 25; Robbery, 10; Manslaughter, 12; Murder, 9; Murder in the first degree, 5. Add the 5 to the 9, and we have Murder, 14; Rape, 3; assault with intent to commit Rape, 7; and Bigamy 5!"

Here is another item; look at it! Of the whole number of 608 now confined in the Ohio penitentiary, there are only 81 owning property; without property, 527! These 527 are "squatter sovereigns" and agrarian levellers, such as you send out from New York and other Free States, armed with *Sharp's Rifles* and *Holy Bibles*, to regulate Kansas affairs, and kill off "border ruffians."

But, I do not propose to entertain this audience with declamation, or round assertions, but with *facts* and *figures*, which never deceive. According to the authorities of your own great city of New York (*turning to Mr. Pryne*), derived from the official report of the police, there were in that city, from May, 1846, to May 1847, *one year:*

"Committed for drunkenness alone	7,453
Drunkenness and disorderly conduct	5,584
Assault and battery	1,771
Fighting in the streets when drunk	1,316
Petit larcenies, to obtain the means of drinking.	2,209
Attempts to kill while drunk	36
Stabbing, in a state of intoxication	16
Murder, committed while drunk	8
Suspicion of murder	4
Threatening life	53
Highway robbery	34
Vagrancy, growing out of drunkenness	1,259
Lodgings to the houseless, (intemperate)	31,203
Total	50,846"

This, fellow-countrymen, was the state of morals in New York *eleven* years ago, and the journals and municipal reports of the city concede that they have annually grown worse, and that the number of ruffians annually committed to prison, have so increased as to keep pace with the increase of the population. They committed for the crimes I have specified, in one year, and that, too, *eleven* years ago, 50,846 persons—more men than we ever had in Mexico, to subdue that Republic!

But I have other items of interest to lay before you. For seven years, ending with 1830, there had been 5669 desertions in the United States army, while 7058 had been tried by court martial during the same period. So says the Report of the Secretary of War, GEN. CASS, then serving under the Administration of Gen. Jackson. The army records, giving the nativity of these deserters, and offenders against martial law, set down 4000 of the deserters as natives of the New England States, and it was in view of their proneness to desert, that GEN. GAINES, at that time, recommended that army recruits be taken from the Southern States!

The *New York Herald* gives a list of the failures of 1857, in which it appears that 884 of these failures are in the Free States, against 75 only in the Slave States! This was during the panic of last fall, and up to the close of the year 1857.

The *Herald* of a more recent date, sets forth the list of failures that have occurred in the United States, from the first of January to the first of April, 1858, giving the number of failures for the *first quarter* of the present year. I give the list entire, and call the attention of my opponent, and through him, of the civilized world, to the figures:

"New York State.....	183	"Pennsylvania State..	104
New York City......	74	Philadelphia City...	27
Massachusetts State.	25	*Maryland State*.....	10
Boston City..........	34	*Baltimore City*......	23

"*Alabama*............	25	"New Hampshire....	13
Arkansas	3	New Jersey........	23
Connecticut.........	20	*North Carolina*	33
Florida	2	Ohio	174
Georgia..............	19	Rhode Island........	25
Illinois...............	195	*South Carolina*.....	11
Iowa..................	93	*Tennessee*............	32
Indiana..............	81	*Texas*	5
Kentucky............	41	Vermont............	19
Louisiana...........	30	*Virginia*	41
Maine................	9	Wisconsin...........	63
Michigan............	74	All the Territories..	19
Mississippi	6		
Missouri	31	Total in U. S....	1405"

I *italicise* the fourteen Southern States, and leave the twelve Free States in Roman characters. Thus it will be seen that out of *fourteen hundred and five failures*, 312 only are in Slave States, while the remaining *ten hundred and ninety-three* are in twelve Free States, as monuments of their superior morality! These failures foot up the round sum of $30,639,000; and to use the *Herald's* own language—"The amount South, is disproportional, showing that it is small concerns there which are breaking down."

I may be told, that the reason of the many and great failures in the non-slaveholding States, when compared with the South, is, that the "enterprizing" men of the country are North, the manufacturing interests, and the wealth and capitalists are there! I deny this; and I propose to throw some additional light upon this subject, by consulting the Federal Census for 1850. The census testifies that Massachusetts, which is the *richest* non-slaveholding State, could divide with each of her citizens $548. Rhode

Island, which is the next *richest* non-slaveholding State, could divide with each of her citizens $526; one other non-slaveholding State, *Connecticut*, could divide with her citizens $321. After this, the Free States fall down to $231; then to $228; and down to $160, and to $134.

On the other hand, including whites and colored, South Carolina could divide $1001; Louisiana $806; Mississippi $702; and Georgia $638, with her citizens. Alabama could divide $511; Maryland $423; Virginia $403; Kentucky $377; North Carolina $367; and Tennessee could divide $248, with each of her citizens.

In a division of all the property accumulated by all the non-slaveholding States, it will give to each citizen $233; while all accumulated by the various Slave States, will give to each citizen $439—*nearly double!* It is not possible, with these facts before us, to believe that slavery tends to poverty.

I call your attention to the Compendium of the United States Census, chapter v. table lxxi. There you will find that there are more free *mulattoes*, than there are free blacks in the Free States. In Ohio, there are *seven* mulatto children for *one* in Virginia, according to the negro population; and in Indiana and Illinois, there are *five* for *one* in Tennessee and Georgia! As the white people of the North do not marry blacks, these mulattoes must have been born out of wedlock. While, then, there are more mulattoes in the Free States than blacks, in the South, on the contrary, there is only *one* mulatto to *twelve* blacks! Look at New York, also, with its tens of thousands of public prostitutes, besides thousands of private ones, and compare this with the proverbial virtue of the white women of the Southern States. The white *men* of the North have had something to do with all this: let them cleanse their skirts, first, of these abominable sins, before they come to the South to lecture us upon the sin of slavery. Let them cast out the beam that is in their own eye, and then they may see clearly to cast out the mote that is in their Southern brother's eye.

Crime, in Northern cities, absolutely keeps pace with *pauperism*. In *Boston*, according to official State Reports, a few years past, and since the taking of the Federal Census, *one* person out of every *fourteen* males, and *one* out of every *twenty-eight* females, was arraigned for criminal offences. According to the Census of 1850, there were, in the *State* of Massachusetts, in a population of 994,514, the astonishing number of 7250 convicts for crime; while others escaped upon *technicalities* of the law, and for the want of sufficient proof, who deserved conviction! In Virginia, the same year, in a population of 1,421,661, there were 107 convictions for crime.

The Federal Census shows that, in the *State* of New York, from which the gentleman hails who follows me in this discussion, the proportion of crime is the same as in Massachusetts!

In the *city* of New York, in 1849, there were sentenced to the *State Prison* 119 men and 17 women; to the *Penitentiary*, 700 men and 170 women; to the *City Prison*, 162 men and 67 women—making a total of 1235 criminals. Here is an amount of crime, in a single Northern city, that equals all in the *fifteen* Slave States together, for any one year! In the *State* of New York, according to the Census of 1850, there were, in a population of 3,097,304, as many as 10,279 convictions for crime; while, in South Carolina, in a population of 668,507, there were only 46 convictions for crime, and *one-fourth* of these were *Northern* men!

The gentleman boasted, last evening, that, on his return home, he would take the stump for *Gerritt Smith.* I suggest to him that he had better take the *pulpit,* and try to improve the morals of his native State!

In New England, one free negro is *blind* for every 807; while, in the Southern States, there is only one blind slave for every 2645. In New England, there is one free negro *insane* for every 980; while, in the South, there is but one insane slave for every 3080! Can any man bring himself to believe, with these facts before him, that freedom in New England has proved a blessing to this race of people, or that slavery is to them a curse in the Southern States? The morals and character of the negroes themselves, are of a far higher grade in the Slave States than in the Free States, although surrounded, in the latter, by the refining and elevating influences of Black Republican society!

It is common at the North to hear men boast of the superior *educational* advantages of the Free over the Slave States, and of their excelling us in common school education, as well as in the facilities for the higher grades of learning. I here give from the *Richmond*

Enquirer, a statement in regard to College education in New York and Virginia. The white population of New York is to that of Virginia *three* to *one*, yet Virginia excels her in college education. Here is a statement of the number of colleges, professors, students, &c, in New York and Virginia:

	New York.	Virginia.
"Number of colleges	8	10
Professors	82	72
Students	883	1,309
Volumes in library	5,500	65,000
Alumni	6,371	6,484

Connected with this subject of education let me here introduce a paragraph from the Philadelphia *North American*, a journal decided in its opposition to Slavery and the South:

"The South, as a general rule, is better represented in Congress than Free States. The best men in the South are willing to go to Washington and to look after the interests of their section, and their constituents keep them there as long as they are desirous to serve. But it really seems as if, in many cases, the North picked out third rate men intentionally to represent them. It is quite notorious that very many who go to one or the other branch of Congress from the Free States are men without education, with only a superficial smattering of knowledge on a few common topics, picked up in a way themselves cannot explain, and who have never, until they found themselves in high place, associated with persons of good breeding. Their only arts are those of the demagogue or the trickster. They are utterly incapable of rising to any commanding views of national policy, or comprehending in its full significance our Constitution, and the principles of our government. The intrigues and management of the petty politician are alone within their scope."

The Legislature of Wisconsin, composed of Anti-Slavery men, not long since closed a protracted and angry session, and has given to the world the report of an "Investigating Committee," setting forth a degree of bribery and corruption in legislation never before heard of in a Christian country, and such as would put rotten Denmark, or unprincipled Russia to the blush! The "La Crosse Railroad Company," a moonshine enterprise, bribed the Legislature. I give the language and figures of the Report:

"Of the bribed Senators, nine were Democrats, who received $135,000; and three were Republicans, who received $30,000. The only Senators who voted against the bill, were six Republicans. They refused all offers of bribes.

"In the Assembly, fifty-seven members received bribes as follows:

38 Democratic members received................	$260,000
19 Republican members..........................	95,000

"Seven members of the Assembly refused bribes; six of whom were Republicans, and one a Democrat. Of other State officers who received bribes, were—

A Republican Governor..............................	$50,000
Democratic Bank Comptroller.......................	10,000
Democratic Lieutenant-Governor	10,000
Democratic Clerk of Assembly......................	5,000
Dem. Assistant Clerk of Assembly................	10,000

"To recapitulate, the account stands thus:

"Number of Democratic members and State officers who were bribed is 51.

Amount received by them........................ $430,000

"Number of Republican members and State officers bribed is 23.

Amount received by them $175,000

"The above exhibit is confined to the members and State officers. When we go beyond that, we find that the Democracy have fairly wallowed in corruption. To a moonshine railroad, of which Democratic Ex-Gov. Barstow was president, $1,000,000 of La Crosse county bonds was given, as its share of the plunder, which was divided out by Barstow and his followers, he receiving $80,000, his private Secretary $52,000, the editor of the Madison *Argus* during Barstow's administration $52,000, and so on. To other outside papers there was paid, for their influence, $246,000; about $40,000 went to Republicans, and the rest to Democrats."

Now the point I propose to make is, that of the *nativity* of these thieves. They are *Northern* men — cradled in opposition to the institution of negro slavery. The reason why the Democrats *outstole* the Republicans is, that they were the most numerous in that Legislature; but all were for making Kansas a Free State, as their resolutions show. What a commentary upon the morality and integrity of Anti-Slavery men, hailing from the New England States!

Look at the journals of Congress, in all time past, and when investigating committees have been raised to ferret out bribery and corruptions, the guilty parties have turned out to be from Free States. For instance, look at your *Mattisons*, of New York! Are $87,000 given by Lawrence, Stone, & Co., to *bribe* Congressmen and Editors to enact a Tariff law to suit the North, Northern Congressmen, and Northern editors get the corruption fund and divide it out among them! Offer a Southern Representative or Senator a bribe for his vote to aid in swindling the Government, and he spits in your face, at the same time that he slaps your jaws! But make the offer to a Northern Representative or Senator, and he looks to the ground — then raises his hang-dog countenance, and articulates, "I *guess* I will take it—you can rely upon me!" This is the difference between Southern gentlemen and Northern Abolitionists!

The New York Senate appointed a "Select Committee" to visit in person the "Charitable Institutions of the State, and the City and County Poor and Work-Houses, and Jails," and report thereon. I find this Report on page 23, of the New York "Journal of Medical Reform," for May, 1857, Vol. V., No. 1; and from this document I take a single extract:

"Who could have imagined that our poor-houses, erected at the expense of our humane and virtuous people, and supported by their money, were thus turned into houses of prostitution, where adultery and licentiousness in their most revolting forms abound, and go unchecked and unpunished. Who *knew* that these poor-houses in our very midst were but so many vile nests of moral and physical pollution?

"The record does not stop here, for we are told that 'the treatment of lunatics and idiots in these houses is frequently abusive. The sheds and cells where they are confined are wretched abodes, often wholly unprovided with bedding. In most cases female lunatics had none but male attendants. Instances were testified to of the *whipping* of male and female idiots and lunatics, and of confining the latter in loathsome cells and *binding them with chains*' * * * 'In some poor houses the committee found lunatics, both male and female, in cells, in a state of nudity. The cells were intolerably offensive, littered with the long-accumulated filth of the occupants, and with straw reduced to chaff by long use as bedding, portions of which, mingled with the filth adhered to the persons of the inmates and formed the only covering they had.' Talk of the horrors of the cells and dungeons of the Inquisition! Utter pious ejaculations over the repulsive aspects of Southern slavery! Send millions of money to 'improve the moral and spiritual condition of the Flathead Indians and the world of heathenism!' What a picture is this for the contemplation of a Christian community! It is *not* a picture of the fancy; it is a stern and shocking reality. The condition of the slave is paradise to the atrocities and suffering and tortures such as are here depicted. Let us turn our eyes and hearts homeward, for here is a field broad enough for the exercise of our superabundant sympathies. Let slavery, which we have not the right or the power to mitigate or remove, occupy less of our thoughts and time and attention, and let us turn to the relief and removal of a system of cruelty and injustice which exists at our very thresholds."

I will now present you a few cases of Northern fanaticism, illustrative of the *Infidel* spirit, and *Infidel* tendency of the Northern mind. A Woman's Rights Convention was held at Rutland, in Vermont, in June last, composed of an equal number of fools and fanatics, of both sexes—representing Free Lovers, Free Soilers, Abolitionists, Spiritualists, Trance Mediums, Bible Repudiators, and representatives of every other crazy *ism* known to the annals of bedlam. The proceedings of this Convention were considered of sufficient importance to be reported in full by the New York city papers.

After resolving in reference to the *Rights of Woman*—that she has a right to be virtuous or otherwise, as may suit her inclinations, the Convention adopted by acclamation the following articles of faith:

1. "*Resolved*, That the authority of each individual soul is absolute and final, in deciding all questions as to what is true or false in principle, and right or wrong in practice. Therefore, the individual, the Church, or the State, that attempts to control the opinions or the practice of any man or woman, by authority of power outside of his or her own soul, is guilty of a flagrant wrong.

2. "*Resolved*, That slavery is a wrong which no power in the Universe can make right; therefore, any law, constitution, court, or government; any church, priesthood, creed or Bible; any Christ or any God that by silence or otherwise

authorizes man to enslave man, merits the scorn and contempt of mankind.

3. "*Resolved*, That the earth, like air and light, belongs in common to the children of men, and on it each human being is alike dependent. Each child, by virtue of its existence, has an equal and inalienable right to as much of the earth's surface as is convenient by proper culture to support and perfect its development, and none has a right to any more.

4. "*Resolved*, That all efforts of Churches and priests to enforce an observance of a Christian Sabbath as of *Divine appointment*, is a flagrant violation of individual right, and must be prosecuted in a dishonest disregard of the spirit and positive teachings of the New Testament.

5. "*Resolved*, That nothing is true or right, and nothing is false or wrong, because it is sanctioned or condemned by the Bible; therefore the Bible is powerless to prove any doctrine to be true, or any practice to be right, and it should never be quoted for that purpose."

What a mixture of woman's rights, land reform, Abolition fanaticism, Sabbath-hating, and Bible-opposing theology. And yet, the sentiments advanced here by this clerical gentleman are in *unison* with these in all material respects.

In May last, a Reform Convention, and a Woman's Rights Society met, numerously attended. The infamous objects of the Society are thus alluded to by the New York *Day Book:*

"Friday, May 14, 1858, was a day that every honest New Yorker — every unperverted man and woman — ought to be ashamed of. For be it known that on that day there met a Convention of men and women, white and black, in this city, and, strange as it may seem, open and undisguised prostitution was advocated! Here, in a country that is sending thousands and thousands of dollars to convert the heathen — to instruct them in the principles of Christianity — there are those who openly promulgate the beastly doctrine of promiscuous intercourse between the sexes! Can this be believed? If not, let the report of the proceedings of the Woman's Rights Convention testify."

I quote once more from the *Day Book*, a conservative and reputable Journal:

"There are no orgies recorded in the annals of Roman degradation more disgusting than the recent meeting of this so-called Woman's Rights Convention. Negroes, mulattoes and mongrels, of all colors and shades of colors, mixed up with men and women calling themselves white—women without delicacy or decency, lost to modesty or shame, and men bold in beastliness made up the staple of this gathering. Even George W. Curtis, a man whom even his enemies would charitably suppose would have not been found in such a place, was there, and disgraced himself by calling the President of the United States 'a pimp.' He advocated the right of suffrage for women, and contributed, by his presence, to lend whatever influence he has to the pernicious doctrines promulgated."

Just in this connection, lest I omit it, I beg leave to introduce an extract from the Report on Home Missions, recently presented at the "Massachusetts General Association," and copied by the New York *Observer*.

"From reliable statistics it appears that in Maine, New Hampshire, Vermont and Massachusetts, not more than *one quarter of the whole population* are in the habit of attending church. There are one million three hundred thousand people in New England, who, so far as attending church is concerned, are, practically, like the heathen. There are twenty-six towns in this State, (Massachusetts,) which have no evangelical preaching."

The gentleman inquired last evening, why we did not teach our slaves to read the Bible? We do, more or less, in every Southern State. But I ask him, why they do not send the Gospel to these "one million three hundred thousand" Northern heathens?

But a few months ago the 25th annual session of the "American Anti-Slavery Society" was held at Mozart Hall, in New York, and the *Herald* has this notice of it:

"The twenty-fifth annual saturnalia of the conglomerated isms composing the Garrisonian American Anti-Slavery Society, commenced yesterday morning, at Mozart Hall, Broadway, with the usual incongruous assemblage. There were 'black spirits and white,' of every shade; strong-minded women, with diminutive hoops, eye-glasses, green spectacles, and unfashionable bonnets; weak-minded men, with a superabundance of hair and an evident predilection for the Grahamite diet, and the usual scattering of old ladies, blue stockings, silly girls, and noisy little boys. Though the meeting was called for 10 A. M., the audience collected slowly, and at twenty minutes after ten, the hour for commencing the performances, the room was nearly half full. After the platform had been partly filled with men, women, and blacks, and the old ladies had subsided into a quiet body of friendly gossip, the President of the Society, Mr Wm. Lloyd Garrison, opened the meeting by reading a detached portion of Scripture, designed to show a biblical opposition to slavery."

The meeting adopted, by acclamation, an infamous string of resolutions, and *Charles L. Remond*, (black) *Wendell Philips*, (white) *Miss Frances Ellen Watkins*, (black) *Wm. Garrison* and *Edmond Quincy*, (white) made speeches, sustaining the following resolutions:

"*Resolved*, That chattel slavery is delineated in its whips and chains, its yokes and thumb-screws, its paddles and branding-irons, its drivers and blood-hounds, its scourgings and mutilations, its bloody persecutions and horrible cruelties, its abrogation of the marriage institution and enforced licentiousness, its athletic assumptions of power above all that is called God, its devilish nature and accursed aim, its thronging perjuries and shocking blasphemies; and the steady growth and constant expansion of a system so frightful, are demonstrative proof that to this nation most justly applies the description of the prophet: 'Their feet run to evil, and they make haste to shed innocent blood—judgment is turned away backward, and justice standeth afar off; for truth is fallen in the street, and equity cannot enter; and he that departeth from evil maketh himself a prey.'

"*Resolved*, That the day has gone by (if it ever existed) here at the North, to frame or to offer any apology in behalf of Southern slaveholders, but, having revealed themselves to be the enemies of freedom universally, merciless and profligate in spirit, desperate and heaven defying in purpose, and bent on eternising their terrible oppression, they are to be classed among the most dangerous and depraved of the human race, and treated accordingly.

"*Resolved*, That we register our testimony against the American church, the popular religion, and the government of the United States—because, by their deliberate consent and active co-operation, four millions of our countrymen are held in the galling chains of bondage, whose emancipation is resisted by them with exceeding obduracy of spirit and malignity of purpose.

"*Resolved*, That the 'revival of religion,' which has swept over the country with contagious rapidity during the last three months, is manifestly delusive and spurious, exceptional cases to the contrary notwithstanding; because it has expressly excluded the millions in bondage from all consideration—has multiplied its converts as readily at the South as at the North."

HENRY WARD BEECHER, the great bell-wether of the New York Anti-Slavery flock, in his "Life Thoughts," says:

"The Bible Society is sending its Bibles all over the world—to Greenland and the Morea, to Arabia and Egypt; but it dares not send them to our own people. The colporteur who should leave a Bible in a slave cabin would go to heaven from the lowest limb of the first tree."

In this, Mr. Beecher is greatly mistaken. There are thousands of "slave's cabins" in the South, where the Bible may be found—where it is read and loved by slaves. In the city where I reside, there are two large Sabbath Schools for the slaves, where they are taught to read, and love the Bible. The one is under the care of the Methodist, the other of the Protestant Episcopal Church. Indeed, Bibles may be left at all the "slave's cabins" of the South, with perfect safety to the colporteur. We really desire our slaves to be furnished with Bibles, and taught how to read them; first, because it will promote their spiritual interests; and next, because in that glorious Book, they are taught to be obedient to their masters; and further, that they are slaves by God's own appointment! To our slaves, and all others, we say of the Bible:

"This sacred book, from Heaven bestow'd,
The apostate world to bless—
A light to mark the pilgrim's road
Through this dark wilderness

"This book reveals a Saviour's charms,
And life and light bestows,
Secures my soul from death's alarms,
Or aggravates my woes.

"I would not let this volume lie
Neglected and unknown;
For it must raise me to the sky,
Or bear my spirit down."

A Southern correspondent of the Philadelphia *Christian Observer*, makes the following sensible and pertinent remarks on the subject of "elevating the colored race." And what he says is but a specimen of what is being done in the South, in teaching the slaves and gathering them into the fold of Christ. By hundreds and thousands, they are flocking into the Church. What are Abolitionists doing for them? What do they propose to do?

But, to the remarks of this correspondent:

> "Georgia has not the honor, as I supposed, of the largest church in the United States, black or white; for Virginia claims that distinction. The Baptist church (African) in Richmond, Va., numbers 2700 communicants!!—truly a congregation to be proud of. The Baptists have 52,000 colored communicants in Eastern Virginia alone. There is is a colored church in Petersburg, Va., of 1800, and another of 1400. In Charleston, S. C., the Presbyterian Synod represents nearly 5000 colored members, Throughout Louisiana, large congregations of slaves are found. In New Orleans, one African Methodist has 1350 members, and six colored missionaries. A devoted Episcopal clergyman, who labors among the people of eleven plantations in Louisiana, says: 'It has never been my privilege to declare the glorious truths of the Gospel of the blessed God to more orderly, quiet, serious congregations;' that 'their hearts are unfeignedly thankful,' and that 'they show forth his praise not only with their lips, but in their lives.' The labors of pious missionaries are gladly encouraged among slaves by their masters—even by those who are not themselves professors."

But, gentlemen, the time I have already occupied admonishes me that I must give way to the gentleman who is to reply to me; and this I shall do after I consume a few brief moments.

The cities and towns, and many of the interior settlements, in the New England and North-western States of this Confederacy, in my honest judgment, open a wider and more inviting field, at this time, for honest, faithful, evangelical missionary labors, than

Hindostan, Siam, Ceylon, China, or Western Africa; for the reason, too, that the natives of these benighted lands, who have been denied the light of the blessed Gospel, cannot be held to as rigid an accountability, in the next life, as those who see the light, like the Free-Soil population of the North, and still love and do the deeds of darkness! I seriously contemplate getting up a missionary organization, to be styled: "THE MISSIONARY SOCIETY OF THE SOUTH, FOR THE CONVERSION OF THE FREEDOM-SHRIEKERS, SPIRITUALISTS, FREE-LOVERS, FOURIERITES, AND INFIDEL REFORMERS OF THE NORTH!" All jesting aside, duty, principle, and expediency imperatively demand that we should send among our deluded Northern neighbors a corps of competent missionaries. I am willing to lead the way, and to open the campaign on Boston Common; and if I shall succeed in converting my brother Pryne from the "error of his ways," I would be pleased to have him go with me as an *exhorter*, and he would then be occupying the same position he does in this debate! May I hope for your conversion? (*turning to the gentleman.*) He shakes his head — he gives me an emphatic No! No, gentlemen, I have no hope of the reformation of the clergy of New England. The Evangelist Luke tells us that it was not until a multitude of the *common people* believed, that the *priests* became obedient to the faith!

Christian masters and slaves of the glorious South cannot remain guiltless, in a coming day, if they fold their arms and look idly on at the heart-sickening spectacle now presented by — not their *brethren* — but their *fellow-creatures* of the North, and do nothing to turn them from their abominations! In addition to their wicked and rebellious course upon the slavery question, they have forsaken, to a very great extent, the true God and the Christian religion, and gone after Spiritualism, Abolitionism, Fanny-Wrightism, Fourierism, Mormonism, Free-Loveism, and the hundred and one *isms* so spontaneously produced by the soil of New England! True, the path of a Southern missionary, in the midst of the isms, cruelties, and crimes of the North, enforcing morality and honesty, would not be strewed with flowers. But let him fall back for consolation upon the sublime sentiment of the poet:

"Am I a soldier of the Cross,
A follower of the Lamb —
And shall I fear to own his cause,
Or blush to speak his name?

"Must I be carried to the skies
On flowery beds of ease,
While others *fought* to win the prize,
And sail'd through bloody seas?

"Sure I must *fight*, if I would reign;
Increase my courage, Lord;
I'll bear the toil, endure the pain,
Supported by thy word.

"Thy saints [of the South!] in all this glorious war,
Shall conquer, though they die;
They see the triumph from afar,
By faith they bring it nigh!"

In conclusion, I will only offer a few criticisms upon the speech of the gentleman last evening, and I will then yield him the stand. He denied that the term *servant* means *slave*, and he sustained his position by a quotation from *Albert Barnes*, an Abolition preacher of Philadelphia. I asserted, and I now repeat, that the word rendered *servants* in the Bible invariably means SLAVES; and I sustained my position by the Bible and the Greek Lexicon. But the gentleman advised you, last night, to trample under foot a Bible that favors the institution of slavery!

Last evening, the gentleman stood here, and with a knowledge that we had bound ourselves not to interrupt each other when speaking, asserted that I had said, the Bible and the Almighty advise the carrying on of the slave-trade; and that, the night before, I had denounced the slave-trade!

Now, whether the gentleman *intended* to make a false impression upon the minds of those who heard him, and who may read the newspaper report of what he said, I will not say; but this I do say, *he has left a false impression.* In my first address, I denounced the African slave-trade as piracy, and the unprincipled traders of New England for engaging in it. In my address last evening, I quoted a passage from the law of bondage written out by Moses, to show that the people of those days *bought and sold slaves*, and held them *as property.* Out of these two *facts*, the gentleman has *fabricated* a charge he ought to be ashamed of, and publicly take back!

The assertion that Christian masters at the South chain their negroes to carts while they go to the communion table, is as destitute of any foundation in truth, as was that unblushing avowal of the Devil to Christ, that he owned all the kingdoms of the world, and could give him a legal title to them!

The assertion by Mr. Pryne, that *Frederick Douglass* and *Sam Ward* are intellectually *his* superiors, I do not doubt, after the exhibition he has made of himself on this stand! But I do not think it follows, as a matter of course, that they are giants in intellect. They may be intellectually his superiors, and still be moderate men! These free negroes hail from Syracuse, I believe, and Mr. Pryne tells me that is the place of his nativity. I will not pause to inquire if anything good can come out of Nazareth, alias *Syracuse*, but I will ask the gentleman one or two questions, and I insist on a reply to them. As he holds these two free negroes in such high esteem, both on account of their integrity and talents; as they have sons, and Mr. Pryne says he has a little daughter — would he be willing to see her united in matrimony to one of these *buck negroes?* Answer the question, and the colored persons here to-night will know how to appreciate your friendship! Show your *faith* by your *works*, and marry your children off to the sons and daughters of these talented negroes!

Finally, I do not expect the gentleman to meet the issues I have presented this evening. To *evade* these, he announced to you last evening what his subject should be this evening. It is much easier for the gentleman to travel the old and beaten path of Abolition slang-whanging, than to fall into the new road I have marked out for him!

REPLY

"To Mr. Brownlow's "Statement."

When the reading of Mr. Brownlow's statement was concluded,

Mr. Pryne rose and said: Gentlemen, I wish to make a brief statement in reply to that which you have just heard.

In the correspondence between my opponent and myself, it was agreed that our speeches in this debate should be of an hour in length; or, should they, under the pressure of any special occasion, go beyond that limit, their duration should not exceed an hour and a half. Every speech of Mr. Brownlow thus far, has extended beyond the time agreed on as the ordinary limit, and has occupied nearly an hour and a half. While I admit that, as a matter of courtesy and discretion on my part, I am at liberty to allow him to consume more than an hour, courtesy and discretion on his part demand that he should not, taking advantage of the privilege stipulated in the correspondence, overrun the limits of the hour on every occasion, and then claim it as a right.

Gentlemen, in this respect I have exhausted courtesy, I have gone beyond its claims, in order to sustain the honor and dignity of my side of the Union. From the South I have been accustomed to expect the extremest courtesy; yet now, what was extended as a privilege, is claimed as a right.

Having exhausted the bounds of courtesy, I fall back upon my rights, and ask him to keep himself within the hour at least half the time. I stand for the hour as the limit of the time.

He says that I have not been interrupted. No; and for the very good reason, that I have not overstrained courtesy and good manners, and demanded that the audience should interrupt me. Nor do I intend to do so.

He says he asks no favors. I have not asked a favor; nor shall I. I ask my rights, and shall maintain them.

He remarks that many gentlemen from the South are here, and have been. I am glad of it; but if this statement is designed as a crack of the whip to intimidate me into giving him more than his rights in this debate, it is utterly futile, for I accept no such intimidation. Whether gentlemen are from the South or the North, I care not. I only ask my rights, according to the agreement, and shall maintain them.

"OUGHT AMERICAN SLAVERY TO BE PERPETUATED?"

NEGATIVE, III. — BY ABRAM PRYNE.

LADIES AND GENTLEMEN,—I rise to fulfil the promise I made last evening, that my argument to-night should be made up very much of figures. I am happy to be able to say that my preparation made, traverses the ground that the gentleman has gone over, perfectly; and I shall not be in the slightest degree at fault, in being able to meet the argument which he has made.

Before I proceed to do so, however, allow me to offer one or two preliminary observations that seem to me to be at this point fitting. The insinuation was thrown out to-night in the preliminary statement of my opponent, that perhaps I and my friends wanted to recede from this debate. I now say, that so long as Mr. Brownlow wishes to repeat with me this debate in the principal cities of the North, giving me half the time, and the selection of place, and making of arrangements which he has had in this case, half of the time, he will find me on hand to meet him, whether on Boston Common or elsewhere.

My opponent in his speech of to-night spoke of my conversion, and wished to know whether there was not a hope that he could make me an exhorter. I have been practising here what I trust is very fair exhortation for a raw hand, and when he shall be converted from the sins I have recounted before him, and which stare him and his people of the South in the face, like the ghosts of centuries of crime, then let him come and ask me for a new strain of exhortation, and he shall have it. I mean to prove "my call," by preaching to the nearest and greatest sinners first, and when he and they show "works meet for repentance" I will begin with sinners of a milder type.

And now a word with reference to general statements. Of course, a man may make an hour's argument professedly based upon facts, and of every other fact the bottom may have fallen out, if it ever had one; yet, in an impromptu reply, one cannot be expected to gather up all these fallacious statements and answer them. So, gentlemen, in regard to many of these statements that have been brought forward as facts, do not take it for granted that I believe them, that they are incontrovertibly true, simply because I do not put my finger in every case on the flaw. Why gentlemen, I have to-night and heretofore, laughed in my sleeve from the perfect consciousness that the veriest schoolboys all over the North are able to understand and to tell the gentleman, that many of the professed facts which are paraded as a marked feature in the argument of my opponent, are entirely without foundation. And gentlemen, as this is not a primary school, and as I will trust the correction of these mistatements with the primary schools of the entire North, do not ask me to consume my time in refuting them.

Something has been said with reference to my language being harsh, as though mine were strange words coming from the source they do. But, gentlemen, I have a harsh subject to deal with—haggard, and fierce, and bloody, and grim — towering upward, in the enormity of its own moral darkness, above all other wrongs that have cursed the world; and am I expected to describe it in dulcet phrase, and with silken words? Give me a pleasant subject, and I will do my best to set it forth in pleasant words. Give me a subject that is all full of horrors, and I will do my best to make those horrors start forth in the words that I employ.

In regard to the remarks of my opponent to-night, I will charge upon the first half of his speech with a single broadside, that can be all gathered up into a single retort, based upon a universally-known fact, and then I shall pass on to the other branch of my argument.

We have had read to us comparative statements of the criminal statistics of the North and the South. I do not, in many cases, accept these statistics as correct; for even without the census report before me, I was able to detect many erroneous statements. Besides, they are gathered up and thrown out in such a general, vague way, that one cannot, in every case, hunt down the misstatement. Like the Irishman's fleas, you put your finger on them, and they are not there. I can well afford to let not a few of his statistical assumptions alone, to sink by their own weight; and it would be folly for me, before an intelligent people, to spend time in hunting them, for the game is not worth the effort, and will break its own neck in the chase if left alone.

But, gentlemen, I can reply to all these criminal statistics in a word. There are, in the Slave States of this Union, 250,000 criminals, who have robbed humanity of three million men, women and children, desolating the cradles, disrupting the marriage relations, breaking up families, and selling many of the daughters to prostitution. These criminals are yet untried, unconvicted, unsentenced. They are on trial before the moral sense of the wide world to-night; and when the moral sense of the world shall have carried out in their case the same principles of law which the North applies to those who violate justice and freedom, then come to me with your prison statistics of the South, adding these 250,000, and I will figure with you. We of the North punish such criminals, while you of the South send them to Congress to make laws.

Now, gentlemen, I shall ask you to listen to an argument of statistics. Such an argument might be, in most cases, dry; but this will, as it seems to me, bear so pat upon the question that I doubt not you will listen with interest. For I am not talking to lazy men and women, who are unwilling to think, but I feel that I address those who are ready to take all the trouble necessary to a just decision of the question discussed. I shall argue to prove that American slavery ought to be abolished because it desolates the fair soil of the South with poverty; because it diminishes the value of the land; because it stands in the way of all material progress; because it impoverishes the whole country over which it spreads.

In proving these positions, I shall make a contrast between the North and the South in all the elements of material wealth, taking my statistics in all cases from the Census Reports, collected and supervised by a Carolinian, who cannot be at all suspected of doing injustice to the South. In what I state my authority shall be De Bow.

The North is usually called the sterile North. The South is denominated (in the language used by Mr. Brownlow in the course of our correspondence — much better language, by the way, than that employed in some other parts of that correspondence) "the sunny South." We of the North are considered as dwelling among bleak hills, where chilling winds sweep over our mountain-tops. The fruits that grow at all are considered to be of little worth, and the grain that we raise is thought to be dug from among the rocks. The South, on the other hand, is "the sunny South." Let us see how they compare in all the elements of material wealth, and then inquire what has caused the difference.

The entire area of the Free States of this Union is 392,062,082 acres; the entire area of the Slave States, 544,926,720 acres; the difference in favor of the Slave States being 152,844,638. The settlement of these various portions of the country was almost simultaneous. In 1850, the difference of population in favor of the Free States was 3,821,946. The natural advantages of the Slave States, if they had been open to settlement on the same terms as were the Free States, and if their institutions had invited settlement, would have caused their population to far exceed that of the North. But no man can enter the South until he has sworn allegiance to Slavery, and done obeisance to its demands. The men who came from Germany—driven out by the waves of European revolution — the hard-handed men from all quarters of the globe, who settle down in our free Northern valleys and grow up in a little while into thrifty, hardy, useful citizens, are all shut out from the South, because her institutions are vitally antagonistic to freedom and free labor; and the European peasant comes here to work with his own hands. He has learned to hate oppression from his sad experience at home, and has no desire to degrade himself by coming into competition with slave labor. It is this class who build our magnificent public works, opening for us the channels of a rich inland commerce, and making our Northern territory a rich network of canals and railroads, bringing the carrying trade of the world to each city and rural hamlet in our half of the Union.

Again, the soil of the South would be worth much more per acre than the soil of the North, were it not for the fact that the institutions of the South have cursed the soil and made its settlement almost impossible. They have overrun their ground with a mere hoe, skimming the surface and extracting the life-blood of the soil by a murderous system of tillage — carrying nothing back to supply the drainage produced by continual crops upon the same ground; while the North plows deep, and farms in a suitable and scientific manner; yet the average value of land at the North is $28.07 per acre, while in the South it is only $5.34, making the difference in favor of the North $22.63 per acre. Is it not slavery that thus depreciates the value of land in the South? While the South has more land than the North by over 150,000,000 of acres, yet her whole soil is worth less in the market than it would have been, if free, and at Northern prices per acre, by $11,988,387,840. This is what slavery has wrenched from the value of Southern soil—being many times the estimated value of the whole slave population of the South. Every slave has cost many times his value in the impoverishment of the soil, the retarding of the settlement and growth of the country, resulting from the institution of slavery which has been there perpetuated.

Astounding as these figures are, they cannot be contradicted. So overwhelming are they, that on the first examination I was myself shocked at their apparent improbability; but careful investigation only confirms them. I charge upon slavery that it has eaten out of the bosom of the sunny South this mighty sum of $11,988,387,840.

What a vast mine of wealth to sacrifice on the altar of slavery! What a sum to sink into the fathomless maw of such a monster crime! all for the purpose of allowing 250,000 slaveholders to lord it over their negroes, keep race-horses, and vary the amusements of gambling, fighting, and drinking, by an occasional dash into politics, to play the game of Southern statesmanship, and, when weary of that, to astonish the waiters and attachées of Northern hotels by blustering about Northern watering-places.

I would now contrast some statistics in relation to New York and North Carolina. In New York, there was assessed for taxes, in 1856, 30,080,000 acres, which were valued at the rate of $36.97 per acre. In North Carolina, the same year, 32,450,560 acres were valued at $3.06 per acre — a difference of over thirty dollars an acre. Between the valuation of the State of New York and that of North Carolina, the total difference is $1,023,332,500. There was just thirty-six years' difference in time of the original settlement of these two States. Sunny Carolina, having altogether the advantage of my own rock-ribbed native State, ought to have been far in advance in the valuation of her real estate. But, thank God, the hard-handed freemen of New York have been able, while gathering wealth from the bosom of the soil by science, and art, and genius, to still pour it back again, that they may gather it, year after year, while the soil still becomes more valuable.

This is your contrast between freedom and slavery. While one steadily impoverishes, the other steadily enriches; and the hard rocks and bleak hills of New York are, under freedom, worth far more than the rich soil of North Carolina, under slavery. But we are told that the products of the South are, many of them, very rich. "Only think," say Southern planters, "of our cotton crop and sugar crop, and our tobacco crop." Let us now examine the statistics as to the value of these great crops. I intend to prove this proposition, that the aggregate value of the cotton, tobacco, rice, hay, hemp, and sugar of the South is outweighed in market value by the single hay crop of the Free States. The total value of all these crops, as given by the undoubted authority on which I rely, is $138,605,725. The hay crop of the North is 12,690,982 tons. That, reckoned at $11.20 per ton (which is the average valuation by the Bureau of Agriculture at Washington, and it often brings $26 per ton in Baltimore), makes the excess in value of the hay crop of the North over the aggregate value of the Southern crops which I have named, $3,533,275.

Gentlemen, shall I not breathe into the words of scorn with which I condemn cotton-worshippers of the North, a deeper sting, when I exhibit this startling fact. This is the great cotton-god, so much worshipped in the North as well as the South! This is the cotton-god that is supposed to be so mighty at a distance!—so rich when he flaunts himself at the North!—so wealthy when he puts on airs in Northern cities and among Northern men!—this cotton-god, weighed in the hay-scales of the North, is found to be worth less in the market, in dollars and cents, than the hay with which we of the North feed our horses.

And why is not the value of Southern productions greater? Because her system of tillage impoverishes the soil; because her laborers are not owners, generally, but work under the lash; because they have no hope of reaping themselves the fruit of their labor, and can feel no interest in its results. These workers of the South are almost called heathen by my friend on the opposite side; and it would take the sublimest type of Christianity to make them care anything for the interests of the man who lashes them in the cotton-field, and does not pay them for their labor.

The entire wealth of the Slave States, as per Census report, is $2,936,090,737. The total wealth of the Free States $4,002,172,108—making the difference in favor of the Free States, $1,166,081,371. Do not these figures warrant me in saying that the sterile and rocky North has a chance yet to make its own living, and get along in the world, and is not entirely

16

dependent upon the patronage of the South, that grows a little cotton, now and then, to help us along; while our hay crop at the North outweighs in value all these great staple products of the South.

Even if cotton should cease to rule the politics and religion, and morality and literature of the nation, may we not hope that the people of the North would be able to get along, and keep from becoming paupers? Let us now contrast the amount of grain raised in the two sections. The North raises, on an average, twenty-seven bushels of oats to the acre; the South raises seventeen. The North raises, on an average, eighteen bushels of rye to the acre; the South raises eleven. Of corn, the North raises thirty-one bushels per acre; the South twenty bushels. Of potatoes, the North raises 125 bushels per acre, and the South 113 bushels. Why this falling off on the side of the South, notwithstanding its great natural advantages? It is merely because of her slave system of tillage.

On all articles of bushel measure, the difference in value in favor of the North, is $44,782,636. On all articles of pound measure, the difference in favor of the North, $59,199,103.

Let us now consider the subject of commerce. The tonnage of the North is 4,252,615 tons; that of the South is 855,517 tons. The annual exports of the North amounted in value in 1855 to $167,520,693; the exports of the South, in the same period, to $107,840,688—a difference of about sixty millions of dollars between the exports of the North and South, and, besides, the exports of the South are carried out in Northern bottoms. The commerce of the South is mainly carried on by Northern vessels; and the greater part of the carrying trade of the South falls into Northern hands. Yet we of the poor, sterile North, are impoverished by our freedom; and gentlemen come here from the South and teach us political economy, and teach us how we can gain a decent living!

Let us now see which section pays the greatest proportion of the expenses of government. The revenue to support the General Government is derived from the duties on imports from foreign nations. The Revenue Tariff fills the United States Treasury from the receipts at the Custom Houses. Of course these receipts will show the comparative amounts paid from each section of the Union into the Treasury.

In 1854, the custom-house receipts of the Free States amounted to $60,010,489. The same year, the receipts from the Slave States amounted to $5,136,969. The difference in favor of the North was $54,873,520! What a fall was that! The South boasts of an extended line of sea-coast, stretching from Delaware Bay clear around the Gulf of Mexico, and far to the north along the shores of the Southern Pacific. But she has no trade, only a magnificent "site" for one, which she lacks the enterprise to build upon. But she is *going* to have a foreign trade! Her statesmen and political economists are *going* to do great things. She is *going* to stop buying goods at the North, *going* to increase her own tonnage, and *going* to do her own importing. But her greatness is all in prospect. It is "distance that lends enchantment to the view" of her commercial importance. Her commerce, trade, wealth, and political glory, are all a series of "dissolving views," growing "beautifully less" as you approach them.

Now, when you remember which end of the Union creates the preponderance of expense for the Federal Government—in whose behalf the wars are made—for whom the fugitive slaves are caught—who kicks up the majority of political rows, about Missouri compromises and Kansas forays—you will see in the above figures, a weighty reason why the North should aim at the abolition of slavery.

Let us now consider the two sections in relation to manufactures. The Northern capital invested in manufacturing is $430,240,501; the Southern capital is $95,029,709. What a contrast! The value of the products of this capital of the North is $842,586,058; the value of the products of Southern manufactures is $165,413,027. What causes the difference? Why, the South cannot be a manufacturing country, because of the system under which she lives. Her natural advantages, taken in the aggregate, are as good as those of the North. But while Northern freemen, with their strong arms, have chained the steam to the car of their machinery, and made the lightning a motive power in their manufacturing operations, causing the hum of their spindles to break out on the morning air, in one harmonious song, almost from one end of Massachusetts to the other, and while the spirit of freedom perforates the mountain for a railroad, bridges the river, that it may be a path for the carrying trade of nations, and produces a network of railroads all over the North, enriching it in every direction—the system at the South has so impoverished that section as to afford the terrible contrast I have presented to you. This contrast cannot be described in better language than that employed in an extract, which I will read, from a book whose author is a North Carolinian, and therefore, it may be supposed, not very likely to do injustice to his native State. I quote the words of Hinton Rowan Helper:

"The North is the Mecca of our merchants, and to it they must and do make two pilgrimages per annum — one in the spring and one in the fall. All our commercial, mechanical, manufactural, and literary supplies come from there. We want Bibles, brooms, buckets, and books, and we go to the North; we want pens, ink, paper, wafers, and envelopes, and we go to the North; we want shoes, hats, handkerchiefs, umbrellas, and pocket knives, and we go to the North; we want furniture, crockery, glass-ware, and pianos, and we go to the North; we want toys, primers, school-books, fashionable apparel, machinery, medicines, tomb-stones, and a thousand other things, and we go to the North for them all. Instead of keeping our money in circulation at home, by patronizing our own mechanics, manufacturers, and laborers, we send it all away to the North, and there it remains; it never falls into our hands again.

"In one way or another we are more or less subservient to the North every day of our lives. In infancy we are swaddled in Northern muslin; in childhood we are humored with Northern gewgaws; in youth we are instructed out of Northern books; at the age of maturity we sow our 'wild oats' on Northern soil; in middle life we exhaust our wealth, energies, and talents, in the dishonorable vocation of entailing our dependence on our children and on our children's children, and, to the neglect of our own interests and the interests of those around us, in giving aid and succor to every department of Northern power; in the decline of life we remedy our eye-sight with Northern spectacles, and support our infirmities with Northern canes; in old age we are drugged with Northern physic; and, finally, when we die, our inanimate bodies, shrouded in Northern cambric, are stretched upon the bier, borne to the grave in a Northern carriage, entombed with a Northern spade, and memorized with a Northern slab!"

Let us now compare the two sections with regard to internal improvements. There are in New York 2700 miles of railroad; in Ohio, 2869; in Pennsylvania, 2907. These three States have 1117 miles more of railroad than the whole fifteen slave States. The whole North has 17,855 miles of railroad; the whole South, 6859—difference in favor of the North, 10,996 miles. These facts are some evidence of the comparative wealth and prosperity of the two sections; and these Northern railroads are all above ground. The underground railroad now traversing the North from all important points, from Mason and Dixon's line to the Canadas, is not taken into the account in this estimate. It is quite probable that my opponent does not regard that great work of improvement with favor, and as I mean to be fair in this argument, I have left that out of my estimate. How is it in regard to canals? New York and Ohio alone have 794 more miles of canal than the whole fifteen slave States. The whole North has 3682 miles of canal; the whole South, 1116; difference in favor of the North, 2566. The North has expended for railroads, $538,313,647; the South, $95,252,581; difference in favor of the North, $443,061,066.

Let us now consider some of the indications of material strength. The military force of the Slave States is 792,876; that of the Free States, 1,381,843. Now who makes the wars, and employs the military force? We have found where the great bulk of the soldiers come from. Who causes the necessity for their employment? The Florida War; a war inflicting the most gigantic wrong upon an heroic tribe of Indians, because, in their affiliation with fugitive slaves, they helped and protected them, cost us in round numbers, $40,000,000. That was a war to catch negroes for the South.

This military force had to be employed in the everglades of Florida to the tune of this amount to fight a few hundred weak Indians, who deserve the plaudits of the world in coming ages for the heroism and magnanimity with which they defended themselves and the fugitive slaves that ran away from American Christianity and American Republicanism, and sought protection in the bosom of their better heathenism.

And the Mexican War came next. I only mention this to indicate who makes the wars. The North, as you see, furnishes the soldiers, and in the end pays the money. While upon this subject, the fact is worth mentioning, that, in the War of 1812, we suffered the disgrace of having the National Capitol burned, because it was on Southern territory, and the militia surrounding it were so busy watching their slaves, for fear they would run to the British army, that they could not beat back the little squad of men that advanced against them.

Let me now give you some statistics with regard to the Post-Office. The total amount of money collected for postage in the North in 1855 was $4,670,725, cost of transportation for the North was $2,608,295, so that the surplus paid by the North over the cost of sending her mail matter was $2,012,430. The total amount of postage collected in the South was $1,553,198. The cost of transportation was $2,385,953. So that the South has failed to pay her postage by $1,632,763, which the North has to pay for her. The rich planters of the South, with the system under which they live, have to take from the Northern end of the Post-Office bag the money to pay their own postage.

The reason of this is found in the fact that she has a population of 4,000,000 blacks and a white population of 512,882 that can neither read or write, out of an aggregate population of 9,612,979; making nearly half of her adult inhabitants who could not read a letter if one was sent them. Besides she is so destitute of internal improvements, and her roads are so bad, that it costs far more to transport her lean mail bags over the same distance than it does the plethoric mails of the North!

What are the figures with regard to schools? In the schools of the North there are 2,769,901 pupils; in the schools of the South 581,861 pupils — a difference of 2,000,000 in favor of the North. The schoolmaster is present in the North, and has been for some time; and while he shall continue to be with this number of pupils under his care, it will take such missionizing as the gentleman gives us here, a long time to convert the North to Southern ethics, political economy, religion, or politics.

Let us see the figures in regard to newspapers, as furnishing a standard of the intelligence of the two sections. In the North there is a weekly and daily circulation of 334,146,281 copies; in the South, $81,038,693.

In general literary intelligence the contrast between a free and slaveholding society is yet more striking. The South is so meagrely supplied with books that it seems almost ungenerous to reveal her literary poverty. But my opponent has, by his onslaught upon the Free States, invited this searching expose; and his slaveholding society shall have the full benefit of the statistical argument.

The South has 695 public libraries in here domain of thought. The North contains 14,911. These libraries of the South contain 649,577 volumes. The number of volumes in the public libraries of the North swells to the respectable number of 3,888,234, a contrast of over 3,000,000 volumes! An immense majority of these books in Southern libraries were written by Northern men, printed in Northern printing offices, bound by Northern hands, and sold by the Northern publishers. The North has opened the heart of her literature to the inspiration of the spirit of freedom. Her works of fiction, her essays on government, her religious publications (saving those of a few fossilized denominational publishing societies, who emasculate the gospel to make it palatable to slaveholders), all breathe the spirit of liberty. The harp of the North, touched by the inspired fingers of her Whittier, her Lowell and her Longfellow, fills the land with the strains of her songs of freedom. Literature cannot live in chains. The muses take their flight from a land of whips and fetters, and the South gropes on in the gloom of literary night, for fear the sun of intelligence will reveal her crimes against humanity.

And, now, we come to the churches. Surely, the

pious South must be ahead of us in this respect, if we are to take the Parson's statistics, or rather if we are to take his exhortations and assertions. The total value of the church property in the North is $67,793,-477; of the South, $21,674,581. But, perhaps, the balance will be made up on the amount given to the Bible cause. Surely, the South will be ahead of us there! The Bible is presented in this debate as the sheet-anchor of slavery. If my opponent is to be taken as authority, almost every page of it is filled with sanctions of slavery. It is presented as the great manual of the peculiar institution. Of course then it is in high favor in the South. We have a right to expect to find it in each slave cabin, and to find each slave pouring over its pages, to reconcile himself to the scourging, branding, starving, and robbing inflicted by its authority. When his hog and hominy fail, he can fill himself with Pro-Slavery texts. When badly whipped, he can find consolation for his smarting back in its patriarchal precedents; and when his wife and children are stolen and sold, he can bind up his broken heart with its sacred leaves, and learn submission from its divine sanction of the villany from which he suffers. Of course, slaveholders will give largely to circulate the Bible. Let us see. In 1855, the North gave to the Bible cause, $319,677; the South, $68,677—only $251,000 difference between the amounts contributed to the Bible cause. Yet Mr. Brownlow is going to get up a missionary effect in the South to circulate Bibles at the North!

But perhaps the balance is made up on the tract cause. The North paid to the Tract Society $131,972, the South $24,725; and yet the Tract Society, I blush to say, at its last annual meeting, in the face of this beggarly account of Southern contributions, toadied to the South so largely in New York city a few months since, as to excite the indignation of all high-minded Christian men. I know that these words which I am using will make me unpopular with a large portion of my audience, but I came here to tell God's truth, and you shall have it.

For missionary purposes for the year 1855, the North contributed $502,174, the South $101,934; a difference of only $400,240 in missionary contributions. But perhaps the South will make up on the Colonization cause. The scheme of taking the free negroes at the South, and sending them to Africa, must certainly be her pet, for she wants to get rid of them, and she has a pious regard for the Christianization of the negro. Let us see how she supports this cause by her pocket nerve.

The North contributed for Colonization $51,930; the South $27,618. The North contributes double that given by the South. I do not mention this as a compliment to the North. I only give it as one of a series of facts tending to show the comparative wealth and readiness to give, as existing in the two sections. For, instead of contributing myself, or encouraging any other person to contribute to the Colonization cause, I would far rather contribute Sharp's rifles, pistols, and bayonets—in order that the negro might be defended in possessing his freedom on our own soil, and living among us, where he has a right to live.

Now, what say you with reference to the comparative pauperism, and the comparative criminality, and the comparative virtue, and the comparative benevolence, and the comparative Christianity, of the two sections of the Union, as shown by these statistics. What makes the difference? What, but the incubus of American slavery, that has settled down over the fair clime of the South, and has sent the virus of its poison into the life-blood of her native elements of strength, and improvement, and progress? But these figures do not at all give the whole view of this question, for who can estimate what has been lost to the world of mind by the suppression of genius, resulting from the system that prevails in the South? Who can tell of the glorious thoughts that have been crushed, of the bright intellects that have been ruined, of the great souls that have withered away in the prison-house of obscurity, who ought to have been in the world like Douglass and other great minds among the colored men, leading their own countrymen out of darkness, by the light that flashes from their brilliant intellects, and by the zeal of their efforts for human advancement? Who can estimate the loss of moral power from this source! Who can measure the loss of power to convert the world to righteousness, and decency and morality, and hasten on the dawn of a better day for humanity! These things cannot be computed by figures. They are beyond the province of the mathematician. No man can tell what has been lost to the world in morals and intelligence by the institution of American slavery.

Slavery disgraces us before the civilized world, not only by this destruction of our elements of material strength, but by the ruffian element that it introduces into our politics, by the manner in which it degrades our statesmanship, by the scenes that brute force, assuming that might makes right, enacts in our Senate Chambers, and by the efforts that it makes to suppress freedom of debate, and crush out the expression of free opinion.

And, gentlemen, I cannot forget in this connection, the glorious Charles Sumner, who with an intellect towering loftily, the depth of which has not yet been measured, and with a moral character as stainless as the garb of an angel, was stricken down for having heroically performed a glorious duty to God and humanity — stricken down by a ruffian hand, and his blood staining the floor of the Senate chamber. Gentlemen, this is the spirit that slavery breathes into the politics of our nation; this is the maner in which it conducts discussion — this is the disgrace into which it brings us before the civilized world!

I ask in view of these things — while Alexander of Russia is setting free his serfs — while the African princes themselves who have held slaves, are giving them their liberty — while Turkey herself is moving in the cause of freedom, and the Ottoman Empire feels the impulses of humanity—I ask in the name of heaven, if it is not time we should shake off the disgrace of being the last among the nations of the earth to recog nize the rights of common humanity, and give man his freedom because he is a man.

Gentlemen, in the name of these great principles, I demand the abolition of American slavery. I cannot consent, nor can you consent, nor can the civilized world long consent, that Republicanism, in its glorious

17

experiment here in the New World, shall be all the time in danger of becoming a failure, and of being wrecked on this terrible rock of wrong. I cannot, as an American citizen, consent that tyrants who shake their bloody sceptres from across the water, should laugh at us living under a government more tyrannical upon 3,000,000 of men than the worst European despotisms. I cannot consent, so far as my poor powers are concerned, to the perpetuation of this system, which is our shame before the civilized world. In the noon of the nineteenth century, when the impulses of the human soul are grasping after a larger freedom, when the spirit of the age is pushing out towards an enlargement of the area of mind — when the very breezes around us are instinct with the influences of intellectual and moral progress — this horrid incubus of slavery settles down upon the bosom of the mightiest, and what might be, the noblest nation on earth, and exerts its crushing power on the elements of intellectual and moral and spiritual and political strength; and it is time that it should be abolished — that it should die.

It is time that we were done with the frippery of this little, pettifogging textual argument. It is time that we were done with its taunts and jeers, and sneers and retorts. It is time that we should march up to this question in a spirit that harmonizes with the gravity of its issues, and argue it, before the civilized world, in the light of the great principles which it involves. It is time that we should cease to be jesters and jokers. It is time that we should cease to play the harlequin, and should take the position of *men* in morals and in politics, arguing this cause on the grand principles that give dignity to this debate — principles worthy of this audience we address, and of the question we discuss.

And, gentlemen, I notify you, that hereafter I shall not descend from these high, broad grounds, to meet sneers and taunts and gibes, and harlequin grimaces, that may come to me in the shape of any language that is read here. I have a greater purpose and a nobler cause, and while I may for a moment turn aside for a good-natured retort, I shall not spend time in picking up the petty quirks and flings scattered loosely through this argumentation.

I demand to enter the merits of this question, and I ask of my opponent that he shall give us the gist of this debate, and put it in form and shape to be met, for I am here to meet it, to question it, and, if possible, to show the matchless wickedness of the slave system, and defend the cause of freedom before the civilized world. I trust that in the succeeding evenings of this debate, we shall be able to lift its tone out of these comparatively low grounds, where it has rested heretofore, and give it the altitude which it merits, as the gravest, and broadest, and profoundest question of the age.

[Mr. Pryne desires to acknowledge his indebtedness to the "Impending Crisis," by Helper, for assistance in preparing the above speech.]

"OUGHT AMERICAN SLAVERY TO BE PERPETUATED?"

AFFIRMATIVE, IV. — BY W. G. BROWNLOW.

AN argument, if not *the* argument of Abolitionism, is, that men cannot hold property in man. The claim is a vile heresy—its consummation a wicked and terrible usurpation. I might content myself with saying, that the institution of slavery is as old as the oldest of human institutions — is recognized by the Scriptures of the Old and New Testaments—and the right of man to hold property in his fellow man, is taught from the opening to the close of the Bible.

I might content myself with the assertion that, even among the Hebrews, the legislation of Moses provided for the event in which a Jew is constrained to sell himself through poverty, and to acknowledge the *right of property in him* by his purchaser. I might content myself with saying, as I now do, that *Christians* of undoubted piety, in the days of Christ and the Apostles *owned* slaves, and their *rights of property in them* were recognized by the Saviour and the Apostles.

In France, Spain, Portugal, and England, slavery was established by legislation at one time or another, and slaves were recognized as *property*. Slavery, in its widest and broadest acceptation, was known to exist in the days of Queen Elizabeth, and the queen was herself the *owner of slaves*. And slaves were protected as *property* by the Common Law of England down to the time of James II. Fifty years after LORD MANSFIELD'S speech in the celebrated "Sommersett Case" of slavery, LORD STOWELL decided the right of a master to his slave, absconding, and his right in him as *property*. LORD STOWELL was at the time in correspondence with JUDGE STORY, of Massachusetts, sent him a copy of his decision, and asked his opinion about it. No man of intelligence will doubt the anti-slavery feelings and proclivities of JUDGE STORY. Here is an extract from his answer to the British Lord:

"I have read, with great attention, your judgment in the slave case. Upon the fullest consideration which I have been able to give the subject, I entirely concur in your views. If I had been called upon to pronounce a judgment in a like case, I should have certainly arrived at the same result."

In France they had a similar system of slavery, calling the slaves *bondsmen of the estate*, because they belonged to the landed estates, and were usually sold with them as *property*. This species of slavery continued in France until 1779, *after* our independence.

As it regards Spain, any one reading her literature for the eighteenth century, will find that her authors never introduce a tale of romance, but what some Moorish or negro *slave* comes up as the inmate of the household, and *property* of the hero!

Turning to our own country, slaves are *protected as property* by the Constitution of the United States. What is this protection? The question is answered on page 671 of 16th Peters, in these words:

"I cannot perceive how any one can doubt that the remedy given in the Constitution, if, indeed, it give any remedy without legislation, was designed to be a peaceful one; a remedy sanctioned by judicial authority; a remedy guarded by the forms of law. But the inquiry is reiterated, is not the master entitled to his *property?* I answer that he is. *His right is guarantied by the Constitution;* and the most summary means for its enforcement is found in the Act of Congress. And neither the State nor its citizens can obstruct the prosecution of this right."

This was Judge M'Lean's language, one of the minority of the Supreme Court of the United States, in the *Dred Scott case.* That entire court, though differing in some respects, concurred, man for man, that the rights of the South are guarantied in *slaves as property*, by the Constitution!

Slavery, outside of the Bible, is the creature of the common law of England, in which country it existed, and was protected by the common and the statute law, as far back as the days of Queen Elizabeth, who, as I have already stated, herself owned slaves. Our ancestors brought the laws and institutions of England to this continent, as their birth-right, and hence slavery was the common law of the thirteen original colonies. At the time of the American Revolution, it was the common law of the western continent. But it is just to the truth of history to say, that slavery was forced upon the thirteen original colonies, as the common law, against the urgent remonstrances of the *Southern* portion, the *North* acquiescing most cheerfully! How, then, can an Abolitionist assert that slavery is not recognized by our Constitution, and that slaves are not *property?*

But I am aware of the difficulty of *driving* historical facts into the heads of Northern Abolitionists and of New England clergymen, as to the slavery or anti-slavery record of this or any other country — this or any other age. Upon the subject of slavery in *this country*, they "stick it out with stomach stout," unless the facts can be found in the Bible. The New Testament begins *Anno Domini*, and does not come down to the formation of our Federal Constitution, the days of Washington, Franklin, and others, and to this, our day and generation.

Abolitionism asserts that the early founders of this Republic were opposed to slavery. This I deny, and denounce as utterly untrue. I quote from the speech of THEODORE PARKER, delivered at the "New England Anti-Slavery Convention," in May, 1858. That speech appears in pamphlet form, "copyright secured." On page 11, the author says:

> "It is now well known that many of the leading men in the conventions, Federal as well as State, were hostile to slavery. I need only mention Franklin, Washington, Madison, Samuel Adams, and John Hancock."

The very *reverse* of what this champion of Abolitionism says, "is now well known" to be true. Let us look into the facts of history.

1. Washington and Franklin put the compact I have been dwelling upon, the *Fugitive Slave Law*, into the Constitution. Perhaps I ought not to disclose this fact until EDWARD EVERETT has done with his oration and his Mount Vernon Fund, as it will stop all contributions by anti-slavery men!

2. GEORGE WASHINGTON & Co. divided the territory of the Union, when the great division was made —

all north of the Ohio to be *free;* all south of that *slave.*

3. WASHINGTON signed Acts of Congress admitting Slave States into the Union. JOHN ADAMS did the same, when they both had the power to *veto* them, and knew that Congress could not take them up and pass them by a two-thirds vote!

4. WASHINGTON, FRANKLIN, RUFUS KING, and others, prohibited, in the Federal Constitution, the abolition of the *African slave-trade* before the year 1808—the memorials requesting them to do so, all coming from the *North!*

5. And JOHN ADAMS signed the Act of Congress which repealed the *Wilmot Proviso ordinance* (organizing the North-western Territory as an anti-slavery Territory), organizing the Alabama and Mississippi Territories *as Slave Territories!*

6. WASHINGTON, FRANKLIN, and ALEXANDER HAMILTON put into the Constitution the provision providing for the *three-fifth* representation of slaves in the House of Representatives, by which the South now gains nearly thirty Representatives!

7. THOMAS JEFFERSON negotiated the purchase of the Louisiana Territory, a slaveholding and slave-abounding territory, larger than the then whole territory of the United States; and, in the treaty with France, guarantied the preservation and protection of "*slave property.*"

Fifty other facts of a similar character, and equally as strong as these, could be cited, to prove what an untruth Abolitionism utters, when it asserts that the early founders of our Republic were opposed to slavery. WASHINGTON, JEFFERSON, MADISON, and MONROE, were all taken from one State, and made Presidents by *Northern* votes, because they were *slaveholders*, and were supposed to be friendly to the slave-trade, by which so many men at the North were making fortunes!

Now, these Southern slaveholding Presidents were *Northern made.* Washington was elected and re-elected without opposition. Jefferson was re-elected by an immense majority, and both times beat *Northern* men by getting *Northern* votes. Madison and Monroe were elected more by Northern than Southern votes.

The existence of slavery in ancient society, from time immemorial, is an unquestionable fact, that, to stand here and argue, would be a reflection on the intelligence of this audience. But the ascertainment of the *numbers* of slaves owned and sold in the different quarters of the earth, and in different ages, is of great importance, for it touches the question of slavery at all points. I cannot be expected to enter into details, however, and will content myself with saying that HUNDREDS OF MILLIONS were sold in the slave-marts of Phœnicia, Assyria, Egypt, Judea, Greece, Italy, Germany, Britain, and Gaul. Out of these millions, none ever rose with indignity and strength to retaliate on their purchasers.

Ancient society, like Southern society, consisted of freemen and slaves; and the *number* of the latter is connected with its constitution, its spirit, and its character. Ancient writers tell us that they were very numerous in Athens, and the cities which, like her, prosecuted the arts of industry and trade. The census of Demetrius returned for Athens 20,000 native-born citizens, 10,000 resident foreigners, and 400,000 slaves! Corinth had 460,000 slaves! Ægina, a rocky strip as barren as the cold North, with its one hundred and fifty superficial miles, had 470,000 slaves! The slaves in Attica were mostly owned by individuals, some owning three hundred, six hundred, and one thousand, whom they hired out and worked on their farms. The Athenian government owned 200,000 slaves, and employed them in working the mines and prosecuting works of internal improvement.

This body of condensed testimonies and select proofs, shows that slavery found its basis in the organization of primitive society; and in my several lectures I have traced it up the stream of time to God's awful mysteries which enshroud the origin of society! Whether I have turned to a long line of monuments, historical, poetical, or philosophical, sacred or human, or to codes and creeds, I have everywhere found the primitive existence of slavery — just such slavery as exists in America — none better — most of it worse!

Voices from the east, and voices from the west; voices from the precincts of Eden, and from the summits of smoking Sinai; voices from the dark and gloomy depths of antiquity, and from the glare of refined and elevated civilization; voices of inspired men from the sanctuaries of God, and voices of bad men from the precincts of cruelty and degradation; voices from every tongue, and every nation that lived upon the tide of time past, proclaim the consistent, primative, heathen, and Christian fact of original slavery!

A grand law of God in nature adapted the several physical characters and constitutions, as well as the respective complexions of the races, to the localities in which they were designed to dwell. To the white race, the descendants of *Japhet*, the northern regions of the earth were given. To *Shem* and his descendants, the copper-colored race, the *middle* regions or temperate clime, north of the equator, was allotted. But to *Ham* and his race was given the burning South!

But who did Ham marry? This is an important question in this age of slavery agitation and excitement about the origin of the races, and their several colors. Ham evidently got his wife from the race of Cain. Commentators generally agree, that in Genesis vi. 2, "sons of God" mean those of the race of Seth; and that "the daughters of men" imply the females of the race of Cain. The word "fair" in our version, applied to these females, does not warrant the conclusion that they were *white women*, or that they were even of a light complexion. It is translated from the Hebrew *tovoth*, being in the feminine plural, from *tov*, and only expresses the idea of what may seem *good* and *excellent* to the beholder; it expresses no quality of complexion or beauty, beyond what may exist in the mind of the beholder.

Cain had been driven out a degenerate, degraded, deteriorated vagabond. As soon as these races intermarried, God became displeased with them—determined to destroy man from the earth—avowing that the "wickedness of man had become great in the earth."

We have no proof that the race has ever improved. All the sons of Ham were born after the flood, and for generations afterwards they kept up the name *Cain*, *Cainite*, *Canaan*. These variations will not be noticed in a language so remote as ours, but linguists and commentators trace them all back to their root, the original of *Cain*. The curse of slavery was imposed on the descendants of Ham, because of this marriage, and they were subjected to be bought and sold. The very name *Cain*, signifies "*one purchased.*"

The descendants of Ham were *black*, and the black man of Africa is of that descent. "And the Lord set a mark upon Cain." This "*mark*" was a *black skin*. Since language was first used to designate the ideas of men, *black* has been applied to sin and wickedness. In the book of *Nahum*, chapter 2d, it is said in reference to this race, "The faces of them all gather *blackness*." The descendants of Ham were *black when born*. His wife, of the race of Cain, was a *negro wench*, inheriting Cain's "*mark*," and that mark was a *black skin*. The wife of Ham was by the name of *Namah*, and the descendants of Ham perpetuated her name in the family, to their latest generation. The name of this *negro woman* was handed down in Scripture, for obvious reasons, while the name of the wife of Noah remains a mystery! And it was before the flood that the degenerate sons of Seth fell in love with the black daughters of the race of Cain. And the degenerate *Sethites* of New England, when they meet with our Southern *Cainites*, illustrate the *habits* of their antideluvian predecessors! *Abram* is a negro name, and thereby hangs a tale!

Abolitionists take the ground that the precepts of the Bible are diametrically opposed to slavery; and that the slave-trade is only evil, and evil continually I have not so learned the precepts of the Bible; and as for the African slave-trade, the revival of which I do not advocate, and have already denounced as *piracy*, I am not sure that it has not always been a blessing, instead of a curse to the African race.

The 28th chapter of Deuteronomy sets forth the blessings and curses promised the Jews, and, I may add, all mankind, for obedience or disobedience to the laws of God. At the 68th verse they were told that they should again be sent to Egypt and exposed for *sale*—that no man should buy them, or that there should not be buyers enough, as the passage may be read, to give them the benefit of being *slaves*—deemed a great blessing, as it alone assured protection and sustenance. This was all verified at the time Jerusalem was sacked by Titus; and in Egypt, as well as many other places, thousands of the Hebrew captives were exposed, *as slaves*, for sale, and thousands of them died of starvation because *purchasers* could not be found. The Romans, always in the market when slaves were to be sold, would not have these Hebrew captives, because they were too stubborn and degraded for their use. Their numbers, compared with the number of purchasers in the market were so great, that the price was only nominal, when a sale was effected; and thousands starved to death, because purchasers could not be had at any price.

This same incident happened to all the Jews, who were freemen in Spain, during the reign of Ferdinand

and Isabella, when 800,000 Jews were driven from that kingdom in one day, half of whom famished to death, because they could not find masters, though anxious to do so, and capitalists were purchasing slaves, where they could be suited in the quality. What are the teachings of the Bible in this case? It predicted this, and its teachings on this subject favor the institution of slavery.

It may be urged by Abolitionism, that this was a curse inflicted upon the Jews for their disobedience, and murder of Christ. Such a peculiar relation of facts, and state of bondage, have not been confined to the Jews alone. In 1376, the Florentines, then a travelling, trading, or commercial people, possessed such infirmities that Christianity was scouted by them, and murder and robbery became mere pastime. The surrounding governments, and the Church, whose patience were almost exhausted by their pillage, delivered them over to slavery, which was hailed as a great blessing by such as met with purchasers; others were punished with death. In the days of Walsingham, in England, a large proportion of the traders were of the same people, while freemen were liable to be put to death by any one, and their effects legally seized upon; in bondage they were protected; and they sought slavery as a remedy—only the better classes finding purchasers. This was in *Christian* England, in accordance with what was then understood to be the precepts of the Bible.

In 1830, John and Richard Lander were sent out to explore certain parts of Africa by the "London African Association." They reported that their hearts sickened at the contemplation of the scenes of horror they met with, and added:—"It is to be regretted that since the abolition of the slave-trade in Africa, slaves have become of little value in that country. That the Africans in many places have *returned to sacrifice and cannibalism*, is also true, and a cause of deep sorrow to the philanthropist; but considering the state and condition of the savages, there is no alternative but a revival of the slave-trade. The slave there, if he cannot be *sold*, is at all times liable to be put to death, either for purposes of food, or of thinning their ranks."

Now, suppose we buy, and then turn them loose there, they will at once become the subjects of slavery, because slavery affords them protection, as long as their savage owners are able to afford them the means of living. Let us present this state of facts to our Christian philanthropists of the North, and ask them to apply their much talked of golden rule, of doing to others as they would have others do unto us; and, in case the slave-trade with Africa had not been abolished, what would they deem it their duty to do for the present, practical, and lasting benefit of these poor victims, whom the misguided, false, and misdirected sympathy of the world has thus consigned to sacrifice and death?

So recently as 1851, our sympathies were excited by an account published to the world, of an African chieftain and an extensive slave-holder, who, during the previous year, finding himself cut off from a market for his surplus of slaves on the western coast, in conquence of the abolition of the slave-trade with Europe and America, put to death 3000 whom he could no longer feed, or profitably employ! The trade with

Arabia, Egypt, and the Barbary States, was going on, and was lawful; but these markets were not sufficient to drain off the surplus numbers on the western coast, and hence, such as were not suited for *food*, were indiscriminately slaughtered! While the slave-trade was tolerated, even cannibalism was checked up, from the fact that one negro would bring in exchange ten times the amount of provisions to be found in the serving up of his carcass, and a greater variety at that.

The blood of these 3000 massacred negroes now cries from the soil of Western Africa unto the Abolitionists of England and America, who enacted laws prohibiting the slave-trade, in the following eloquent, touching, and as I think, appropriate terms:

"Gentlemen, apply, oh! apply to suffering and degraded Africa, the Bible doctrine of the golden rule, and relieve us poor African slaves from starvation, massacre, and death. Come, oh! come; buy us from our savage owners, who, as cannibals eat us up, or thin our ranks by indiscriminate slaughter, when we become so numerous as to be a burthen to them. Come, oh! come; buy us, that we may be your slaves, either in the West India Islands, or among the cotton, tobacco, rice, and sugar plantations of America, and have some chance to learn that religion under which you prosper! We prefer the Southern overseer's task, with enough to eat and to wear, to starvation and death in our native land! Then, in the language of your Bible, 'we shall build up the old wastes,' 'raise up the former desolations,' and 'repair the waste cities, the desolations of many generations.' 'And strangers shall stand and feed your flocks, and the sons of the *alien* shall be your ploughmen, and your wine-dressers.' 'Then ye shall be named the Priests of the Lord; men shall call you the MINISTERS OF OUR GOD.'"

The Church of Christ, did, at all times, during its early ages, consider the existence of slavery, and the holding of slaves, compatible with a religious profession and the practice of Christian duties. No other proof is necessary on this point, than the sermons of St. Paul and St. Peter. These sermons will be found in Corinthians, Ephesians, Colossians I., Timothy, Titus, Philemon, and 1st Peter. These Scriptures distinctly teach the doctrine of the Christian Church; and no doctrine therein taught stands out in bolder relief than the lawfulness of *owning* and *dealing* in slaves.

Some suppose Abolitionism, as held in England and America, an ism of modern origin. Not so, however; it is as old as the Council of *Nice*, and was taught in the year 325, when Constantine was Emperor.

The "illustrious predecessors" of our New England Abolitionists, were the *Gnostics* and *Manicheans* of Asia Minor. These *fanatics* denied the lawfulness of *marriage*, and contended for our New England theory of "Free Love;" they enacted a prohibitory wine-law, similar to our "Maine Liquor Law;" they required by law, all men to enter religious societies, and attend church, as did the "Blue Laws" of Connecticut; they decried the lawfulness of slavery; they denounced slave-holders as violating the laws of God and man, just as our Abolitionists do; they aided slaves in deserting their owners, just as the officers of our "underground railroads" do; and in all things they assumed to be more *holy*, more *perfect*, and more *spiritual*, than other men, just as do the unmitigated Anti-Slavery hypocrites of our New England States!

The criticisms of the gentleman, touching the terms *servant* and *slaves*, lead me, now while the subject is on my mind, to notice these terms, although I consider I was sufficiently explicit in a former speech.

The English words *servant*, *to serve*, and *service*, *serving*, &c., have descended into our language from the Latin word *servus*, A SLAVE; and these words, when first introduced into the language, as distinctly carried with them the idea of slavery, as does now any term we can employ, and will continue to do so wherever the English language and slavery prevail. In no slaveholding country has the word *servant* ever been applied to a freeman as a legitimate term of description; but in non-slaveholding communities, these words are occasionally used in a different sense, but in every instance erroneously; because they are without adherence to their derivation and analogy. These words, when found in the present authorized version of the Scriptures, are in the majority of instances translated from some Greek word that included the idea of slavery. I could give examples in which errors exist, in this particular, in our translation of the Christian Scriptures; such as John xviii., 36. Mark xiv., 54. John xviii., 18. Hebrews iii., 5. He that seeks the truth must keep in mind the distinction between the different terms in our Scriptures, called by the same name, "*servants*," and not suffer his mind to be influenced by any bias which has been produced by other agencies.

St. Paul commences his epistle to the Romans, to the Philippians, and to Titus, with the appellation of *servant*. In the first case he calls himself the servant and apostle of Christ. In the last instance, he terms himself the servant of God, and apostle of Jesus Christ. Peter, in his second epistle, styles himself a *servant* and apostle; Jude, the *servant* of Christ. In all these instances the word means *slave*, as any linguist will testify, and is used commendatively, but figuratively, to signify their entire devotedness to the cause in which they are engaged, and to their Leader, as a good slave is to his master. And it is proper to remark, that the professing Christian is indebted to the *institution of slavery*, which was approved by the inspired Apostles, for the lesson of humanity and devotedness here so plainly taught him; and without which, perhaps, he never could have been taught this duty, in these particulars, so pertinently and clearly. The humility and devotedness of the Christian are illustrated by the institution of slavery, as set forth in John xv., 20: "Remember the words that I said unto you, the *servant* (or *slave*) is not greater than his Lord."

But, in this connection, the inquiry naturally occurs, how happened it that St. Paul found it necessary to inform Timothy that the law forbade the stealing or enticing away of other men's slaves? By consulting his epistles to the Gentile churches, it will be seen that there had grown up among them some new and villanous "Free Soil" doctrines, which his office as an apostle made it his duty to reprehend in unmistakable terms. These doctrines were the abolition of marriage, and the abolition of *slavery*, as will be seen by examining the 7th chapter of first *Corinthians*. Some of the Gentile Churches advocated the doctrine that, if a man or woman of the *faith* married to one not of the faith, that said marriage should be abolished; so also, that a slave of the *faith* should be set free, and especially by a *believing* master; so also, the believing child should be discharged from the authority of the unbelieving parent. The promulgation of these doctrines filled society with disorder where the apostles labored, and the Church with confusion.

In his instructions to Timothy, St. Paul complains of the *New England* doctrines, taught by Hymeneus and Alexander, two unmitigated "freedom-shriekers," and denounces them as *blasphemous.* What were they? The most odious of them was the *abolition of slavery*, and for which he "delivered unto Satan" these two reckless anti-slavery champions, as he would my *reverend opponent*, if he were here, and could hear his arguments. It is notorious, moreover, that St. Paul in his instructions to Timothy, to Titus, to the *Colossians*, to the *Ephesians*, &c., denounced the Abolitionists of his day, and warned his ministerial brethren against them. Consistency of character, to say nothing about his independence in avowing his sentiments, warrants the conclusion, that in all his sermons to the masses, and such as were not published, he kept up a fierce fire upon these anti-slavery men, warning the common people, including the *slaves themselves*, against their wicked and seductive influence.

I have already established the doctrine and action of the Church, as connected with the subject of slavery, by learned writers in the three or four first centuries; men who were renowned for their piety, and claimed to have been governed by the immediate teaching of Christ and his apostles. During every century, suffice it to say, from the crucifixion of Christ down to the present time, by far the greatest portion of the world has been flooded with slavery and slaves; and, in all of these various portions of the earth, the slave trade was carried on. According to BEDE, Britain furnished other nations with slaves, as far back as the year 577. And in the midst of all the feeling of rivalship between the Jews, the Pagans, and the Christians — and, in truth, between some of the different Christian sects, as to their systems of religion, they all agreed more or less in the right to own and trade in slaves. They differed in their opinions as to *who* should hold slaves, and they regulated the traffic by laws very different in their character. The law of the Roman empire, in force throughout Italy and Sicily during the fifth century, enjoined that slaves who were Christians could not be held by those who were not of the same faith. In India, the creditor could take the children of the debtor, and keep them as his *property*, and as his *slaves*, until the debt was paid. Among the Gentiles this same right was in existence, with the further provision, that the child could be subjected to *perpetual slavery.*

I repeat a sentiment I have already avowed and argued, that it is a great popular error, which supposes all of our species to be born equals. I do not believe one word of it. It involves the absurd proposition that each one also possesses the same faculties and mind, and to the same extent. Through the whole animal world, as with man, the amount of mental power each one possesses, is in exact proportion to the development of the nervous system and animal structure. The highest grade of development is found among the Caucassian species of man. Physiologists assert that the African exhibits, in maturity, the imperfect brain of a

Caucasian *fœtus*, two months before birth. The Malay and Indian exhibit the same at a period nearer birth; while the Mongolian, that of the Caucasian infant after birth. The *beard*, the attribute of a full maturity among men, largest in the Caucasian, does not exist among the lower grades of the African. COLOR is also found the *darkest* where the development is the least perfect, and the most distant from the Caucasian. Hence, a particular tribe of Arabs, on the banks of the Jordan, from their intermarriages among blood relations, have so degenerated in intellect, as to have become as black as negroes! And it is a well-known physiological fact, that Caucasian parents too nearly related, exhibit offspring of the Mongolian type. There is truth in the ancient adage — "the fathers have eaten sour grapes, and the children's teeth are on edge." Whether, therefore, we view the tribes of ocean, earth, or air, we behold a regular gradation of power and rules, from man down to the *atom*, demonstrating the truth of the lines by Pope:

> "Whether with reason or with instinct blest,
> All enjoy that power that suits them best."

> "Order is heaven's first law; and this confess'd,
> Some are, and must be *greater* than the rest."

A few remarks upon certain issues he raised last evening, and I conclude this speech. First, the gentleman said my mention of the South being represented here, was a crack of the whip intended to intimidate him, but that it would fail! How absurd such an inference from such a remark! Does not every man of sense know, who has listened to these discussions, that, from first to last, *three* or *five* of the audience to *one*, have been against me, and with my competitor, in sentiment and feeling? Has he not been surrounded by newspaper reporters friendly to his side of the question, while I have had none to report or write letters? Is not the entire press of this city on his side? Do they not give long reports of his statistics and points, while they crowd my speeches into twelve or fifteen lines, as preliminary to what they say in praise of him? Last, but not least, has he not had a horde of free negroes and fugitive slaves here all the time clapping for him, and *hissing* me? I wish to intimidate *little Abram Pryne*, from McGrawville, New York, an unscrupulous Abolition missionary! How utterly ridiculous the idea! If I could successfully brow-beat him, it would be no credit to me.

But, the gentleman bantered me to repeat this debate —*where?* "In all the principal cities of the North; both parties agreeing as to time, place, &c." This is a beautiful challenge, characteristic of the gentleman! If he will so amend his challenge as to make it read thus, I am in for the war: "Repeat it in all the principle cities of the North and South, time about each side of the line; Pryne selecting the Northern, and Brownlow the Southern cities." Here is a fair offer— one which will give him a chance to enlighten the South, whilst I enlighten the North!

He made a flourish last evening over the falling off of the South, in her contributions to the Tract, Sunday School, and Bible cause, and boasted that the North doubled the South in her contributions.

The American Tract Society has been involved in a

controversy for some time, the South charging some of its vile Abolition managers with publishing rank Abolitionism in their tracts. The South does not choose to contribute to any such dirty work.

As it regards the Sunday School cause, whose head-quarters are in this city, its Treasurer, a pious Anti-Slavery man, has proved a *defaulter* to the tune of about *eighty thousand dollars*, by speculating in *Morus Multicaulis*. The South has no money to embark in this sort of enterprise.

As it regards the Bible cause, the people of the South glory in promoting *that*, but we are growing indifferent towards keeping so many in offices, upon high salaries, while they distribute as many Abolition documents, as they do Bibles and Testaments!

His statistical comparison of the North and South, I will not only meet to-morrow evening, but I will show that the *reverse* of what he said is true, and as a fair debater I notify him of it, and call on him to come prepared to sustain himself with the proof. I shall *prove* what I say on the subject.

He notified us last evening, that this being a great National question, he would not stoop to answer questions of low ribaldry. Indeed! On what strange meat has this our hero fed, that he has grown so great! The question I propounded to him is, and I now repeat it—Would he be willing to see his daughter married to the son of such distinguished *buck negroes* as Sam. Ward or Fred. Douglass? This may be a *dark* question, but it is a great *Domestic* question, intimately connected with the great National question! I still call for an answer. Let him say Yes or No! If he will not consent to a union of this character in his own family, why is he so loud, and apparently so earnest in his arguments to persuade others to do so? Does he preach a doctrine he is not willing to practice? Does he ask me and others to introduce gentlemen of color into our domestic circles, and is unwilling to say whether he would extend to them a similar courtesy? A want of candor in refusing to answer the question, shows a want of faith in the correctness and propriety of his own theory. "Thou believest that there is one God; thou doest well: the *devils also believe*, and tremble. But wilt thou know, O vain man, that faith without works is dead?" These are the teachings of the New Testament (James 2d and 19, 20), a book, by the way, which sanctions slavery, and which, in consequence thereof, the gentleman thinks is only fit for a foot-ball!

Will he do it? No, not him! He will answer it as he has answered all my arguments, by going off on some side issues. He promised to reply to my scriptural arguments, and to meet the express passages I laid before him; but he has never done it, and never will.

He concluded by declaring that it was high time that slavery was abolished in the South, and by *inuendo* intimated that it would be done. And as he avowed his determination to labor in the cause, shoulder to shoulder with others of his kind, perhaps it will be gratifying to him to know *when* the good work will be accomplished. I am able to tell him the precise time when his labors will terminate, and he can communicate it to his co-laborers. When the angel Gabriel sounds the last loud trump of God, and calls the nations of the earth to judgment — then, and not before, will slavery be abolished south of Mason and Dixon's line! Work on, brother Pryne, in the good cause — there is a good time coming, and I hope you may be there to see it!

The gentleman's denunciation of the late Mr. Brooks, of South Carolina, and his application of the term *ruffian* to him, were in very bad taste, since that gifted and brave man is in his grave, and has been for a length of time. Mr. Brooks was an honorable, generous, and high-minded gentleman; and he who says otherwise is the *slanderer of the dead*, and the perpetrator of a *falsehood* unworthy of a professor of the Christian religion!

As I am still within my time, I will say a word as to his comparison of the soil and extent of territory in New York and North Carolina. Why single out North Carolina? She is a gallant State. The first blood in defence of American liberty was shed there, and the first Declaration of Independence was issued there. God bless North Carolina! But she is an old and small State, compared with others in the South, and much of her soil is thin and worn-out. Why not call up Texas, side by side with the great State of New York. Texas will make *three* such States; and between the soil, as to fertility, and the climate, as adapted to agricultural pursuits and stock-raising, there is no comparison.

Why not call up Arkansas? According to the records of the general land-office of Arkansas, she has an area of 55,000 square miles, equal to THIRTY-FIVE

MILLIONS OF ACRES! And this is exclusive of her territory covered by rivers, lakes, and unexplored swamps, which will, in the course of a few years, be in a high state of cultivation, and covered over with Southern negroes, cheerful, contented, and happy, as all Southern negroes are whose minds are not poisoned by the false representations of such unprincipled Abolitionists as the one who will follow me in a short time! Let me tell him that Arkansas alone is equal to the States of Rhode Island, Connecticut, Massachusetts, Vermont, New Hampshire, New Jersey, and Maine! Or, if the gentleman please, Arkansas is as large as the great State of New York, with New Jersey and Connecticut thrown in!

But, gentlemen, you shall hear from me to-morrow evening, as to the extent of the territory of the South, and her vast capabilities. The wealth of a people is to be estimated by their surplus productions. All the enterprises of peace and war depend on what a nation is able to spend. The Reports of the Secretary of the Treasury show, that the exports of the United States amounted last year to $270,000,000, exclusive of gold and foreign merchandise re-exported. Of this amount, the productions of the South are $185,000,000. In addition to this, we sent to the North, from the Slave States, $35,000,000 of our surplus productions, worth, when manufactured, $220,000,000, equal to $16.66 per head of our population, supposing it to be twelve millions — a dividend which no nation on earth can show! I thus advertise the gentleman of what is coming, that he may prepare to meet it!

Thanking you for your attention, I yield the stand to our hero of freedom and amalgamation, whose style can but remind you of the lines of Wordsworth

> "Among the rocks and winding crags—
>   Among the mountains far away—
> Once more the Ass has lengthened out
> More ruefully and endless shout,
>   The long dry see-saw of his horrible bray!"

"OUGHT AMERICAN SLAVERY TO BE PERPETUATED?"

NEGATIVE, IV. — BY ABRAM PRYNE.

LADIES AND GENTLEMEN: — Permit me, before I proceed to my argument of this evening, to brush away from the track of this debate two or three little incidental matters which have been introduced by my opponent.

In the first place, allow me to say that the coarse, vulgar, and brutal allusion to myself and my family, I shall not touch in definite terms, nor stoop to answer. Gentlemen, I stooped quite enough when I engaged in this debate.

Let me say, however, that under the instructions of their own good mother, my children are taught the principles of freedom and humanity; and should my daughter, on reaching the years of womanhood, be asked for her hand by any lordly stripling of the lash, she would answer in the language of Whittier's Yankee Girl:

"With a scorn in her eye which the gazer could feel,
And a glance like the sunshine that flashes on steel.

"Go back, haughty Southron! thy treasures of gold
Are dim with the blood of the hearts thou hast sold;
Thy home may be lovely, but round it I hear
The crack of the whip and the footsteps of fear!

"And the sky of thy South may be brighter than ours,
And greener thy landscapes and fairer thy flowers;
But dearer the blast round our mountains which raves,
Than the sweet summer zephyr which breathes over slaves!

"Full low at thy bidding thy negroes may kneel,
With the iron of bondage on spirit and heel;
Yet know that the Yankee girl sooner would be
In fetters with them, than in freedom with thee!"

A single word as to the practical question of the mixture of the races. I believe it was Henry Clay who computed what number of years it would take, according to the progress of Southern amalgamation, to bleach the whole slave population white. If gentlemen wish to see where this evil prevails, let them look at the variegated colors in the South.

During this discussion, there have been repeated allusions to Northern men, and they have been held up to scorn as guilty of pusillanimity and hypocrisy. Mr. Garrison (with whom I do not agree, but whom I honor as a noble and true man), and Henry Ward Beecher and others, have been made the objects of such attacks. Why, gentlemen, if this anti-slavery enterprise had done no other good than to bring into public view those lofty and glorious characters that lead it, realizing once more the old heroic age in their manifestations of moral heroism, it would be well worth all it has cost.

And, gentlemen, although Northern men have sometimes been altogether too much disposed to cringe to the South, I believe that Pennsylvania has had a man [Grow] who, in the last Congress, was able to show that Northern blood, although slow in rising, is, when once up, quite able to protect its rights.

Criminal statistics with reference to the North have been given by my opponent; and he has laid great stress on the number of criminals in the State of New York. In passing I would merely remark, what you all doubtless understand, that the city of New York being the great *entrepot* of the continent, the mass of foreigners from all nations flock there; so that, of course, whatever may be the other conditions, there will be more criminals there. Besides, the very class of criminals that the North punishes, go unwhipped of justice in the South.

We send to prison our robbers, thieves, and murderers — our violators of female chastity — our defrauders of the laborer—our ruffians who commit assault —our abductors of young girls from their homes and parents; while the South sends to Congress her ruffians who commit rape—her robbers of cradles—her violators of wives, sellers of maidens—her maimers of men, and whippers of women. Besides, the single State of New York has a population one-third as great as all the Slave States, counting in their slaves; so that in criminal statistics, she ought to balance *five* of the largest Slave States. Lock up your criminals in these five States, and then we will count with you.

Northern infidelity has been much harped on in the speeches of my opponent. Gentlemen, there are two kinds of infidelity. There is one kind that prays — and steals negroes; that sings psalms — and whips women; that cants theology — and robs cradles! However sound Southern theology may be in its *theory* — practical infidelity, scorning the rights of man, disregarding the claims of humanity, trampling on the laws of God, is the general *practice* of the South; and its theology will never be able to fill the wide chasm between its profession of religion and its practices. If we must have infidelity of either type, I much prefer that type of unbelief which is questionable in its theory, to the most orthodox theology, when so cruel, wicked, and inhuman in its practices.

My opponent has thought proper to scorn, and flout at the Methodist Church of the North. I am not a Methodist, nor a defender of the Methodist Church North; but let me say that, whatever there is of right and of power in that church, it has reared itself into the respect and esteem of the Christian world, because of the recent movement among the Methodists North against American Slavery. All through central New York—by virtue of the efforts of the Methodist Anti-Slavery paper, started on an independent basis — the spirit of Abolitionism is rising so high in the Methodist Church North, that, if the next General Conference should not cast out every slaveholder within its bounds, there will be another division, and one that will purify the Methodist Church North, and make it Anti-Slavery.

I have found it difficult to get from my opponent the material of this debate, and have been compelled to allude, in my previous addresses, to many arguments not yet offered by him, but which are usually urged on the Pro-Slavery side of the question. I shall pursue to-night the same course.

One argument often urged against the Anti-Slavery men of the North, is, that the agitation of the freedom of the slave tends to violate the compromises — the guarantees to the South, entered into on the formation of the American Constitution. Where are those guarantees? Are they really found in the Constitution, or do they exist only in the brains of Southern men? Are they in the preamble, which I read and commented upon the other night? Are they in this clause?

"No person shall be deprived of life, *liberty* or property, without due process of law."

Yet three millions of persons have, without the shadow of a shade of legal process, been deprived of liberty, and even of the right to own property, by the South, which claims a right to do this, guarantied by the Constitution. What is "due process of law" but a trial by jury? Is it "due process of law" when a man is imprisoned or placed in bondage, even before he is accused? Is it "due process of law" when the lash is laid upon him without a legal trial? Carry out this clause of the Constitution in its proper spirit, and so far from being a guarantee of slavery, it will prove a guarantee of freedom, and will sweep American slavery from the nation.

"'*Due process of law.*' This phrase (a technical term in law) means indictment and trial by jury, for some alleged crime, and verdict and sentence in open court. For this definition we have the authority of Lord Coke, Judge Story, (in his Commentaries,) and also of Judge Bronson. (Hill's Reports, IV., 146.) By the latter two, the definition is made to apply to the Constitution of the *United States.* And Judge Bronson's decision sets aside a *State enactment*, on the ground that it takes away property without this 'due process of law.' Then *liberty* cannot be taken away without the same 'due process of law,' even though a *State enactment* could be produced in support of it. The writ of *Habeas Corpus*, as before shown, secures this 'due process of law' for all who are held in slavery, and the process would release them all. No slave in America was ever reduced to slavery by 'due process of law.' It is impossible thus to enslave men, for though persons may be imprisoned for crime, under 'due process of law,' and, to that extent, deprived of liberty, yet they cannot thus be reduced to 'goods and chattels personal,' or made the 'property' of their fellow-men. There is no legal process for this; nor can it be done, even when, 'in cases of invasion or rebellion, the public safety may require' 'the writ of habeas corpus' to 'be suspended.' There is neither law nor valid precedent for any such process."—*National Charters, Goodel.*

But where, in the Constitution, will we find these guarantees in favor of slavery? In that clause which declares that the *habeas corpus* shall not be suspended —that glorious writ that the stern old barons wrung from the tyrant King John, and which our fathers wove into the Constitution of the United States—that writ under which every man restrained of his freedom has the right to appeal to the courts, and have an investigation into the cause of his detention. Let that writ be issued by the Judges of the United States Courts, as they are bound to issue it, under the Constitution, on the complaint of every slave in this nation. Under that clause which provides that "no person shall be deprived of life, *liberty*, or property, without due process of law," let them inquire why these slaves are held in bondage, and let them find the law for American slavery. Under the writ of *habeas corpus*, tried by a judge worthy of the bench, every slave in the nation would be set free; for the Constitution of the United States would bear him out in that decision.

It may be replied, perhaps, that Judge Taney has made the Dred Scott decision, in which he says that black men have no rights which white men are bound to respect. I admit that when a judge descends from the dignity of the judicial station, prostitutes his high office, and becomes the mere caterer of a political party, turns the United States Court room into a political caucus, makes his decisions under the pressure of political influence—you cannot trust him to carry out the Constitution, or anything else. But when we have such judges, we are not without redress. Men do not live always. We shall, I hope, get very soon a better set of judges upon the bench of the Supreme Court; and then, under those clauses of the Constitution that I have named, American slavery can be and will be abolished. Gentlemen, I have no apology to offer for bringing to bear upon men in high places who are derelict in their duty, as scathing a rebuke as I would direct at the humblest mechanic in Philadelphia, did I deem him guilty of as flagrant an offence.

Judge Taney's decision is based upon the historical fiction, that when the Constitution was framed, no considerable body of people in the country regarded the negro as having any rights, and therefore the Constitution, whatever its language, cannot be supposed to recognise any rights for him. I explode this assumption by quoting from the history of the times immediately preceding the adoption of the Constitution.

William Pinckney said in 1789, the very year the Constitution was adopted:

"Sir—Iniquitous and most dishonorable to Maryland, is that dreary system of partial bondage which her laws have hitherto supported with a solicitude worthy of a better object, and her citizens by their practice, countenanced. Founded in a disgraceful traffic, to which the parent country lent its fostering aid, from motives of interest, but which even she would have disdained to encourage, had England been the destined mart of such inhuman merchandise, its continuance is as shameful as its origin."

In the Convention that drafted the Constitution —

"Mr. Madison declared, he 'thought it wrong to admit in the Constitution the idea that there could be property in men.'—3 *Mad. Pap.*, 1429.

"On motion of Mr. Randolph, the word 'SERVITUDE' was struck out, and 'SERVICE' unanimously inserted—the former being thought to express the condition of SLAVES, and the latter the obligation of FREE PERSONS."—*Ib.* 3., p. 1569.

In the Virginia Convention to ratify the Constitution, Patrick Henry argued "*the power of Congress, under the United States' Constitution, to abolish slavery in the States*," and added:

"Another thing will contribute to bring this event about. Slavery is detested. We feel its effects. We deplore it with all the pity of humanity."—*Debates Va. Convention*, p. 463.

"In the debates of the North Carolina Convention, Mr. Iredell, afterwards a Judge of the United States Supreme Court, said—'When the entire abolition of slavery takes place, it will be an event which must be pleasing to every generous mind, and every friend of human nature.'"—"*Power of Congress*," &c., pp. 31–2.

And yet Judge Taney says nobody believed at that time that the negro had any rights to be respected.

Another defence offered by the South against the abolition of their slave system is, that their slave property cannot be interfered with without the violation of State sovereignty. What is State sovereignty? Is it the unrestrained power to inflict wrong in the name of law? Sovereignty has its own natural limits. God himself is not a sovereign in such a sense that he has a right to do wrong; nor is any State sovereign in such a sense. The sovereignty of the States is bounded by the objects and purposes for which States are instituted, and only sweeps the area of their legitimate power, which is to protect the rights of man. When a State, under its claim of State sovereignty, wields its power, not for the protection of the rights of man, but for the destruction of the rights of more than half its inhabitants, such an act, so far from being in harmony with the principles of State sovereignty, is in harmony only with the principles of State *villany*. I deny the existence of any State sovereignty which confers a power to do wrong.

Cromwell, when charged with wanting allegiance to the king, in demanding the execution of Charles, replied:

> "No, I am true in my allegiance to the king. Bring me a king, and I am ready to bow down to him, to do him reverence, to obey his authority. But this *thing* that you have here is a beardless, effeminate boy; there is no kingship about him, no royalty in his soul, nothing kingly in his person or his life; and by virtue of all my regard for true kingly dignity, I am bound to see that this *thing* be displaced from the seat of the king."

So say I with reference to State sovereignty. I am ready to bow to State sovereignty, and pay her allegiance. But when you bring me in the presence of State villany, and demand, in the name of State sovereignty, that I shall do her homage, I answer, "This thing to which you ask me to bow, is not State sovereignty; it is State villany; State sovereignty demands the freedom of every slave."

Besides, State sovereignty must be limited by the other clause of the Constitution:

> "Congress shall guarantee to every State of this Union a republican form of government."

The States, I take it, have no sovereignty that overrides this power of Congress to guarantee to every State a republican form of government; and if slavery is at all points antagonistic to the true idea of republican government, the very guarantee to each State of a republican form of government would sweep slavery from the nation.

Another objection to the Anti-Slavery movement often made by Southern men, is, that the agitation of this slavery question will drive the South out of the Union. Well, what of it? What if the agitation should drive the Southern States out of the Union? Who cares? Not I. What interest has the North in the Union? Of what value is the Union to us when we have been used to catch the slaves of the South — when the Union has tied us to the incubus of American slavery? Of what value is it to us when what the South wants of us is that we should help her fight her battles for slavery? Though I am not a disunionist, yet I cannot, by any demonstration, be made to shrink from affirming that if the question be, whether slavery shall be abolished by the dissolution of the Union, or shall continue without its dissolution, I am, such being the terms, no defender of the Union.

But, gentlemen, I am not in the least afraid that the

South will go out of the Union. Visiting the county poor-house before I left home, I saw the paupers, who were most of them cripples or infirm, eating their comfortable dinner, everything around showing that they were well cared for. I cannot but think that this threat of the South that she will dissolve the Union, has just as much pith and weight as would the threat of those county paupers, that if they could not have their own way, they would dissolve the union with the county. I rather think that the county could get along without them, and that the North would survive a dissolution of the Union.

All this bluster about going out of the Union is not worth the wind it costs. It reminds me of a story I have heard. A young man, who wished to be considered a great fighting character, rushed into a crowd with much bluster and noise, and wanted to whip somebody. His father, pretending to be fearful that he might do some damage, rushed in after him, caught him and held him, calling on others to assist him, declaring that he was a terrible fellow in a fight. Presently, a brawny Yankee stepped forward and squared off, exclaiming, "If that fellow wants to fight, let him come on!" The noisy bully did not like the looks of his eye, and had no notion to fight, only intending to get a reputation for courage cheap; and frightened by this unexpected turn of affairs, in an agony of fear cried out to those around him: "Hold that other fellow! hold that other fellow, some of you! I guess dad can manage me." So the South will cry out, when she sees that the North is ready to leave the Union: "Hold that other fellow, some of you! I guess dad can manage me."

Let me, in this connection, relate another anecdote. A tall six footer in Western New York was in the habit of getting drunk occasionally. In one of these drunken fits, he determinined that he would frighten his wife, by making her believe that he intended to smash all her crockery-ware. So, when he reached home, he put on as solemn a manner as he could command, and said to her: "Polly, set all the dishes out on the table, for I am going to break them all — every one of them." Polly at once set them out, and then, taking an old cracked pitcher, she dashed it upon the hearth, breaking it into a hundred pieces, and called out to him: "Come on, Seth, I'll help you." "Polly," says Seth, "I guess you can set up the dishes for the present." So the South is ready to make a great noise, and threaten to break all the dishes, so long as she thinks she frightens the North; but let the North show a disposition to meet her half-way, and she will say: "Polly, I guess you can set up the dishes."

My opponent has asserted that the right of property in man is a universal right acknowledged in all nations. I answer him in the magnificent sentences of Lord Brougham:

> "Tell me not of rights; talk not of the property of the planter in his slaves. I deny the right; I acknowledge not the property. In vain you tell me of laws that sanction such a claim. There is a law above all the enactments of human codes — the same throughout the world, the same in all times: it is the law written by the finger of God on the hearts of men; and by that law, unchangeable and eternal,

while men despise fraud and loathe rapine, and abhor blood, they shall reject with indignation the wild and guilty phantasy that man can hold property in man."

I am satisfied to offset the sentiments of Brougham against the assertion of my opponent. The assumption of the right of property in man is too plain a case to argue. Some things cannot be made more plain by argument, and the right of man to self-ownership is an axiom.

Reference has been made to the testimony of the the Fathers, as being in favor of slavery. We have been told that Washington and Jefferson, and the other founders of the Republic, supported the slave system.

I read the testimony of Gen. Washington. In a letter to John F. Mercer, dated Sept.–, 1786, Gen. Washington says:

"I never mean, unless some particular circumstances should compel me to it, to possess another slave by purchase, it being among my *first wishes* to see some plan adopted by which slavery, in this country, may be abolished by law."

I could give you extracts from other letters quite as pertinent; but it is unnecessary to detain you with reading them.

Let us hear the voice of Jefferson:

"There must doubtless be an unhappy influence on the manners of our people, produced by the existence of slavery among us. The whole commerce between most of slaves is a perpetual exercise of the most boisterous passions — the most unremitting despotism on the one part, and degrading submissions on the other."

* * * * * *

"And can the liberties of a nation be thought secure, when we have removed their only firm basis — a conviction in the minds of the people that these liberties are of the gift of God; that they are not to be violated but with His wrath? *Indeed, I tremble for my country when I reflect that God is just; that His justice cannot sleep forever;* that, considering numbers, nature, and natural means only, a revolution of the wheel of fortune, an exchange of situations, is among possible events; that it may become probable by supernatural interference! *The Almighty has no attribute which can take sides with us in such a contest.*"

I could multiply quotations from Jefferson to the same effect.

What is the voice of Madison? Advocating the abolition of the slave-trade, he said:

"The dictates of humanity, the principles of the people, the national safety and happiness, and prudent policy, require it of us. It is to be hoped that, by expressing a national disapprobation of the trade, we may *destroy* it, and save our country from reproaches, and our posterity from the imbecility ever attendant on a country filled with slaves."

Monroe says:

"We have found that this evil has preyed upon the very vitals of the Union, and has been prejudicial to all the States in which it has existed."

Hear the language of Patrick Henry:

"It would rejoice my very soul that every one of my fellow-beings were emancipated. We ought to lament and deplore the necessity of holding our fellow-men in bondage. Believe me, I shall honor the Quakers for their noble efforts to abolish slavery."

John Randolph, in a letter to Wm. Gibbons, in 1820, says:

"With unfeigned respect and regard, and as sincere a deprecation of the extension of slavery and its horrors, as any other man, be he whom he may, I am your friend, in the literal sense of that much-abused word. I say much abused, because it is applied to the leagues of vice, and avarice, and ambition, instead of good-will toward man from love of Him who is the Prince of Peace."

Thus I could go on, and give you page after page of similar testimony, from men of the South as well as the North. But I will only add the testimony of the "Old Dominion"—of Virginia herself—before she found that she could make money by breeding slaves.

The "Virginia Society for the Abolition of Slavery," organized in 1791 (in those days, they had an Abolition Society in Virginia!), addressed Congress in these words:

"Your memorialists, fully aware that righteousness exalteth a nation, and that *slavery is not only an odious degradation, but an outrageous violation of one of the most essential rights of human nature, and utterly repugnant to the precepts of the Gospel*, which breathes 'peace on earth and good-will to men,' lament that a practice so inconsistent with true policy and *the inalienable rights of men*, should subsist in so enlightened an age, and among a people professing that *all mankind are, by nature, equally entitled to freedom.*"

The first General Congress of the colonies assembled in Philadelphia in September, 1774. Preparatory to that measure, the Convention of Virginia assembled in August of that year, to appoint delegates to the General Congress. An exposition of the rights of British America, by Mr. Jefferson, was laid before this Convention, of which the following is an extract:

'THE ABOLITION OF DOMESTIC SLAVERY is the greatest object of desire in these Colonies, where it was unhappily introduced in their infant state. But, previous to the enfranchisement of the slaves, it is necessary to exclude further importations from Africa. Yet our repeated attempts to effect this by prohibitions, and by imposing duties which might amount to prohibition, have been hitherto defeated by his Majesty's negative; thus preferring the immediate advantage of a few African corsairs to the lasting interests of the American States, and the rights of human nature, deeply wounded by this infamous practice.". — *Am. Archives*, 4th series, vol. i. p. 696.

The Virginia Convention, before separating, adopted the following resolution:

"*Resolved*, We will neither ourselves import, nor purchase any slave or slaves imported by any other person, after the first day of November next, either from AFRICA, the WEST INDIES, or ANY OTHER PLACE." — *Ibid.* p. 687.

North Carolina also held her Provincial Convention in August of the same year, and

"*Resolved*, That we will not import any slave or slaves, or purchase any slave or slaves imported or brought into the Province by others, from any part of the world, after the first day of November next." — *Ibid.* p. 735.

Georgia spoke as follows:

"We, therefore, the Representatives of the extensive District of Darien, in the colony of Georgia, having now assembled in Congress, by authority and free choice of the inhabitants of said District, now freed from their fetters, do resolve:

"To show the world that we are not influenced by any contracted or interested motives, but a general philanthropy for ALL MANKIND, of whatever climate, language, or complexion, we hereby declare our disapprobation and abhorrence of the unnatural practice of slavery in America (however the uncultivated state of our country, or other specious arguments, may plead for it), a practice founded in injustice and cruelty, and highly dangerous to our liberties (as well as lives), debasing part of our fellow-creatures below men, and corrupting the virtue and morals of the rest, and is laying the basis of that liberty we contend for (and which we pray the Almighty to continue to the latest posterity), upon a very wrong foundation. We, therefore, Resolve, at all times to use our utmost endeavors for the manumission of our slaves in this colony, upon the most safe and equitable footing for the master and themselves." JAN. 12th, 1775.—*Ibid.* p. 1136.

You will now agree, I think, that the testimony of the Fathers is on my side, not that of my opponent.

In the course of this debate, much has been said against the efforts to abolish slavery, because of the degraded character and mode of life of such colored persons as have escaped to the North; and my opponent has given you the horrors of the state of society in Canada. It has been affirmed that the slave is unable to take care of himself. How happens it, then, that he takes care of himself and his master? for his master does not work. Poor fellow! he must have a hard task to take care of himself, with a half-dozen lazy whites hanging to the skirts of his tattered garments to filch their living out of him. What is it but adding insult to injury, when you thus load him with fetters, steal his wages, and then affirm that he cannot take care of himself?

But let us see whether the slaves that escape to the North are able to take care of themselves. Let us see what is their character with the people of Canada. I read an extract from the *Toronto Journal:*

"The colored people of Toronto are an example in point of industry, sobriety, and morality, to their white neighbors. Out of 5346 persons committed to Toronto jail, last year, 5268 were white men and women!!! Out of 1057 ladies committed, only eight were colored. *We judge people by their conduct, not by their color.*"

Let me read to you also the testimony of an ex-sheriff in Canada:

"I have also great pleasure in stating, that so far as my knowledge of the colored population of Toronto is concerned, great credit is due to them for their general good conduct and industry, and that during the long period in which I continued to hold the office of Sheriff, fewer convictions for offences took place in the Superior Courts and Courts of Quarter Sessions, which I had to attend, than, when compared with the white population, might have been expected.

"I remain, Sir,

"Your obedient servant,

"W. B. JARVIS,

"Formerly a Captain in the Queen's Rangers and Ex Sheriff."

Let me now make a few remarks, suggested by the speech my opponent has given you to-night. He has given us a rehash of that long historical story, which he went over on the first evening of the debate, about the existence of slavery from the first ages until the present time. I replied to him on the evening when this course of argument was first offered; and I will only give in substance the same answer to-night. Is a giant wrong any the less a wrong because its locks are gray with age? Supposing it to have existed through all ages, does that fact change the blackness of its infamy to the whiteness of innocence? or does it not rather deepen its dark stains of damning guilt before the moral sense of the whole world? Does it make murder right because it began with Cain, and has existed from that day to this? So slavery (even admitting that it has existed in all ages and all nations) has existed as an outrage upon man, and gains no sanction of justice because it began its atrocities almost with the creation of the human race.

It has been urged on the other side that Africa has been blessed by slavery, or rather, that Africa is such a horrid place that it is a blessing to the slave to bring him here. Let me tell the gentleman what made the coast of Africa so desolate, and what has contributed so much to the ruin of the people along the coast. They were as happy and contented as are those in the interior, until the slave-traders of the *civilized* world came to them with the vices of the slaveholders of the South, dealing out whiskey among them; inciting the tribes to war one with the other; scattering the firebrands of destruction among them; exciting them, by appeals to their cupidity, to conquer their fellows and sell them into slavery. That dark, deep heathenism, which is to be found on the coasts of Africa, has gathered the blackest tinge of its enormity from the slave-trade, and from the efforts of the South and other portions of the world, to gain slaves from that region.

Read the travels of Dr. Livingston. Has he not found in the interior of Africa a people who, not having been cursed by this horrid trade, are far advanced in enlightenment, and farther advanced in humanity than a great many professed Christians of America. They have built large towns, have rich agricultural districts, and are in a position to command the respect of the world as much as any nation destitute of the blessings of Christianity.

Admitting that the condition of Africa is bad enough, how is it bettered by slavery and the slave-trade? Is it not rather injured, depressed, made infinitely worse by the continued existence of American slavery?

The Bible argument has again to-night been touched on. I shall not weary you by a textual argument, but permit me to offer a few reflections founded on the genius and spirit of true Christianity, shedding the light of its glorious principles upon this dark subject.

Christianity sustains slavery—does it? Jesus came among us to hang the world in chains—did he? The law that he proclaims justifies robbing mothers of their children and wives of their husbands—does it? What is the language of that law? The whole sum of Christianity is thus condensed into a few sentences:

> "Thou shalt love the Lord thy God with all thy heart, and with all thy soul, and with all thy mind, and with all thy strength;" and "Thou shalt love thy neighbor as thyself."

And when the commentary on this passage is given in the story of the Good Samaritan, we learn that our neighbor is he who is in distress, who has fallen among thieves. In short, our neighbor is the slave, who has fallen among the thieves of this nation.

The very genius of the command I have quoted requires that we should act the part of the Good Samaritan towards the slave—should see that his wounds be bound up, and that he be protected in his rights against the thieves that would despoil him.

Do you ask me to believe for an instant that Jesus,

as he looks down from heaven to-night over the broad expanse of the South—as His ear catches the piteous cry of the babe bereft of a mother's care, because that mother is under the lash—as He hears the deep groan of the poor slave who, on his hard couch is mourning the bitterness of oppression—as He listens to the shrieks of maidens, writhing under the whip, because they will not submit to lust,—do you ask me to believe that our glorious Saviour, as His view takes in this whole horrid scene of brutality, and outrage, and cruelty, is not only indifferent to its horrors, but even throws the shield of the Divine sanction over a hell on the face of God's earth.

If you ask me to believe this, you ask me to cease to be a Christian, and turn infidel! You ask me to change names between God and the devil; for Satan himself, if there is left in his dark heart one particle of susceptibility to good and true emotion, cannot be indifferent to the wrongs of the slave. Yet I am told here in pious phrase, backed up with canting quotations from hymns, that the religion of the Bible, which Jesus Christ came into the world to teach, sanctions, and shields, and throws its halo around American slavery!

Infidelity, indeed! Why, if the alternative is to be either to accept a religion of this kind or to sink into blank infidelity, who wonders that infidelity makes progress in the world? Who wonders that men of mind and heart should refuse to swallow a religion which demands that they shall accept the American slave-system as impregnably holy?

No, gentlemen; as an humble servant of God, I feel proud to do what I may to shield his glorious character from the imputation of being an abettor of man thieves. I am glad to have the opportunity of proclaiming here that the blackest blasphemy ever uttered by the lips of man is the declaration that God sanctions American slavery.

On such a question as this, I cannot stop to bandy texts. Slavery is an attack broadly levelled at the very intuitions of our common consciousness. The great principle of freedom is so clearly mirrored in the depths of the human soul, that there is no need for me to cite Bible texts and historical incidents, or enter into a minute examination of the question of races. Even the brutes of the field know that the ethics of American slavery are false. The horse can detect in a moment the presence of humanity; he knows the difference between a creature possessing a soul, and a piece of furniture — "goods and chattels personal." Yet the religion, the ethics, the politics of the South, and, I regret to say, of a portion of the North, have not yet attained to the perceptions of the horse!

In my view, it does not need philosophy, it does not need learning, it does not need quotations from the Bible, or from any other source, to settle a question so plain as this. The simple fact that God has given each man into his own hands — that He has stamped His own image on his brow — that He has given him the consciousness of his own individuality—that He has bestowed on him the power to think, to will, to act, and the desire to take care of himself—this is God's own testimony, written upon the very foundations of human nature, declaring that man is entitled to liberty, that freedom is his birthright, and that whoever lays hands upon him to prevent its enjoyment, is violating the commands of the Spirit of God himself.

This is a question which it seems to me affords but little ground for argument. It is not more argument that the world wants to be convinced of the iniquity of American slavery — it is more heart to feel for humanity. The difficulty is not a want of intellect, of learning, of historical research, of knowledge in regard to the races, but it is a want of soul to appreciate the dignity, and beauty, and glory of humanity — to understand the sacredness of that type of God which he has vouchsafed to us in each other's form — to feel the influence of the great law of human brotherhood. We have been told that American slavery will not be abolished until the judgment day. Let me say that the man holding such an opinion, but little knows the spirit of the age. Put your ear to the ground, my friend, and you will hear the low, muttering, rolling swell of the on-coming wave of humanity and intelligence, that shall ere long sweep from the earth every vestige of this horrid system. Understand the spirit of the age —the impulses of human progress, and the enlargement of human sympathies; catch something of the spirit which rises up among our Northern hills, and finds its manifestation throughout Northern society; and then you will come up to the faith that the day is not far distant when every slave on this continent shall be set free.

The whole land has within a few days been in a jubilant state of excitement, because of the successful laying of the great Atlantic Cable. The world is becoming a net-work for the communication of intelligence that shall thrill along the nerves of the electric wire from America to Europe, and make the circuit of the globe. In this enlightened day, great thoughts, great impulses, and great aims cannot be restrained; and the spirit of American slavery can no more defend itself successfully against them than prevent the plunge of Niagara over the fall. The time is hastening on, when by virtue of the enlarging impulses and vigorous growth of the human soul, American slavery shall be abolished.

Look back even for a few years. In your own city, not very long ago, such thoughts as I have uttered would have been received with showers of brickbats and rotten eggs. It was then as much as a man's life was worth to testify to the truth. I come into the Anti-Slavery enterprise at too late a day to understand the full force and beauty of this martyr spirit. The men who in those days stood true to the glorious cause, who lifted up the banner of righteousness, and marshalled the better heart of the nation to see the wrongs of the oppressed—these men deserve to be embalmed in the memory of future generations; the gratitude and love of the world should settle down upon them in one benediction.

What! stop the impulses of humanity, and prevent the abolition of American slavery! A great idea never stops; a glorious human impulse never belittles itself, and immortality speaks out in the birth of every noble thought. The intuitions of humanity, ever gaining breadth and strength, go onward and inward; and truth, proving that

"The eternal years of God are hers,"

moves forward in strength and power to final triumph.

I have no fears for the success of this enterprise—no doubts that the slave will be set free—no dread that the jubilee will not come, for the hearts of this mighty nation have caught the impulse of freedom, and you can never turn back the tide. I have only to say, that if in this debate I shall aid in the humblest way in giving impetus to the glorious cause, I shall feel richly repaid, and shall rejoice to the last day of my life in having had the proud privilege to strike one blow for God and man!

"OUGHT AMERICAN SLAVERY TO BE PERPETUATED?"

AFFIRMATIVE, V.—BY W. G. BROWNLOW.

GENTLEMEN, having concluded my remarks last evening fifteen minutes inside of my time, I may exceed my limits to-night a few minutes, but it shall be very few.

There is nothing more common in this age of polemic warfare, than for every combatant who assails the motives, calling, doctrines, or, if you please, the *character* of another, to claim the right to do so, because (as he says) he acts on the *defensive*. The reason of this must be obvious to every reflecting mind. He who acts in the defensive is entitled to the sympathies of the public, because he is supposed to have been unjustly assailed; and these sympathies will justify the *defender*, while the *aggressor* would justly deserve the opprobrium of the intelligent, and the frowns of the candid. But, as both the advocates and opponents of the South claim to occupy this ground, it is of the utmost importance that this controversy should be settled, and that the candid and conservative men, both North and South, should be at once enabled to decide to whom this high claim belongs. It seldom occurs, in a family or neighborhood quarrel, a Church controversy, or a dispute between nations, or even sections of the same nation, that both of the parties to the dispute are acting on the defensive. Some one *commenced* the war; some one is the *aggressor;* some one is to blame more than another for the existence of said quarrel, or controversy. So it is in the present controversy which divides, distracts, and agitates this great Nation, from the cod-fisheries of Maine, to the Gulf of Mexico, growing out of the slavery question. Who is at fault, the North or South? It is my purpose in this, my last of this series of addresses, to set forth who is at fault.

To *defend* one's self, presupposes an unwarranted attack from another — not merely an *attack*, but one for which there was no just cause. I may attack an enemy of mine — a sworn and uncompromising foe — with all the violence of which my nature is capable, and still I may act on the defensive, if the *previous* conduct of that enemy, including his threats of personal violence, were such as to render my assault necessary to my future safety. You, gentlemen, any of you, may attack an enemy in like manner, and still act on the *defensive*, if the previous threats of that enemy were such, in the eyes of the law, as to make that attack necessary to your future well-being. Nay, it is a principle in municipal law, both in this country and in England, that if an evil-disposed person threaten your life upon sight, you are justified in shooting him down upon sight. This was the principle acted upon by the gallant PUTNAM, when he assailed the *wolf* in his den. Putnam made the *attack*, but it was in *self-defence.* The *howlings* and *prowlings* of the "*varmint*" in the neighborhood, to say nothing of his depredations among the live stock of the farmers, could no longer be tolerated. The vile wolves, attired in "sheep's clothing" in Abolitiondom, upon whom Southern farmers are visiting a righteous retribution, have howled about the borders of the Slave States long enough. They have prompted insubordination among our domestics; they have stolen others, and run them off upon an under-ground railroad; and they have resisted laws passed by Congress to restore to us our property. When we declared the War of the Revolution, we were acting on the defensive. We *declared* the war, but we did it in *self-defence*. In the language of the Declaration of Independence, Great Britain "kept among us, in time of peace, standing armies, without the consent of our Legislatures," &c., &c.

Now, fellow-countrymen, how stands the case as between the Anti-Slavery men of the North, and the Pro-Slavery men of the South? Who commenced the "war of words and fight of quills," that has raged between the opposing sections of North and South, for lo! a quarter of a century past? Who has kept up the strife, and added fuel to the flame? In the language of the time-honored instrument already quoted, "let *facts* be submitted to a candid world."

The Anti-Slavery men of the North, have perseveringly refused us the exercise of those rights the Bible, the Constitution, and laws of our country guarantee to us, and to our children. Act iv. sec. 2, of the Constitution of the United States, declares that,—"No person held to labor or service in one State, under the laws thereof, escaping into another, shall, in consequence of any law or regulation therein, be discharged from such labor or service, but shall be delivered up on claim of the party to whom such service or labor may be due." But this preacher of Abolition "righteous ness," has avowed upon this stand, that he intends to stump the State of New York in favor of *Gerritt Smith* for governor, because he is pledged to call out the militia of that State, when any attempt is made to arrest a fugitive slave. The gentleman is said to own stock in the under-ground railroad, and to be associated with his *colored superiors*, Douglass and Ward, and other negro-stealers of Syracuse. This will account for his zeal in this infamous cause.

Now, the Fugitive Slave Law is based on the foregoing clause of the Constitution of the United States; and the Supreme Court of the United States, the highest judicial tribunal known to this government, has declared this Fugitive Slave Law to be constitutional. Yet, Anti-Slavery men at the North resist this law, and thereby rebel against the Constitution and civil authorities of the country.

Four years after the declaration of American Independence, Pennsylvania and Massachusetts emancipated their slaves; and, *eight* years thereafter, Connecticut and Rhode Island followed their example.

Three years after the last-named event, an *Abolition Society* was organized by the citizens of the State of New York, with John Jay at its head. *Two* years subsequently, the Pennsylvanians did the same thing, electing Benjamin Franklin to the Presidency of their association — *he declining to serve! Thirty-eight* years after Pennsylvania struck off the shackles from her slaves, *one-third* of the convicts in her Penitentiary were free negroes; and *one-half* of New Jersey's convicts were free persons of color. Am I called upon for the proof in these cases, I cite the "Boston Prison Discipline Society's Report," for 1826–7.

The records in Massachusetts, Connecticut, and Rhode Island, did not show such a proportion of colored convicts, and for the best of reasons. The negroes were not there. Before the laws emancipating them could take effect, the pious Abolitionists hurried them round to Virginia, and the Carolinas, and sold them for the cash.

Thus are we of the South on the *defensive* in this controversy. And against whom do we wage war? It is against the sanctimonious hypocrisy of a band that, with words of pity on the lips, with wailing in the tone, with woe upon the visage, and *bigotry* where the *heart* should have been, continue to agitate this question as they have been doing for years, both in and out of Congress.

The question really is, whether the teachings of the Bible, the provisions of our National Constitution, and the decisions of the Supreme Court, on the one hand, or the dictation of demagogues, on the other, shall rule the destinies of the South, and of the Union. Hence, our stand is taken, and our purposes immovably fixed. We have a right to peace under the provisions of the Constitution, the acts of Congress, and the decisions of the Supreme Court; and we desire peace; but we see no prospect of quiet, but, on the contrary, that of everlasting agitation!

I need not here pause to speak of the threats these agitators have uttered, respecting the abolition of slavery in the Southern States. One of the file-leaders, who represents the party, SENATOR SEWARD, said at a mass-meeting in Ohio, only two years ago:

> "Slavery can be limited to its present bounds; it can be ameliorated. It can be—and it *must* be—ABOLISHED, and you and I can and *must* do it."

Only a few months since, Senator Wade, of Ohio, declared that the North was the lord and master of the South; that the South would be compelled to obey her lord and master, whether so inclined or not. Senators Wilson, Hale, &c., followed in a like strain, until the victorious jubilations were concluded. Similar scenes occurred in the House of Representatives very often last session; and from these blustering threats, this gentleman defiantly ventured to utter his boast last evening, of a similar character. In his fanatical outbursts of wild and fierce denunciation of the South and everything Southern, he is but the *echo* of such demagogues and incendiaries as I have named. Nay, he is the *sattelite* of Seward, Smith, & Co., and revolves around them as his primary! Their cardinal principles are as wicked, as revolutionary, and as vile, as are those of the Father of Evil; and they have these unblushing, unscrupulous, and unprincipled clerical hacks, and others, giving out their hostilities over the country!

And those who counsel resistance to the laws and to the Constitution of the Republic, like Mr. Seward, the people of the South will hold guilty of a high misdemeanor, and they will ever treat them as disturbers of the public peace, nay, as enemies of the independence, the perpetuity, the greatness, and the glory of the Union, under which, by the blessing of Almighty God, we have hitherto so wonderfully prospered!

But why disturb a system that is beneficial to the physical and moral welfare of the negroes? Why remove them from the restraint of Christian and civilized life, and turn them back to savage barbarism, penury, want, and starvation, merely for the sake of saying they are *free?* Of what advantage is freedom, if men are not competent to use it, to their own and their neighbors' good? Why take away the comfort they now enjoy, and turn them out to starve, or steal, or to be destroyed by a superior race? Why all this noise about freedom, when that boasted freedom would bring anarchy, poverty, suffering, moral and physical desolation to the negro? Is there any of the spirit of Christianity in all this agitation? The examples of the French Revolutionists, and the acts of British emancipationists, particularly in the West India Islands, should be a warning to all American Abolitionists!

Negroes in a state of slavery are comfortable and prosperous beyond any peasantry in the world, and even beyond the most opulent serfs of Europe; but emancipate them, and you irretrievably consign them to barbarism. Emancipate the slaves in the Southern States, and the white population would either leave the negroes to "one long day of unprofitable ease"—leave them to dream of happiness, or their abolition sympathizers to dream for them—or they would require the negroes to leave the country.

Really, the only way to civilize and Christianize benighted Africa is to annex that vast continent to the United States, and let our people reduce them to slavery, set them to work, and thus develop the resources of Africa. Their lands are the finest in the world, and adapted to the culture of *coffee*, above all other lands. The English, French, and Spanish people, are not the people to own and direct African laborers—they exercise too much cruelty. God looks to the people of the United States to develop the resources of Africa, and I honestly believe he requires us to do that work. Talk about *fillibustering*, and the unlawful seizure of territory in possession of others! The Africans have forfeited their country, by refusing to labor, and to develop its resources. Men must labor. If they will not do so of their own choice, they must be compelled to do so, or starve. The negro will not work without some one to make him do so. Man is doomed to eat bread in the sweat of his face. This he cannot reverse. He may dream of ease without labor, but, while he dreams, the laws of nature, all against him, are sternly at their work. Indolence benumbs the feeble intellect of the negro, and inflames his vile passions, driving him into the extremes of savage barbarism. Indolence brings upon the negro, poverty and want; it surrounds him with temptation; and then, vice, with all her long train of blighting evils, winds her deadly coils around him, and makes him the willing slave of the Devil, to do his will upon a scale of savage barbarity, revolting to the finer feelings of the soul! He dreams of peace and liberty, without labor, but he reaps a harvest of starvation, poverty, disease, and death. The blossoms of his paradise are *fine words* spoken by Abolitionists, but its fruits are *death*. Like the fabled apple of the Dead Sea, beautiful without, but *ashes* within!

I repeat, there is no call for the re-opening of the

African slave-trade among us: a sufficient stock of negroes are in our Southern States, to answer *our* ends, as well as the ends of Providence, which, shocking as the sentiment may be to your ears, are in perfect *harmony! Hamitic* service is now a blessing to these United States, and it is a blessing to the slaves in bondage, though the *mode* of its transplantation was an abomination!

In future, then, the theatre for the achievement of the happiness of the African race, is not the United States—it is *Africa. Utopia* is not the field—it must be abandoned. Let us seize upon the vast territory of Africa, cultivate its rich soil, and force its millions of indolent, degraded, and starving natives, to labor, and thereby elevate themselves to the dignity of men made in the image of God! Christian men at the South, who take a correct view of this question of slavery, will no longer make provisions in their wills, or otherwise, for the emancipation of their negroes, and cast them helpless, upon the frigid charities of the Anti-Slavery men of Ohio, Indiana, Illinois, and the New England States. Let them sell their slaves to Southern planters here, and direct the proceeds to be applied to the opening up of new *slave* States in Africa, where we may settle down, and compel the natives to labor, thus causing civilization and Christianity to spread over a few millions of its population, and the moral effect would be irresistible!

What next? According to the doctrines advanced here, by my not very worthy competitor, "Abolition" is the Christian's mission in this our day and generation, and it is his ONLY mission! It again becomes necessary for me to recall the fact, that slavery of the worst sort existed throughout the Roman Empire in our Saviour's day, and in the days of his immediate successors in office—and that neither Christ nor his Apostles ever were known to preach an "Abolition" sermon, deliver an "Abolition" lecture, or offer up an "Abolition" prayer; but, on the contrary, everywhere taught, "servants obey your masters." I do not mean to say, that Christ was passionately fond of slavery, or made a business of defending Roman slavery, which was more cruel and barbarous than American slavery, for I have no express declarations of Holy Writ to bear me out in saying so; but, perhaps, I have good ground to say the very reverse. But I do mean to say, that Christianity, in the days of Christ, consisted in rendering unto Cæsar the things that were Cæsar's, and in letting civil and servile institutions alone.

When Christ was on earth, He rebuked *sin* of all classes and kinds, and dared to rebuke the haughty Jewish priests in their temple, where they were guilty of sin; but, while slavery, cruel Roman slavery was all about Him, and He was daily in the midst of it, neither He nor his Apostles were ever known to preach an "Abolition" sermon. The slavery Christ saw daily was that under which a master could sell his slave, work him as many hours as he pleased in twenty-four, or PUT HIM TO DEATH if he thought proper to do so. Yet, Christ never preached a sermon in favor of abolishing even this kind of slavery!

A Roman slave could not contract a marriage; and if he had children, with or without marriage, no legal relation between him and his children was recognized. A free woman having children by a slave, was at once reduced to bondage as a punishment for the offence.

By way of parenthesis I take occasion to say, that the Boston matrimonial register shows, that during the past year of our Lord, 1857, there were no less than *sixty* amalgamation marriages; and, singular to say, they were all *white women* to gentlemen of color, mostly fugitives from the Slave States. The white ladies of Boston have singular tastes, and can but feel proud that they are not living in the days of Christ and the Apostles, who endorsed a law that would have made them slaves! I name this fact upon the authority of the *New York Dispatch*, to show the growing degeneracy of New England. When WOMAN, the safeguard of virtue and purity, stoops thus to degrade herself, the degradation of man, as a necessary consequence, must follow.

What next? Under the laws regulating the slavery Christ tolerated, a slave could have no property. A runaway slave could not be lawfully received or harbored by a second or third person; to conceal him was death. The master was entitled to pursue him wherever he pleased, and it was the duty of all authorities to give him "aid and comfort" in his efforts to recover the fugitive. Persons became slaves by capture in war, without any regard to rank, color, or sex. And yet, these were the laws that Christ and the Apostles exhorted Christians to reverence and obey; and this was *the* slavery against which they obstinately refused to preach a single sermon!

The immense number of prisoners captured in the constant wars of the Roman Republic, and the increase of wealth and luxury in the days of Christ, augmented the number of slaves to a prodigious extent. Roman citizens, not a few, owned as many as 10,000 and

20,000 slaves. A freed man, under Augustus, after losing much property and many slaves in the civil wars, at his death disposed of 4116 slaves! The games of the amphitheatre required an immense number of slaves. The gladiators in Italy, only 73 years before Christ, were not defeated by the Romans till 60,000 slaves were slain in battle. Regular slave-dealers accompanied the different contending armies, and, after a battle had been gained, the successful party threw thousands into the market, and sold them at very cheap rates.

In the midst of this system of slavery the Christian era was inaugurated. Christ came in contact with it every day, recognized it as proper, preached sermons in which he urged obedience to these slave laws, and obedience to masters by slaves, but never delivered the first sermon in favor of the "Abolition" of slavery! Christians owned slaves, and both bought and sold them, under the very *noses* of Christ and the Apostles; and they, in turn, sanctioned the traffic, by receiving both the slaves and their owners into the Church, and administering its ordinances to them. What I mean to infer from these facts is, that if slavery were the sin and crime the Abolitionists of this day say it is, Christ saw it in a worse point of view, and never preached a sermon against it; never warred upon the government that protected it by law; but, on the contrary, taught obedience to that government, and reverence for its civil and domestic institutions. His mission was to call *sinners* to repentance—not to concentrate the public mind upon the abolition of slavery, nor to divide churches, and distract society upon that question, as do the hypocrites and demagogues of New England!

I would like to impress upon my brother preachers of the North the example of Christ when on earth, in the midst of Roman slavery — in itself almost indefensible, because of its atrocities; I could then make them useful in ameliorating and Christianizing African slavery in the United States. If Northern Anti-Slavery men would only reason with, instead of *cursing* and *villifying* the people of the South, some practical good to the slave, his owner, and the country generally, as well as to the Church, might be accomplished; but their SLANDER and ABUSE, and their OFFICIOUS INTERMEDDLINGS, have drawn tighter the bonds of slavery in the United States, and caused the slaves to be treated with more severity than they otherwise would have been.

What next? Let us consider, briefly, some of the *effects* of this crusade against the South. The principal watering-places at the North have not met with their usual success during the two or three seasons last past, — while those of Virginia, Tennessee, Kentucky, Georgia, North Carolina, and Alabama, have been overrun. Heretofore, Saratoga, Newport, and Cape May, have been the grand centres of attraction for the fashionable society of every section of the Union. At these, and other points, the wealth and fashion of the South have assembled in crowds, filling their vast hotels to repletion, while gold from the South, the product of slave labor, was poured out with a most lavish hand, such as the liberality and elegance of Southern people alone, could do! My information is, that the hotels at these celebrated watering-places, the two past seasons, were but half filled, and scarcely a Southern family was in attendance at any of them. Southern gentlemen now in this city, will attest the truth of these sayings.

May we not pause here, and inquire into the cause of this sudden, and almost general desertion? No one can be mistaken as to the *cause*. The South has been, for years, reviled and insulted by Northern Abolitionists, and their vile presses. No terms of reproach were low enough to apply to us — negro-drivers, slave-killers, heartless-murderers, outside barbarians, and every vile epithet that could be coined, was heaped upon the heads of the Southern people, without distinction of age or sex. The very *elite* of the South, including the most refined and virtuous females, have been grossly insulted at the tables of these Northern hotels, by insolent free negroes, acting as waiters and hired servants. Beside all this, the entire North, where these watering-places are located, in the late Presidential contest, voted for "Fremont and Dayton;" a miserable *sectional* vote, indirectly given for a dissolution of the Union.

Hence it is, that the Southern people, heretofore the wealthy and liberal patrons of Northern watering-places, remain at home, go to Europe, or visit the superior springs of their own native mountains.

Nor is it the watering-places alone, that have been injuriously affected at the North; this is but a small item in their losses; many of the manufacturing towns at the North, have been sadly crippled in their business. Boston, the hot-bed of sedition, and Abolition slang-whanging, has done a little more than *half* her usual business with the South, the two last seasons. In the meantime, Boston has turned her attention to a new set of Free-Soil customers in the North-west, and these failing to meet their liabilities when the panic set in last fall, many banks and business-houses suspended, and not a few went by the board! Such are, to some extent, at least, the effects of this Abolition crusade against the South. They are fast destroying their whole trade with the South, in their pious efforts to steal a few negroes, and to set others free.

These Abolition vagrants, Kansas-sympathizing, Freedom-shrieking, Union-hating hypocrites, have gone out to *shear*, and returned home most gloriously *shorn*. And this decrease in business will continue from year to year, the South will build up a foreign trade, establish Ocean steamboat lines from our Atlantic cities to the entry-ports of Europe, and thus convey our own products to the European markets, instead of sending them North, and paying a double commission for their transmission abroad, and that, too, to our bitterest revilers, and most unmitigated calumniators. Indeed, the South can do nothing less than to withdraw from all entertainments prepared for her by Northern fanatics.

But the question arises in this connection. What are the capabilities and resources of the South? Upon this point I desire to be heard with attention. We have already an immense line of railroad, and an equally extensive line of steamboats in successful operation, and thousands of miles more projected. We have capacious ports and harbors strung along the Atlantic coast, from the Gulf of Mexico, to the Chesapeake and Delaware Bays, including Sounds and Rivers, to head of tide, amounting to 23,803 miles, and more than *doubling* those of your boasted North! Our inland water communications are unequalled. Look at the following tables, and tell me, does the South lack facilities for commercial intercourse?

Table showing the shore line of States on the Atlantic coast and Gulf of Mexico.

STATES.	Shore line of coast washed by sea.	Shore line of coast washed by bays, sounds, &c	Shore line of rivers to the head of tide.	Total sea coast, and shores of bays, sounds, &c.	Total sea coast, and shores of bays, sounds, &c., and of rivers to head of tide.
	Miles.	Miles.	Miles.	Miles.	Miles.
Maine	427	1,599	427	2,026	2,453
N. Hampshire	13	37	24	50	74
Mass.........	209	865	832	1,074	1,906
Rhode Island.	55	153	232	208	440
Connecticut...	14	239	1,074	253	1,327
New York....	114	886	1,057	1,000	2,057
New Jersey..	118	702	151	820	971
Pennsylvania	....	....	106	......	106
Delaware....	29	136	506	165	671
Maryland....	44	1,008	3,401	1,052	4,453
Virginia.....	148	735	1,690	883	2,573
N. Carolina...	299	1,549	932	1,848	2,780
S. Carolina ..	192	356	708	548	1,256
Georgia.....	76	410	468	486	954
Florida......	1,020	3,005	860	4,025	4,885
Alabama....	33	284	313	317	630
Mississippi..	42	206	137	248	385
Louisiana....	616	1,595	936	2,211	3,147
Texas.......	353	1,284	432	1,637	2,069
Totals....	....	....	14,286	18,851	33,137

Total Northern........................	9,334 miles.
Total Southern........................	23,803 "
	33,137 "

Number of harbors in the different States on the coast, and the principal ones on rivers to the head of tide. [*Incomplete.*]

States.	Number of harbors (not including all upon rivers.)	
Maine	52	
New Hampshire	3	
Massachusetts	51	
Rhode Island	7	
Connecticut	32	
New York	27	
New Jersey	14	
Pennsylvania	3	
	—	189
Delaware	3	
Maryland	11	
Virginia	22	
North Carolina	52	
South Carolina	21	
Georgia	15	
Florida	66	
Alabama	4	
Mississippi	10	
Louisiana	33	
Texas	12	
	—	249
Total		438

The table of harbors is incomplete, but the full table will only increase the number of those of the South, and show her still greater relative superiority. With railroads and rivers traversing every portion of her territory; with safe and ample harbors indenting her coasts; and with thousands of miles of her shores washed by the ocean, what does the South lack in the way of facilities for transportation? Nothing, literally nothing. If, then, the South shall be forced to establish a separate and independent government, by the continued aggressions of the North, would her geographical position shut her out from intercourse with the world? No, verily, she is throughout her whole extent, by the act of God, in contact with the commercial world.

Our coal and iron, copper, lead, zinc, and other valuable minerals, are exhaustless; and the produce of an empire can now most readily be entered at any port in the South.

But, with us in the South, "cotton is king;" and, in the language of Professor De Bow:

> "It is the cotton-bale that makes the treaties of the world, and binds over the nations to keep the peace."

Behind the cotton-bale, in time of war, our armies take shelter; while, in time of peace, our cotton-bales employ the shipping of at least half the American commerce; feed the looms and spindles of the entire North, adding all the wealth and opulence enjoyed by their great marts. And while we enjoy the right of Hamitic servitude, guarantied to us by the Constitution of our country, and by the Divine laws of God, with our superior soil and genial climate, no competition on earth will be able to stand before us. And these rights we intend to enjoy, or to a man we will die, strung along Mason and Dixon's line, with our faces looking North! Leave us in the peaceable possession of our slaves, and our Northern neighbors may have all the paupers and convicts that pour in upon us from European prisons, the getters-up of "hunger meetings" at the North, and the propagators of most of the irreligious and impious *isms* of the day!

The productive wealth of the South, her agricultural and mineral resources, her population and extent of territory, are greatly underrated by the politicians of the North, and the reckless agitators of the slavery question, such as this gentleman!

There are NINE HUNDRED AND TWENTY-NINE THOUSAND SQUARE MILES of territory in the South—an area as large as that covered by Great Britain, France, Austria, Prussia, and Spain. The North, even after the admission of the two large Territories of Kansas and Minnesota, will fall MORE THAN ONE HUNDRED THOUSAND SQUARE MILES short of the South. This does not include the territory lying west of the Rocky Mountains, which will never come into antagonism with the South.

There are TWELVE MILLIONS OF INHABITANTS in the slaveholding States of this Union, and of this number FOUR MILLIONS are slaves; and their aggregate value, at present prices, will amount to SEVENTEEN HUNDRED MILLIONS OF DOLLARS! This item of Southern wealth he left out of his calculation! This gives us an aggregate population larger than that of Great Britain when she struggled against NAPOLEON and the combined armies of Europe! The population of the slaveholding States of this Confederacy is *five times* that of the United Continental Colonies; it is *three times* that of Sweden and Norway; and *greater* than that of Belgium, Portugal, Holland, Denmark, Switzerland, and Greece combined! We have a population *five times* as large as that which conquered our independence, and a thousand-fold as strong! We have ONE MILLION OF MEN upon our muster-rolls, and not 792,876, as Mr. Pryne asserts! At any time, upon short notice, the South can raise, equip, and maintain in the field a larger force than any power on earth can send against her—men, too, brought up on horseback, and in active life, with guns in their hands—men who will not *desert* their colors, as some of your Northern men have done, in Mexico and elsewhere!

Through the heart of the Slave States runs the mighty "Father of Waters," into whose bosom are poured THIRTY-SIX THOUSAND MILES of tributary streams. And in the great "Valley of the Mississippi" is to be the seat of the world's empire! We have a shore-line of over three thousand miles, and so indented with bays, and crowded with islands, as to make the whole measurement twelve thousand miles! We have the best soil and the best climate anywhere to be found, in an equal extent of territory, on the face of God's green earth!

In his contrast between the soil of the South and that of the North, he singled out North Carolina. Why not call up Tennessee, Kentucky, Alabama, Mississippi, Arkansas, Louisiana, and Texas? No soil in the North will compare with these States!

The exportable products of the fifteen Slave States amount annually to $270,000,000, exclusive of gold and foreign merchandise re-exported; and their annual demand for the productions of other countries is about $225,000,000.

There are 80,000 cotton plantations in the South, and the aggregate value of their annual products is

$128,000,000. There are 16,000 tobacco plantations, and their annual products amount to $15,000,000. There are 2600 sugar plantations, the products of which average annually $13,000,000. There are 700 rice plantations, which yield annually a revenue of $6,000,000. Breadstuffs and provisions yield 78,000,-000; the products of the forest amount to $10,700,000; manufactures yield $31,000,000; and the products of the sea yield $3,356,000 — exclusive of $30,000,000 we send to the North.

The facts and figures I have submitted in the foregoing remarks, rest mostly upon the authority of the *Southern Cultivator*, *De Bow's Review*, and the speeches in Congress of SENATOR HAMMOND and REPRESENTATIVE KEITT, of South Carolina. But I am happy to find all the leading facts I have submitted sustained by the Secretary of the United States' Treasury, in his late Report. I will read his statistics of exportation, as they show which section of our Confederacy furnishes them. This statistical report was laid before Congress by JAMES BUCHANAN, and by him endorsed:

"The Secretary of the Treasury, in his late Report, sets down the exportation of domestic produce, exclusive of specie, at $266,438,051. Of this amount, cotton, which is exclusively from the South, furnishes $128,382,351; tobacco gives $12,221,843; and rice yields $2,390,233 — both of which, also, are exclusively Southern; breadstuffs and provisions are estimated at $77,686,455; products of the forest at $10,694,184; of manufactures at $30,970,992; of the sea at $3,356,797. Now take $128,382,351 for the value of cotton, and $12,221,843 for tobacco, and $2,390,233 for rice, which are exclusively Southern staples, and we have the sum of $142,994,427, which the South contributes to the exportation of the country in three staple products, which, in the

Union, are only raised within her limits. But her contribution does not stop here. Of the $77,686,455 furnished by breadstuffs and provisions, she contributed at least $25,000,000; of the products of the forest, in the shape of lumber, etc. she contributed about $5,000,000, or one-half of the exportation. These $30,000,000, added to the $142,994,427 which we have already shown was furnished by cotton, tobacco, and rice, make up $172,994,427, out of the $266,438,051 to which the whole domestic exportation amounts. This would leave $93,443,624, for the domestic exportation from all the Free States. But this is more than they are entitled to. Of the $30,970,992 contributed by domestic manufactures, at least $10,000,000 is the value of the raw material not grown at the North. This leaves only $83,442,624 as the contribution of the Free States against $172,994,427, as the contribution of the Southern or Slave States to the domestic exportation of the country."

Where are your boasted statistics now, Mr. Pryne? It will be seen, from the foregoing, that the South furnishes *more than two-thirds* of the exportation of the Union, after all your boasting at the North, and your erroneous arguments to prove that slavery destroys the industrial pursuits of a country. Shame on your array of false statistics!

Talk about the patriotism of the North, and the devotion of her people to this Union! The first blood shed in defence of liberty, and in opposing English oppressions, was in the *South* — yes, in the much-abused, slave-holding, and slave-dealing South! The State of North Carolina — the glorious "Old North State" — the Rip Van Winkle of the South, whose poverty you have here derided, is entitled to the honor! It was during the gubernatorial administration of the notorious GOVERNOR TRYON, the English governor at the time, who built one of the most splendid palaces in either North or South America, at Newbern, North Carolina, with the proceeds of taxes imposed upon the people for that purpose, and to resist which the people rebelled, just as did the men of Massachusetts afterwards. The battle took place in the year 1771, and is narrated by Wheeler in his "History of North Carolina." On the 16th of May, in that year, the battle was fought between the Americans, called the "Regulators," and the British troops, under the control of the Governor, on the banks of the Alamance river, in what is known now as the county of that name. The British forces, including militia called out by Tryon, amounted to *eleven hundred.* The American forces amounted to *two thousand.* The Royal forces had the advantage in discipline and arms, but, after an action of two hours, came out of the contest with *sixty* killed and wounded; while the Americans had twenty killed and several wounded. Wheeler says:

"Thus ended the battle of Alamance. Thus and here was the *first blood spilled,* in these United States, in resistance to exactions of English rulers and oppressions by the English government. 'The great wolf of South Carolina' showed his blood-barbarity. He hung Captain Tew the next day, without trial, on a tree.

"It was in this case, as Byron truly says in one of his poems —

"'For Freedom's battle once begun,
Bequeathed from bleeding sire to son,
Though sometimes lost is ever won.'

"Thus we see that it was at the battle of Alamance, and not at Bunker Hill, that the first American blood was shed in the cause of liberty. 'Honor to whom honor is due.'"

What next? Talk to me about the North having furnished the great men of the country. This will do to tell to the marines. If we look into the history of the past, we shall find names in the South that will certainly live as long in history, and in marble, as in the North. Aye, there is one Southern name with which there is none to compare, either in the North or in the civilized world. I pronounce the name of the "incomparable WASHINGTON," a celebrated old Virginia slave-holder, and I call upon EDWARD EVERETT to testify, that the Northern colonies were eager to make him commander-in-chief of their forces in the war of the Revolution, and *unanimously* elected him the first President of the United States. Of the fifteen Presidents of the United States, *nine* of them were Southern men. And who will say that the names of Washington, Jefferson, Madison, Monroe, Jackson, Harrison, Polk, and Taylor, are not quite as illustrious as those of the Adamses, Van Buren, Fillmore, Pierce, and Buchanan?

If the North has produced a Samuel Adams, a Hamilton, a Franklin, a Story, and a Webster, the sunny South has given birth to a Patrick Henry, a Clay, a Calhoun, a Marshall, and others of eminent talents. If the North has given to the country more than her share of distinguished authors and scholars, the South has yielded more than its share of the most distinguished generals, statesmen, and politicians.

In conclusion, I am no alarmist; I am no spiritual dreamer; I am no prophet; nor am I the son of a prophet; but allow me to say, there exists among the villanous agitators of the slavery question at the

North, a determination to doom to utter extinction both the rights and institutions of the South. It is quite impossible that the signs of the times can be misconstrued. A dissolution of the Union is what a large portion of Northern Abolitionists are aiming at. No longer ago than the 4th of August, 1858, the "Liberty Party," as they style themselves, held a Convention at Syracuse, and nominated *Gerrit Smith* for governor. My friend, REV. ABRAM PRYNE, figured largely in that meeting. He was the chairman of the committee on resolutions, and of course *wrote*, as well as *reported*, what was adopted. I quote one of his resolutions, adopted with great eclat by the Convention:

> "*Resolved*, That American slavery is a *crime against God and man*, of such matchless magnitude that no forms of law can change its *infernal character* — no limitations or selections of its territory or its power can reconcile us to its *continued existence;* but we raise our voices in the name of God and humanity to demand its *eradication from every foot of the soil of our country.*

I can tell the gentleman, and all who are of like resolution, that if their great-grand-children live to see "American Slavery" eradicated from the States South, where it now is, by the sanction of law and the provisions of our Constitution, as well as with the approbation of God himself, they will live until their heads are as grey as a Norwegian rat. We came honestly by our slaves at the South — we are treating them as the law of God directs—and before we will have them seized and carried off by Abolitionists, we will pour out our blood as freely as we would water. The South is able to take care of herself, and she intends to do it at all hazards, and to the last extremity.

The opposers of the South, by these *ultra* measures, seek to drive us out of the Union, that they may appropriate to themselves, when war comes, if come it must, the army and navy, and the contents of the national treasury! But we of the South intend to fight you *in* the Union, not *out* of it! And when your *blue-bellied Yankees* come South, with "Sharp's rifles and Holy Bibles," to seize upon our slaves, let me say to you, that they will not find themselves in *Kansas!*

What next? Abolitionists at the North are ignorant of the South, in all material respects. Those only who reside there, or who have travelled extensively through the Southern States, know their people, their soil, climate, and capacities. Cast your eyes to the "sunny South," my countrymen, and what a glorious prospect meets the view! Search creation round, and where do you find a land that presents such a scene for contemplation! Look at our institutions, our agricultural and commercial interests; and above all, and more than all, look at the gigantic strides we are making in all that ennobles human kind!

Yes, gentlemen, ours is the land of chivalry, the land of the muse, the abode of statesmen, the home of oratory, the dwelling-place of the historian, and of the hero; the scenes of classic recollections and of hallowed associations lie south of Mason and Dixon's Line; and when the South is prostrated, (which God in his mercy never intends,) the genius of the world will weep amid the ruins of the only true Republic ever known to civilized man!

In saying this, I am not for separating from the North, or dissolving the Union. I am willing to live and die for America, as she is, and has been; but America without the South, and blight, ruin, and decay come upon us; and we bid a long farewell to the last remnant of earth's beauty and the light of heaven!

Who can estimate the value of the American Union? Proud, happy, thrice happy America! the home of the oppressed! the asylum of the emigrant; where the citizen of every clime, and the child of every creed, roams free and untrammelled as the wild winds of heaven! Baptized at the fount of Liberty, in fire and blood, cold must be the heart that thrills not at the name of the American Union!

When the old world, with "all its pomp, and pride, and circumstance," shall be covered with oblivion — when thrones shall have crumbled, and dynasties shall have been forgotten—may this glorious Union, despite the mad schemes of Southern fire-eaters and Northern Abolitionists, stand amid regal ruin and national desolation, towering sublime, like the last mountain in the Deluge — majestic, immutable, and magnificent!

In pursuance of this, let every conservative Northern man, who loves his country and her institutions, shake off the trammels of Northern fanaticism, and swear upon the altar of his country that he will stand by her Constitution and laws! Let every Southern man shake off the trammels of disunion and nullification, and pledge his life and his sacred honor to stand by the Constitution of his country *as it is*, the laws as enacted by Congress, and interpreted by the Supreme Court. Then we shall see every heart a shield, and a drawn sword in every hand, to preserve the ark of our political safety! Then we shall see reared a fabric upon our National Constitution, which time cannot crumble, persecution shake, fanaticism disturb, nor revolution change, but which shall stand among us like some lofty and stupendous Appenine, while the earth rocks at its feet, and the thunder peals above its head!

Contemplating our country and her Northern foes, a specimen of whom is here before us, may I not exclaim with the poet:

> "Country! — on thy sons depending,
> Strong in manhood, bright in bloom,
> Hast thou seen thy pride descending,
> Shrouded to the unbounded tomb?
> Rise! — on eagle pinion soaring —
> Rise! — like one of God-like birth —
> And, Jehovah's aid imploring,
> Sweep the *spoiler* from the earth."

In conclusion, I shall bestow but a few moments' reflections upon the speech the gentleman delivered last evening. He said he would not attempt a reply to my arguments, because they were not what he expected to hear—they were not the arguments he had known Southern men to use — he therefore would state the arguments used by Southern men, that he might apply to them the answers he had prepared before he left home! This humiliating confession his pride of character should have prevented him from making before a public assemblage, even of Abolitionists. He would *make* an argument for the South, and then overthrow it! This is the course of Abolitionists. They *make* all they assert, or charge against the South, and nine times out of ten, they assert and charge what is false. But enough as to this humiliating confession!

My *extension* of the Scriptural argument in favor of slavery, he met with the sweeping assertion, that it was a rehash of my former speech; and with a tirade of abuse, and a collection of profane words and ideas, he wound up in a style disgusting to any decent, not to say Christian gentleman. If he could believe, for a moment, that the Bible sanctioned slavery, he would have no use for its teachings, and would only regard it as fit for a foot-ball! If he could believe that Jesus Christ sanctioned slavery, he would cease to be a Christian, and turn infidel, and would be in favor of changing the name of *Jesus* to *Devil.* This blasphemous language, in mercy to the cause of Abolitionism, even the newspaper reporters have suppressed! This wicked language excited the disgust of every truly decent man in the Hall; its monstrosity, bad as are the meaner portion of Abolitionists, must have been revolting to them!

He next entered upon the Dred Scott decision — denounced the President and his Cabinet — villified the Judges of the Supreme Court, from Taney down — charged them with personal corruption, and official delinquency—and thanked God that they would not live always! Gentlemen, is he not a pretty disciple to call in question the correctness of the decisions of the United States Supreme Court! In what law school was he brought up? He had better withdraw his man Gerritt Smith from the race for Governor, and run him for President, and *if* elected, he will select this *Lawyer* Pryne for his Attorney-General, or appoint him to the Supreme Bench. What a dignified judge he would make! With what an ease and grace he would discharge fugitive slaves, when arrested!

The truth is, there are but a few thousand persons in the Empire State, who swallow the monstrous doctrines of Smith, Douglass, Pryne, and Co. The Republicans and Americans have recently nominated their candidates, and refuse to support Smith. The monstrous character of the sentiments held by this gentleman, are not fully understood. He pretends to take offence at my asking him whether he is willing his daughter should marry a negro or not, when, in fact, he is an *amalgamationist* in sentiment, if not in *practice*. You have heard his eulogy upon Frederick Douglass, and his full endorsement of that arrogant and vulgar negro's sentiments. Then, to get at the real *sentiments* and *feeling* of Abram Pryne, you have but to know those of Douglass, whom he acknowledges to be his superior, and to whom, as a matter of course, he looks up. Here is an extract from a newspaper report of a speech by Douglass, published in the *Chicago Times*, where Douglass spoke during the late Presidential contest:

* * * "There were white men and sooty wenches, and black men and white women, all listening with open mouths to this negro, who boasted that white and black people were disappearing, and mulattoes were fast increasing. He rejoiced that this amalgamation was progressing, and his white and black audience responded with cheers and tumultuous applause to the disgusting sentiment.

"Fair white maidens were there, smiling upon the champion of freedom and Fremont, and applauding with their gloved hands his earnest wish that the distinction between the white and black races would be lost, and instead of them there would soon be but one race—the descendants of white women and black men—black women and white men. He thanked God that the mulatto race was on the increase in Chicago, and his audience cried—Amen!"

As great as is his aversion to answering my questions, I again propound several to him, and I know this audience would like to hear him say yes or no. Does h believe the negro to be the equal of the white man? If so, is he in favor of amalgamation?

Again: is he not a stockholder in the Syracuse underground railroad? Has he never, directly or indirectly, aided fugitive slaves in escaping from their lawful owners? Would he, if an opportunity were to offer, assist a runaway slave in making his escape? If he have thus assisted, he is a negro-stealer! If he have not, but would do so, if an opportunity were to offer, he is a negro-thief at heart, and is condemned by the law of God!

One other remark, and I take my seat. The gentleman had the brazen effrontery to stand here last evening, and say that he "had stooped very low when he engaged in this debate." This *pretence* is set up now as an excuse for not agreeing to meet me south of Mason and Dixon's Line, or debating this question time about, on each side of the line! What a fanatical outburst of *pretended* respectability! To be candid—and I deal in nothing else—Mr. Pryne never was known beyond the smoke of his own chimney, until I brought him into notice by accepting his challenge! He has lived thirty-six years in this present evil world, without ever having been elevated above the dignity of a *brakeman* or *conductor*, on an underground railroad! I deny the possibility of his stooping at all. A man must first *elevate* himself before he can *stoop*, and this he has never done, unless his associations here with free negroes have elevated him!

He attributed remarks to Henry Clay last evening, that Henry Clay never made. If they were ever uttered at all, they were uttered by some one else. I repeat, he read a *forged* extract upon Henry Clay. I make this announcement because Mr. Clay is not here to set himself right! Not only did Mr. Clay never utter the words or sentiments you have attributed to him, but I believe they never were uttered by any one else. I repeat the charge of *forgery*, and it remains for you to produce your authority, or remain under censure. With this distinct avowal, I would let this matter pass, but I choose to go further; I dare to assert, that in his rejoinder he will not "stoop" to notice this matter, and for obvious reasons!

The *Evening Journal* of to-day, in a *pretended* report of the discussion of last evening, prefaces the same with these editorial remarks:

> "In the course of his remarks, Mr. Brownlow took occasion to reflect upon the reporters for the press of this city, saying that they were prejudiced against him and his cause, and had embraced every opportunity to misrepresent him in his speeches. We have been assured that these remarks were not meant to refer to the reporters of the EVENING JOURNAL, the only paper in the city which has presented full and accurate accounts of the discussion thus far.

Now, permit me to say, that I never "assured" the *Journal*, or its reporter, that my remarks were not intended for it, nor did I authorize any one else to give such assurance. On the contrary, I meant the *Journal* above all other papers in the city. Its reporter came to me for my manuscript this morning, and I told him in the presence of others, that I would decline furnishing it, on account of the one-sided, illiberal, and false reports given. His reply was that he desired to give my speech in full, that justice might be done me. Upon these express terms I gave it to him. And in the very paper from which I take this false extract, *less* than one column is occupied in reporting my speech, while *three entire columns* are devoted to the speech of Mr. Pryne! I have no respect for any such journals, and I have no apologies to offer their reporters for any offence I have given them!

Finally, it is customary on such occasions as this for the disputants to express their admiration of the patient and protracted attention. For the general decorum and most exemplary behavior of the decent portion of the audience, I return my sincere thanks. To the opposite class, largely in the majority, my competitor will no doubt make suitable acknowledgments!

His illustration of Southern Christianity in the case of a master chaining a slave to a cart, while he himself went to the communion-table, I must notice briefly, and then I am done. I have denied that any such case ever occurred in any Southern State, and I repeat this denial. He has been called upon by a medical student in this city, to say if the case he pretends to give had occurred in Florida, and if his Presbyterian clergyman were *Henry Cherry*. His answer was, that it occurred in Florida, and that Mr. Cherry was the minister. Now, the whole story is without foundation in truth.

This man Cherry is a Northern Abolitionist — he was once a missionary in India, as my information runs — he studied Divinity with *H. Ward Beecher*, and settled in Florida, near to the Georgia line. He was turned out of the Presbyterian ministry for drunkenness. He went in debt in Thomasville, Georgia, to all who would credit him, until he owed the business men near two thousand dollars, which he owes yet, as he escaped from the country between two days, the favorite time for starting trains on underground railroads! He is now, if still living, in his congenial North, and is a fit subject to slander the high-minded and hospitable people of the South. And in every instance where names are given up, as to the cruelties of slave-owners in the South, the witnesses will turn out to be in keeping with this fallen minister, degraded hypocrite, and vile Abolitionist. Nay, in nine cases out of ten, the *retailers* of these slanders are of "the same sort" themselves!

For the truth of what I here say, as to Cherry, and this slander of a Florida slave-holder, I refer to Rev. H. W. Sharp, and Major John D. Edwards, of Thomasville, Ga., and to Captain James E. Edwards, and R. R. Evans, of Newport, Florida!

"OUGHT AMERICAN SLAVERY TO BE PERPETUATED?"

NEGATIVE, V. — BY ABRAM PRYNE.

LADIES AND GENTLEMAN:—Before entering upon my argument of this evening, allow me to refer to two or three extraneous matters, belonging to the courtesies and proprieties of this occasion — matters in which others than the disputants in this debate are interested.

In the first place, I desire to acknowledge the courtesy, kindness and liberality of the Philadelphia press. In the published reports, both sides have, so far as I know, been treated fairly — except that sometimes Mr. Brownlow's speeches could not be obtained in full. My opponent last night spoke complainingly of the reporters. Allow me to say that my intercourse with this class of your citizens has impressed me with the fact that they are well-behaved gentlemen. The enterprise of the press which has published these speeches entitles it to the good consideration of Philadelphians.

And now, lest it should be thought by some that I consider Gen. Small as in the slightest degree responsible for any of the sentiments uttered in this debate, allow me to say that I regard him as having acted like a high-minded and liberal gentleman, in consenting to read the addresses of my opponent; for, without such consent, the debate could not have proceeded. I know nothing of Gen. Small's political views, nor do I care what they may be; for in my intercourse with him during the progress of this debate, he has acted in so gentlemanly a manner as to put himself above all questions of politics and partizanship, and commend himself to my warm regards.

My opponent has made some remarks as to my speeches being prepared before I left home. I have only to say that an allusion of this kind comes *with marked grace* from a gentleman who came here with every one of his speeches written out—except the tail-end! He must have taken me for a verdant young man from the "rural districts" if he supposes I would come here unprepared to meet him. Prepared, certainly: he gratuitously and blusteringly advised me, in our correspondence, to come well prepared, and I have taken his advice.

On a previous evening I offered to repeat this debate with my opponent in principal cities of the North. In reply, he asked whether I would discuss the question with him South as well as North. In order that you may understand my position in regard to this matter, let me state a few facts.

Mr. Brownlow, nearly a year ago, threw out a challenge which he caused to be published in Northern papers, that he, Parson Brownlow, intended to come North on a missionary tour; that he intended to spend the summer in debating the slavery question with whatever Abolitionists would dare to meet him, and mentioning Theodore Parker, Henry Ward Beecher and others; that he intended to show himself on Boston Common, and that he could speak to a ten acre lot full of people, if such a congregation chose to assemble. It was in the *North* that all this was to be done; it was the *North* in which he challenged the North to meet him. Without claiming the dignity of representing the North, I have met him here in Philadelphia, and offered to continue the debate with him as he advances in his missionary tour through the North. He now attempts to slip through my fingers by asking me to go South with him half the time — a proposition which formed no part of his original challenge to the North.

The reason why I cannot accept his proposition to debate with him on Southern territory, is because the South dare not let me utter, in freedom, my sentiments. Every citizen of Philadelphia knows that this is the truth. The *brave* South meets Northern ministers with mobs. Let a man attempt to address to the Southern mind, sentiments with which the people of that section differ, and the *brave* South gathers hundreds of her roughest citizens to *argue* him down with brickbats, and bowie knives, and pistols, and bludgeons. I cannot be expected to stand up against the mobs of the South with such *arguments* as they employ. In a debate with such weapons as the South is accustomed to use, a mob of thousands of her *brave* citizens would be too much for me. I appeal to brains, not bludgeons. I deal with truths, and not with revolvers. An audience of Camanches or Root-Diggers, would be too much for one clergyman, alone, in debate, if they used the usual arguments of Southern mobs. They meet reason with brickbats and pistols, and settle questions of ethics and logic with *gutta percha* canes, even on the floor of the Senate; and my opponent shows his courage by inviting me to meet such a crowd as would be gathered in the South to hear us. A fair and equal fight that would be! A Southern mob of thousands in arms against a single minister. Brave South! The South will not let me, on her own ground, utter, unmolested, my own free thoughts; and therefore I call upon my opponent to abide by his original challenge, or I shall hold him up before the press of the country as having receded from his former position.

I shall now reply briefly to some of the remarks which you have to-night heard from my opponent, and shall then sum up in a general way the arguments on my side of the question.

An attempt has been made to show that the North is the aggressor in this Anti-Slavery war. Ask the four million slaves of the South who is the aggressor! The South, having stolen the slave from Africa, stripped him of his rights, put him under her heel, now stands in the attitude of crushing him to the earth, and when the North, in the name of reason, and justice, and humanity, and God, protests against the outrage, she is the aggressor, is she? A ruffian has grasped your little child by the throat, and as it looks imploringly to you, you rush forward to defend it, when the wretch cries out, "Go away, you quarrelsome fellow; don't try to get me into a fight; you are the aggressor!"

In regard to this slavery controversy, the aggression commenced when the fatal wrong of slavery began; and the North, together with the entire civilized world, now stands in the defence of humanity, demanding the freedom of the slave.

Through the whole history of the slavery dispute in this country, the South, as you know, has been the aggressor; the aggressor in efforts for the extension of slave-holding territory—the aggressor in procuring the repeal of the Missouri Compromise — the aggressor in attempting to sway, by unworthy influences, the politics of the country — the aggressor in trying to fill, not only the Presidential Chair, but all the offices of the departments and of the army and navy, with her own citizens. The advance of slave-holding interests, and the increase of slave-holding power, has been, for years and years, the grand aim and purpose of her political action; and now, when the free spirit of the North is at last aroused to protest against these aggressions on the rights of the North, and the rights of man, we are to be called the aggressors, are we, and to be put out of the controversy on that ground?

Let me now make a brief reference to that clause of the Constitution which has been cited as the basis of the fugitive slave act. The clause reads thus:—

> "No person held to service or labor in one State, under the laws thereof, escaping into another, shall, in consequence of any law or regulation therein, be discharged from service or labor, but shall be delivered up on claim of the party to whom such service or labor may be due."

This clause of the Constitution, I contend, forms no basis for a fugitive slave law. In the first place, its language is, "no *person* held to service or labor." The Southern doctrine is, that slaves are "goods and chattels personal." In order to apply to the slave, it ought to have said, according to Southern doctrine, "no *property* held to service" — "no *chattels* held to service" — "no *goods* held to service." The personality of the slave must either be admitted altogether or denied altogether. You cannot shift your ground. You must not attempt to give him personality when you want to catch him, and deny him personality when you want to buy or sell him. The fact is, that, in the eye of Southern law, the slave is not a person, but a thing. The distinction between personality and property causes here a gap, broad and deep as that between Dives and Lazarus, which the South must overleap before it can make this clause apply to the slave.

Again, the words are, "no person held to service or labor in one State *under the laws thereof.*" I have, on a previous evening, proved to you that no Southern State has on its statute-book any law under which the master can claim the right to hold his slave. I have given you Senator Mason's statement that no such law could be produced. The slave is not held under the sanctions of law. Mere possession, mere power to hold — brute force — is all the law that the master can show in support of his claim. Thus, we have another reason why this clause cannot apply.

The words "person held to service" do not *legally* describe a slave. They describe a Doctor of Divinity under contract to "serve" a church, or a salaried clerk, or a free chambermaid, as well. A legal description must be definite, in order to be binding. If you contract to sell an "animal" on your estate for five dollars, and the other party claims your best horse under the contract, and you offer him your dog, claiming that you thus meet the contract, a court would decide the contract to be void for indefiniteness. So, a contract to deliver up a "person held to service" cannot apply to a chattel, a piece of goods, held by no contract, and under no legal obligation. On this point Daniel Webster said, in his place in the Senate, March 7, 1850:

"It may not be improper here to allude to that — I had almost said celebrated — opinion of Mr. Madison. *You observe, sir, that the term slavery is not used in the Constitution. The Constitution does not require that fugitive slaves shall be delivered up; it requires that persons bound to service in one State, and escaping into another, shall be delivered up.* Mr. Madison opposed the introduction of the term slave or slavery into the Constitution; for he said he did not wish to see it recognized by the Constitution of the United States of America, that there could be property in men."

The Supreme Court of the United States has decided that —

"Where rights are infringed, where fundamental principles are overthrown, where the general system of the laws is departed from, the legislative intention must be expressed with *irresistible clearness,* to induce a court of justice to suppose a design to effect such objects. — *United States* vs. *Fisher,* 2 *Cranch,* 390.

Again, this clause provides that the person escaping shall be delivered up on claim of the party *to whom such service or labor may be due.* You must prove that there is labor *due* from the slave to the man who is chasing him through the North. But, according to Southern law, the slave can hold nothing, can own nothing, can *owe* nothing; and, if the slave cannot *owe* anything, how can there be any labor *due* from him?

My opponent asks me tauntingly whether I have not stock in the "underground railroad?" — whether I would assist a fugitive slave in making his escape? I answer, without hesitation, that, if a poor negro, fleeing from Southern oppression, should come to my door at night, asking for shelter and a bed, I would give him the best bed in my humble house; and should any kidnapper come in pursuit of him, I happen (though not a man of war) to have in my possession an old rifle, which would do good service in defending him.

My opponent has used the name of Benjamin Franklin to give weight to his side of the controversy. He has told you that Franklin—whose bones, honored and reverenced, as they ought to be, lie among you—declined to act with the Abolitionists of Pennsylvania; refused to co-operate with the Society that elected him its President. I happened to have in my vest pocket, at the moment when this assertion was uttered, a copy of a petition for the abolition of slavery, addressed to the Congress of the United States, signed by Benjamin Franklin, and offered by him on the floor of Congress. I will read a single passage from this memorial:

"From a persuasion that equal liberty was originally the portion, and is still the birthright of all men, and influenced by the strong ties of humanity and the principles of our institutions, your memorialists conceive themselves bound to use all justifiable endeavors to loosen the bands of slavery, and to promote a general enjoyment of the blessings of freedom."

This is my sufficient answer to the imputation that Benjamin Franklin was in favor of American slavery.

We have had warmly described to us the sea-coast of the South, the extent of her harbors, her facilities for commerce and navigation. I have no disposition to deny any of these statements; I myself have told you that the South is far ahead of the North in natural advantages. But how does she improve her magnificent endowments? What advantage is it to her that the waters of the ocean wash her long-extending seaboard? The harbor of Beaufort, N. C., is, in natural advantages, second to none, perhaps, of which this continent can boast. The town was settled, if I remember rightly, almost as early as Boston, and the harbor is nearly equal to that of Boston. Yet make a contrast between Boston and the little village of Beaufort, N. C., with its magnificent harbor and its dilapidated houses, the grass growing in its streets, and you see at once how the spirit of freedom improves the natural advantages that she bestows on the North; while the South, with the waves of the ocean dashing on her extended coast, and her spacious harbors inviting commerce; with a seaboard extending from Delaware Bay around the peninsula of Florida, and along the northern shores of the Gulf of Mexico and far up the south-west, where the Pacific hurls her thundering waves against the land of gold, her coast is made desolate by the spirit of slavery, checking the enterprise and genius that might make the most of these great natural blessings. The point which I make is, that the North is ahead in wealth and power, not in consequence of her superior natural advantages, but in spite of the superior natural advantages of the South.

And here let me read a single extract. Hear how a North Carolinian describes your Southern harbors:

"How is it with Beaufort, in North Carolina, whose harbor is said to be the safest and most commodious anywhere to be found on the Atlantic coast south of the harbor of New York, and but little inferior to that? Has anybody ever heard of her? Do the masts of her ships ever cast a shadow on foreign waters? Upon what distant or benighted shore have her merchants and mariners ever hoisted our national ensign, or spread the arts of civilization and peaceful industry? What changes worthy of note have taken place in the physical features of her superficies since 'the evening and the morning were the third day?' But we will make no further attempt to draw a comparison between the populous, wealthy, and renowned city of Boston, and the obscure, despicable little village of Beaufort, which, notwithstanding 'the placid bosom of its deep and well-protected harbor,' has no place in the annals or records of the country, and has scarcely ever been heard of fifty miles from home." — HELPER: *The Impending Crisis.*

And here is the description of Southern dependence on the North:

"Reader! would you understand how abjectly slaveholders themselves are enslaved to the products of Northern industry? If you would, fix your mind on a Southern 'gentleman'—a slave-breeder and human-flesh monger, who professes to be a Christian! Observe the routine of his daily life. See him rise in the morning from a Northern bed, and clothe himself in Northern apparel; see him walk across the floor on a Northern carpet, and perform his ablutions out of a Northern ewer and basin. See him uncover a box of Northern powders, and cleanse his teeth with a Northern brush; see him reflecting his physiognomy in a Northern mirror, and arranging his hair with a Northern comb. See him dosing himself with the medicaments of Northern quacks, and perfuming his handkerchief with Northern colognes. See him referring to the time in a Northern watch, and glancing at the news in a Northern gazette. See him and his family sitting in Northern chairs, and singing and praying out of Northern books. See him at the breakfast table, saying grace over a Northern plate, eating with Northern cutlery, and drinking from Northern utensils. See him charmed with the melody of a Northern piano, or musing over the pages of a Northern novel. See him riding to his neighbor's in a Northern carriage, or furrowing his lands with a Northern plow. See him lighting his cigar with a Northern match, and flogging his negroes with a Northern lash. See him, with Northern pen and ink, writing letters on Northern paper, and sending them away in Northern envelopes, sealed with Northern wax, and impressed with a Northern stamp." —*The Impending Crisis.*

In regard to the figures which my opponent has given to-night, let me say that his statements touched only one side. He offered figures to prove the greatness of the South; but he did not, step by step, give the Northern balance, as I did in my statistical argument. The reason he did not do so, is that he is ashamed to. Had he done so truthfully and faithfully, the terrible balance against the South would have overwhelmed him, as did my argument on that subject the other night; for my figures, taken from the Census Report, cannot be controverted.

Washington has been again alluded to, this evening, as a friend of the Union, and as a slaveholder. Yes, gentlemen, Washington was a friend of the Union. So am I. If any of you understood me last night as being in favor of a dissolution of the Union, you mistook my meaning. The purport of what I said was, that if we must either have slavery eternally, or have a dissolution, I would consent even to dissolution in the end, in order to get rid of slavery. But I have no belief that it will be necessary to dissolve the Union to secure the abolition of slavery. On the contrary, I believe that the glorious spirit of humanity rising in the North will yet dig a channel, through the ballot-box, for the abolition of slavery, without the necessity of resorting to dissolution.

The name of Washington has been again used to add sanction to slavery. The name of the Father of our Country, from whatever portion of it he came, let me speak with all due reverence, and that reverence will be only heightened as I read these noble words of his to the Marquis de Lafayette on the subject of slavery—

> "The scheme, my dear Marquis, which you propose as a precedent, to encourage the emancipation of the black people in this country from the state of bondage in which they are held, is a striking evidence of the benevolence of your heart. *I shall be happy to join you in so laudable a work;* but will defer going into a detail of the business till I have the pleasure of seeing you."

Every time my opponent attempts to cite Washington, or any of the Fathers, as favoring American slavery, I can answer him with such a quotation as this in black and white.

A matter which I cannot fail to notice, as a prominent feature of this debate, is the effort upon the other side, to change the issue. We came here to discuss the question, "Should American Slavery be perpetuated?" My opponent was to support the affirmative of this question; but instead of offering arguments tending to that end he has given us bitter denunciations of the North, alleging that it is a horrible land, full of hypocrisy, pauperism and crime. But if all this be true, how does it affect the question whether slavery ought to be abolished? It does not make the difference of a hair in the decision of the question. It strikes me that the pot, when it called the kettle black, did not whiten itself much, and that it was so conscious of its own infernal blackness that it wanted to relieve itself by getting the kettle in its company.

The taunts against Northern religion, so repeatedly thrown out, do not affect the issue. If we are all a set of hypocrites, is that any reason why the South should be all a set of baby-stealers? Whatever evils prevail in the North are not *caused* by freedom, nor are they inseparable from it.

My opponent has told us of the kindness of masters. Supposing it to be proved that masters are most kind, how does that change the result of the question whether the relation of master and slave is right? How does that prove that the chattel principle is founded in justice? But I do not acknowledge that masters are kind. I would not admit the kindness of the master, though he should dress his slave in silks, and fill his stomach with the choicest viands of the land. When a man lays his hand on my personality, and blots it out "at one fell swoop" — when he takes the keeping of my own soul and conscience into his tyrannical hands — and then cantingly turns to me and talks about kindness, I hurl back the insulting assumption that he may, without guilt, trample on my dearest rights.

Again: The argument has been trailed all through this debate, that God allowed the Jews to hold slaves. I have shown that the word "servant," as used in the Bible, does not mean "slave," and that, therefore, the argument does not at all cover the ground. But even supposing that God did allow the *Jews* to hold slaves, how does that touch the question whether the *Yankees* have a right to do so? Suppose it true that God did permit, in that age, a system of servitude that was wrong; so did he allow polygamy; but does that fact prove that polygamy is right now? Many things were allowed under the Old Testament dispensation, which the clearer light of Christianity has swept away — of which the better day that dawned with the coming of Jesus has shown us the error and enormity. Christ, at His coming, brushed away all those remnants of a darker age, giving us that glorious Gospel, the very genius and spirit of which puts all humanity on one common level, and makes us all brothers. When the growing light of Christianity has shone for eighteen hundred years — when ages of human progress have gathered their results for our instruction — shall we — as we view slavery in the light of its horrid consequences, shown over the track of centuries, in the light of its desolating effects, marked out through the whole pathway of history — shall we pronounce it innocent and God-sanctioned, simply because we read that some of the ancient patriarchs, in the darker ages, held servants? Why, gentlemen, if I had not quoted a single text, if I had not stopped to reply to my opponent's Scriptural argument, such considerations as these would be all sufficient to sweep it away forever.

Let me now recapitulate briefly the points which I have endeavored to establish by my several arguments in this debate. I have shown that slavery began in murder and piracy; that, such being its illegitimate and villanous birth, it ought to have died at the first; and that the retribution of an incensed God and the just moral sense of the world have been hunting it from that time to this. I have shown that slavery has existed without the sanction of genuine law; in defiance of the Declaration of Independence; in violation of the Constitution of the United States; in conflict with the letter and spirit of the common law, and in the utter absence of any statutary enactment giving it creation or sanction. I have swept away all the vestiges of legal seeming that have been gathered around it, and revealed it to your gaze standing forth in all the horrid features of outrage and barbarity that marked it at its birth through the slave-trade. I have brought to bear on this question not only considerations of morals, but considerations of politics, showing how it disgraces our nation before the civilized world. I have urged against this evil, arguments drawn from the letter and spirit of the gospel of Jesus Christ. I have exhibited the crushing weight of slavery upon the material wealth and progress of the nation. These are the several points which I have sought to bring before your minds.

In reply to what I have said in regard to the Old Testament it has been urged that the New Testament itself sanctions slavery. I remark, in reply, that slavery locks the Bible, places shackles upon the conscience of the Christian, and therefore the New Testament is against it.

My opponent has, from time to time, thrown out taunts at Romanism, because of its retarding influence on the enlightenment of the world. He told us that the most cruel slaveholders in the South were Romanists. I am no Romanist, or defender of the Romanists; still, I do not understand this to be true. And I would remark that slavery, in the course it pursues with regard to religion, in locking up the mind of the slave, in taking the Bible from his hand, in controlling his conscience with the lash of the slave-driver, in driving him from his Sabbath school, in forcing him into a religion that he loathes, and out of a religion that he would love, if he were not obliged to have it crucified and crushed by the enormities practised upon him by its professors; slavery, in doing all this, develops the darkest features of the spirit of Romanism.

The severest complaint that we can make against the Roman Church bears more overwhelmingly against the spirit and practice of American slavery, for suppressing the Bible, for shackling the rights of conscience, for persecuting ministers of the gospel who attempt to preach God's word, for mobbing John G. Fee, for murdering Charles T. Torrey, for inflicting upon the brave and good men who have attempted to preach through the South the words of Jesus, the same ruffian-like persecution with which Romanism, at some eras of the world's history, has met Protestantism. When a man comes here prating about the evils of Romanism, while at the same time he defends and strives to perpetuate a system in the South which is even worse in its relation to religion, he is, to say the least, capping the climax of inconsistency and absurdity.

My opponent seems to think that I have slandered the people of the South in speaking of them as going to the communion table while their negroes are chained to carts. Why, gentlemen, it is but a short time since

I heard the story of such a transaction related in the city of Syracuse, by a Presbyterian deacon who had been to Florida to work for a year or two, and had been driven out on account of his expression of anti-slavery sentiments. He related that one day, going home from Presbyterian church, accompanied by a member who had just partaken with him at the communion-table, he looked over the garden-fence of that member as he approached his house, and saw one of his slaves chained to the cart-wheel. Being asked the reason, this church member answered, that when he went to meeting he dare not leave this slave unless he were chained up, for fear that he would commit some depredation. So, here was your Florida saint sitting at the communion-table while his negro was chained to the cart-wheel at home! Shall I not say that I have done no wrong to the spirit of that religion which sanctions the holding of slaves?

We have been told (and I suppose the gentleman expected it would frighten us) that, because of the growing Anti-Slavery spirit of the North, our Northern watering-places are failing to receive, of late years, the same amount of Southern patronage that they once enjoyed; and that our great commercial cities are fast losing the custom of Southern buyers. He shakes his poor, lean Southern purse at us — as if we cared for your pimps that frequent Northern watering-places, as if we were so extremely anxious for their money that, to secure it, we would trample on the rights of man and crush four millions of slaves! Why, gentlemen, if the heart of the North should be enlarged with humanity sufficient to procure the liberation of the slave, what though our haunts of fashion, with their varied wickedness be all desolate? what though our sales of merchandize be somewhat lessened? But I take the liberty of saying that the statistics to which the gentleman has referred in regard to this matter are entirely untrue. Our Northern watering-places and our Northern commercial cities are frequented by the South as much now as ever before. The number of Southern gentlemen in Philadelphia to-night, buying goods, proves it. And they will undoubtedly continue to frequent the North. So far as this argument is concerned, the crack of the cotton-god's whip will not, I take it, have any great effect in suppressing the humanity of the citizens of Philadelphia, or in crushing the free spirit of the whole North.

As another reason for the abolition of slavery, I refer to its spirit as exhibited in the history of Kansas. The efforts of the South to push slavery into that territory and spread it upon that virgin soil, are so horrid a development of its spirit of ruffianism, that even were there no other exhibition of it, it is time that we should exert ourselves to abolish slavery.

My opponent has, in the course of his speeches, sneered at the Maine Law spirit of the North. That he should do so, is not surprising; for how, in the name of reason, can you carry out your system of ruffianism in Kansas without *whisky?* How can you accomplish the purposes and aims of the slave power, without its terrible ally, the rum power? These two monster spirits of wickedness have stood hand in hand and shoulder to shoulder in this whole controversy. Slavery ought to be abolished, if for no other reason, because it affiliates with the terrible vice of drunkenness.

A member of Congress from my own State was once asked how it was that a certain great statesman (whom I will not mention because of respect for the name he once bore) was brought down into the position that he took with regard to the South in one of the great issues on the slavery question. The answer which this gentleman gave was, that just at that time the saloons about the capitol were filled with the most villanously drugged brandy that ever he knew to be there; and although he did not think that this great statesman drank any more than had been his habit previously, yet the liquor was so bad that it upset his brain, and he went in for the whole demands of slavery, the overturn of the Missouri Compromise and all.

And let me tell you an incident in regard to the passage of the Nebraska bill — a story of shame that should tinge the cheek of every American of spirit. On the night when that iniquitous measure was consummated, the Governor-General of Canada sat in the House of Representatives until midnight, beside Gerrit Smith, (who, as the newspapers said, ran home and did not vote, but who, in truth, was there and did vote.) In the midst of that shameful scene — while half the members were too drunk to stand up to vote, and the others too drunk to hold them up — while the click of pistol locks was heard at times, and the gleam of bowie knives gave occasional threatenings of a fight—during the enacting of this mortifying spectacle, brought on by the spirit of slavery controlling the Congress of the United States, the Governor-General turned to Mr.

Smith and said: "I have witnessed *almost* as disgraceful scenes as this in the British House of Commons." Thus did the courtly foreigner seek to soften the shame which tinged the face of Mr. Smith, in view of his country's disgrace, by a half apology for the drunken row. And thus the spirit of rum and slavery, until they be conquered, will over and over again bring us into this position of contempt before the civilized world.

Again: slavery ought to be abolished, because it seeks to destroy the freedom of the ballot-box. The men in Kansas who wanted to vote like freemen, for a Constitution of their own, were driven back by slavery's bristling bayonets in drunken hands; and that too, I am afraid, with the spirit of the National Administration, under the control of the slave-power, sustaining their ruffianism. Our right of free suffrage at the ballot-box, the very core and essence of all our rights, is either to be encroached upon more and more until it be finally and fatally lost, or we must abolish American slavery.

And let me tell you, freedom in Kansas was secured by a firm resistance to this spirit of slavery. Do you think it was Congressional speeches that secured freedom in Kansas? You are greatly mistaken; it was glorious old John Brown with his armed men. The Demon of slavery was beaten back, because he and his brave band were on the ground to let her minions know that they had caught the spirit of '76, and were ready to fight for freedom.

While on this subject, excuse a little seeming egotism. I am proud to say that before John Brown went to

Kansas, I had the privilege, in an Anti-Slavery Convention at Syracuse, of moving a resolution to buy rifles for his "boys." I made a speech in favor of the resolution, and though it did not escape opposition, it was carried through enthusiastically; the collection was taken up, and John Brown and his "boys" were assisted to buy rifles.

It is the same spirit of firm opposition to the iniquities of American slavery — even to the extent of fighting for freedom if necessary—that is indispensable to save the liberties of our country.

Southern religion has been presented to us as the highest type of Christianity. Let me bring to your mind a picture, unfortunately not a vision of the imagination. On the broad lagoon of some African river are seen the masts of the slaver, towering above the tropical vegetation:

> Hark! from the ship's dark bosom,
> The very sounds of hell!
> The ringing clank of iron—
> The maniac's short sharp yell!
> The hoarse, low curse, throat-stifled—
> The infant's starving moan—
> The horror of a breaking heart
> Poured through a mother's groan!

Now, see that slaver as she approaches her Southern port, the tall church spires of which rise in the distance. Now, look into one of those churches. Remember that its leading members are the owners of this vessel; remember that they provide the market for the negroes she has stolen; and buy the human chattels which she brings across the water; remember all this, and then tell me whether, in the view of God's clear-eyed justice, the slave ship in the lagoon, with its shrieking victims smothering in the hold, is not as worthy the name of *church* as this dome-capped edifice, where, in profanation of religion's name, these traffickers in immortal souls assemble.

Christ regards all his children alike. God, the Father of us all, is acceptably worshipped by fidelity to the great law of human brotherhood. Can a man love Christ, and at the same time treat as a brute one of those precious immortals for whom Christ died?

Suppose there is a man, who calls himself my friend, who, on every occasion, in every place, is profuse in expressions of friendship and of praise. Suppose that to-night, while I am far from my home, my little flaxen-haired boy of four summers has wandered out into the darkness, and as he grows bewildered and weary, a storm comes on, the lightnings flash athwart the heavens, and the clouds pour out their rain. As he wanders on, the storm beating upon his defenceless head he sinks helpless into the mire, and must soon perish. Just at this moment, my pretended friend comes riding along, he who has praised me often and often, and been lavish in professions of love. He sees my poor, helpless child, and what does he do? Of course, he will get down and take him into the warm, snug carriage. No! he drives ruthlessly over him! Suppose that wretch shall come to me to-morrow, renewing his false professions and claiming still to be my warmest friend —what shall I say to him? Shall I not answer, "No! quit my sight, you heartless hypocrite! Had you loved me, you would have loved my child, and tenderly cared for him when in distress."

Now let me make the application. God is the father of us all; and his poor children, the stricken, heart-broken slaves, are groping and struggling in search of freedom; the storms of oppression are beating upon them: and yet they are trodden down and over ridden by the *Christians* of the South, who are at the same time shouting the praises of God, claiming to love him devoutly and to be his sincerest worshippers. Will not God, as their praises rise up to him from hollow hearts, answer, "Inasmuch as ye have failed to do it unto the least of these, my poor little ones on earth, the door of Heaven's kingdom is closed against you. Your praise is a mockery; your professed devotion a sham. I scorn your oblations and your fastings. An acceptable fast is 'to undo the heavy burdens, and to let the oppressed go free, and to break every yoke.'"

Yet we are told that clergymen at the North who plead for the rights of the slave, are derelict in their duty—false to the holy religion they profess. What! are only they true ministers of God's gospel who can lend the sanction of His word to the barbarities of slavery?

Just God!—and these are they
  Who minister at Thine altar, God of Right!
Men who their hands with prayer and blessing lay
  On Israel's ark of light!

What! preach—and kidnap men?
  Give thanks—and rob Thine own afflicted poor?
Talk of Thy glorious liberty—and then
  Bolt hard the captive's door?

What! servants of thine own
 Merciful Son, who came to seek and save
The homeless and the outcast—fettering down
 The tasked and plundered slave!

Pilate and Herod, friends!
 Chief priests and rulers, as of old, combine!
Just God and holy! is that church which lends
 Strength to the spoiler, Thine?

Paid hypocrites! who turn
 Judgment aside, and rob the Holy Book
Of those high words of truth which search and burn
 In warning and rebuke.

And now, my friends, my argument is done. Without fear of being contradicted by the warmest friend of the slave, I say, *I have done my duty.* According to my own poor ability, and with whatever strength God has given me, I have done my duty to the four millions of stricken ones whose wail comes to us on the Southern breeze—to the voiceless maidens, sold in Southern shambles—to the strong-armed men, rendered mute by chains. Could all the slave population of the South hear me to-night, I would venture to stand before them and say that at least to them, my poor, crushed and outraged brethren, I have, in this debate, whatever may have been my faults, done my duty as a brother man.

I have also, as well as my humble powers enabled me, done my duty to the cause of freedom. I have given up my heart to her glorious inspiration, and put all my energies in accord with her noblest instincts and loftiest aims. If I have failed of the success that might have been wished, the cause must be found in my own lack of power. But, gentlemen, I have been successful. I stand here, with all you men of heart and intelligence to sustain me, when I affirm that, in the argument of this debate I have been most eminently successful.

I have done my duty; will you do yours? Will you raise the standard of humanity in this broad land? Will you be true to the aims and purposes of freedom? Will you give up your heart to the moving and growing impulses which are urging the world up to higher light and broader truth, and nobler brotherhood? Will you, taking the sentiments I have uttered, and the principles I have advocated, weave them into your lives, and work them out in your relation to the politics of the country? We need a holier politics, as well as a holier religion — a higher type of statesmanship, a nobler motive of political union, the recognition of government as coming from God, and deriving all its sanctity from the Divine command. Let us engage in the performance of civil duties as men and Christians; and then, when we shall appreciate the glory and dignity of true human government, recognizing God as its author, and His principles as the guiding light in administering the affairs of a nation, we shall cleanse our land from the foul wrong of American slavery, so that we shall no longer be the scorn of the civilized world. Then it will be no longer true that

"While every flap of England's flag
Proclaims that all around are free,
From farthest Ind to each blue crag,
That beetles o'er the Western sea;"

our own America, with her boasted republicanism, and liberty, and religion, is a land where four millions of slaves sigh for freedom. And they will obtain their freedom as they ought to have it. Then, indeed, may we boast of the glory of our land. Then will the heart of humanity look upwards. Then will the eye of God light up with a more kindly smile as he looks down upon us. Then will the world be blessed, not only by the example of the fathers, but by the glorious deeds of the sons of the glorious fathers who achieved the American Revolution.

"So let it be! In God's own might,
We gird us for the coming fight,
And, strong in Him whose cause is ours,
In conflict with unholy powers,
We grasp the weapons He has given —
The light, and truth, and love of heaven!"

THE END.

www.ingramcontent.com/pod-product-compliance
Lightning Source LLC
LaVergne TN
LVHW020239110826
845151LV00003B/968